IMAGES
of America

WEST ADAMS

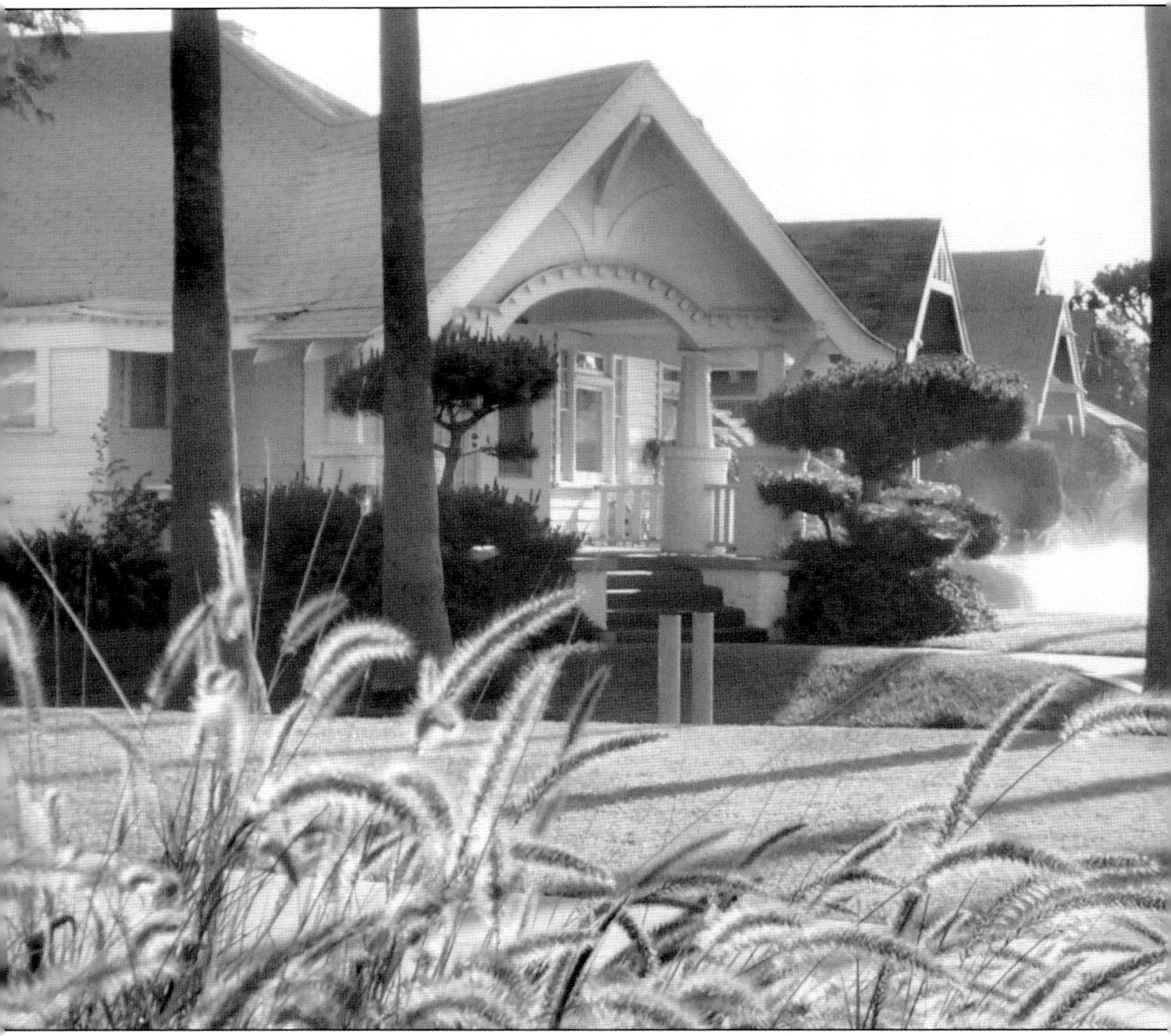

WEST THIRTIETH STREET BUNGALOWS. The palm trees have grown tall on one of the many residential streets of West Adams. Although the mansions and their inhabitants are much more famous, blocks of tidy bungalows have a timeless appeal.

ON THE COVER: It is the summer of 1917, and this attractive young lady modeling the new automobile is in front of one end of the Ezra T. Stimson mansion at 839 West Adams Street. It was designed by noted architect Frederick Roehrig, who also designed the Hotel Green in Pasadena. (Courtesy of Don Lynch.)

IMAGES
of America

WEST ADAMS

Suzanne Tarbell Cooper, Don Lynch,
and John G. Kurtz

ARCADIA
PUBLISHING

ISBN 978-0-7385-5920-9

Published by Arcadia Publishing
Charleston, South Carolina

Printed in the United States of America

Library of Congress Catalog Card Number: 2008926393

For all general information contact Arcadia Publishing at:
Telephone 843-853-2070
Fax 843-853-0044
E-mail sales@arcadiapublishing.com
For customer service and orders:
Toll-Free 1-888-313-2665

Visit us on the Internet at www.arcadiapublishing.com

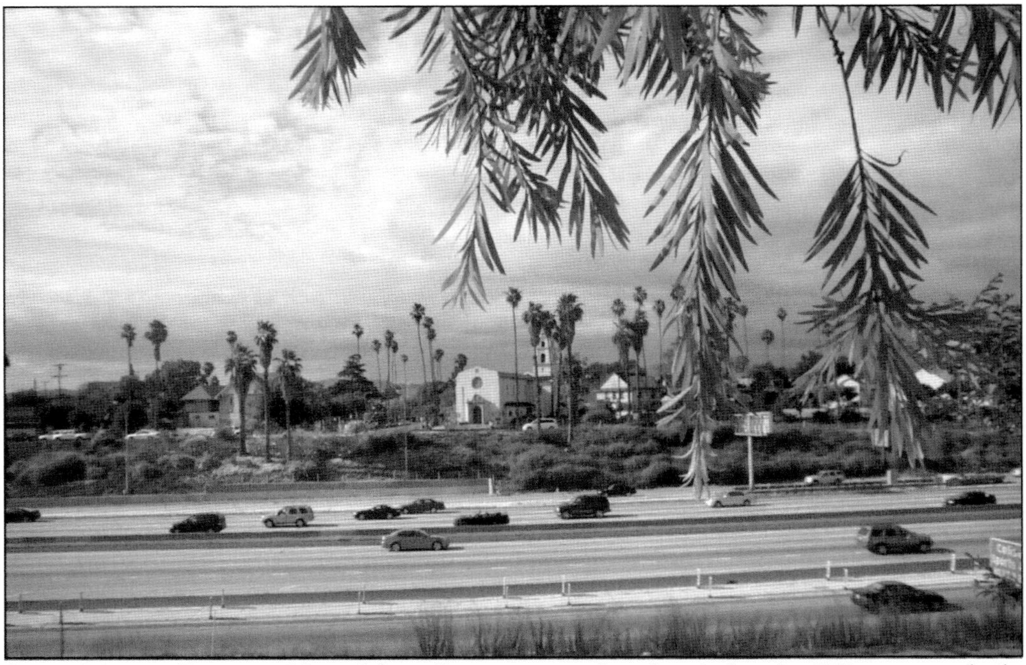

SANTA MONICA FREEWAY. Most of the millionaires moved out long before the 10 Freeway was built, but it ran through areas filled with historic homes. Only the ghosts of the fine houses that were once there remain under concrete filled with the thunder of automobiles. Visible in the distance is the Congregational Church of Christian Fellowship at 2085 South Hobart Boulevard.

Contents

Acknowledgments

Our deepest thanks to all of our friends and neighbors who supplied pictures, information, and encouragement. Most especially deserving thanks are the wonderful Marc Wanamaker, Rory Cunningham, Wally Matsuura, Elizabeth C. Sutherland, Joe Ryan, Jean Cade, Dace Taube of the University of Southern California, Frank Cooper, Amy Ronnebeck Hall, Jerry Roberts, Lyn Gillson, David Saffer, Barbara Dupuy Hammer, Capt. Larry Schneider, ITT Corporation, the UCLA's William Andrews Clark Memorial Library, and Logan Cooper, a West Adams kid who thinks cemetery tours are more fun than house tours.

Unless otherwise noted, all photographs are from the authors' collections. A handful of modern photographs are by Frank or Suzanne Cooper.

INTRODUCTION

Los Angeles has always held a whiff of freedom, promising the ability to change—or make—one's fortune. Postcards of flowers and palm trees in winter made it seem like a magical place where anything was possible, especially at a time when most of the country was shivering under snow. At the end of the 19th century, the wealthy and powerful chose to make the West Adams neighborhood their home and, in doing so, entwined its history with that of Southern California. They came from everywhere, bringing with them a strong dash of pioneer spirit. Some had made fortunes elsewhere, and others arrived with little more than the clothes on their backs. Some were the children and grandchildren of families that had received Spanish land grants. Others were veterans of the Civil War, fleeing colder climates for the benevolent Southern California sun. Some were born here. Some retired here only to find their retirement was busier and more productive than their earlier life had been. At least one chose Los Angeles based on the flip of a coin. Men, and a very few brave women, founded businesses in the city and then took their money home to West Adams, an area roughly bounded by Figueroa Street, Jefferson Boulevard, Pico Boulevard, and West Street.

Transportation was the key to the growth of West Adams. Streetcars and early automobiles encouraged the men who worked downtown to build their mansions here, making it one of the first streetcar suburbs in Los Angeles. Outside the city, there was space to imagine anything. And imagine they did: homes took every form, from Victorian, to arts and crafts, to Spanish Revival, and even a castle that would be right at home in medieval Britain.

Eventually, though, the car became the downfall of what the *Los Angeles Times* termed "the silk stocking district" of West Adams. The rich moved west, and more ordinary, but nevertheless fascinating, individuals took up the story. Smaller, middle-class bungalows had always coexisted with the mansions, but in the 1920s, apartments and businesses became an important part of the neighborhood. The Depression, and a growing student population at USC, turned mansions into boardinghouses. Two grand movie theaters opened, and a few well-known stars and film people moved in, but small neighborhood theaters, shops, and residents with no particular claim to fame were far more common.

By the early 1960s, the Santa Monica Freeway had cut through the heart of the neighborhood, and West Adams went through hard times. Mansions were neglected, subdivided, or torn down, and without the money to maintain them, many houses crumbled from neglect. Politics and the rise of big oil led the city, in its infinite wisdom, to remove the streetcars. The main streets running through West Adams took on the abandoned look of rather downtrodden commercial districts full of potholes. Off every major street, however, stable pockets of homeowners have kept the neighborhood alive, well maintained, and vital. It is not unusual to find homeowners who have lavished loving care on their house for 50 years or more.

Today West Adams is the most diverse neighborhood in the country. Partly because the rich moved out, rather than remodeling history into oblivion, the area has one of the finest collections of dawn-of-the-20th-century architecture imaginable. West Adams was where the housing covenants that restricted ownership on the basis of race were first challenged and among the first places where they fell. It is now one of the most racially and culturally diverse neighborhoods in the country. Any given street may house an elderly Japanese American woman living next door to an African American family whose children grew up here, next door to a young Latino household with toddlers in the yard, next door to a gay couple planting a new garden, next door to, well, you name it, and they probably live in West Adams.

In recent years, historic architecture has been discovered by a whole new generation. Old houses have a quality of craftsmanship and level of detail in even the most modest bungalow that is not found in modern homes. People are beginning to realize that our history is valuable and worth saving. West Adams currently has more Los Angeles City Historic-Cultural Monuments than anywhere else in the city and many Historic Preservation Overlay Zones. A number of people have moved to West Adams because they love the houses, and they have banded together with longtime residents to solve the problems inherent in an urban environment.

Several streets have changed names over the last century. A prominent example is West Adams, which was originally West Adams Street and is now Boulevard. Both names have been used interchangeably in the press between 1913 and 1983. Depending on the time period being discussed, this book uses both. Less ubiquitous changes generally merit the inclusion of both names.

History is written by, and usually about, the powerful. This book focuses strongly on the mansions of West Adams, but the stories of those of more modest means are equally valuable. The area is so rich in history that no one book could detail it all. Look around. Admire the arch of a roofline, or marvel at the size of a house being freshly painted. Add to the story that is West Adams. Enjoy the exploration.

One

From the East to Bankers' Row

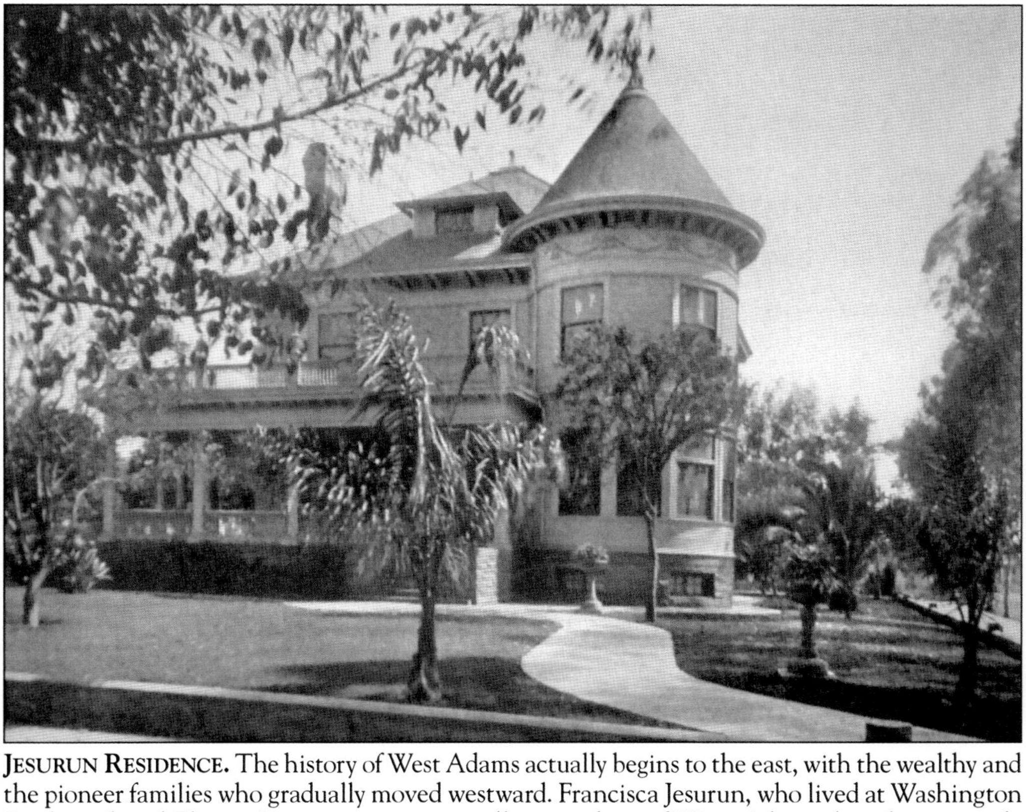

Jesurun Residence. The history of West Adams actually begins to the east, with the wealthy and the pioneer families who gradually moved westward. Francisca Jesurun, who lived at Washington Boulevard and Flower Street, was not actually a resident of West Adams, but she certainly exemplified the history, and penchant for scandal, of Southern California. She was born the daughter of Don Antonio Maria Lugo, owner of a huge land grant. As a child, she witnessed enough battles to recall having her skirt pierced by bullets as she played in the courtyard. After the death of her second husband, Dr. Frederick McDougall, during his term as mayor, she married again. She was a 50-year-old grandmother; her new husband, Edward Jesurun, was 20. Two years later, she sued him for repayment of a $22,000 loan. The man sensibly moved to Antelope Valley, claiming that if she chose to join him, he would provide for his wife "as well as he can, and be good to her." She chose to stay where she was, suing several more people before her death in 1926.

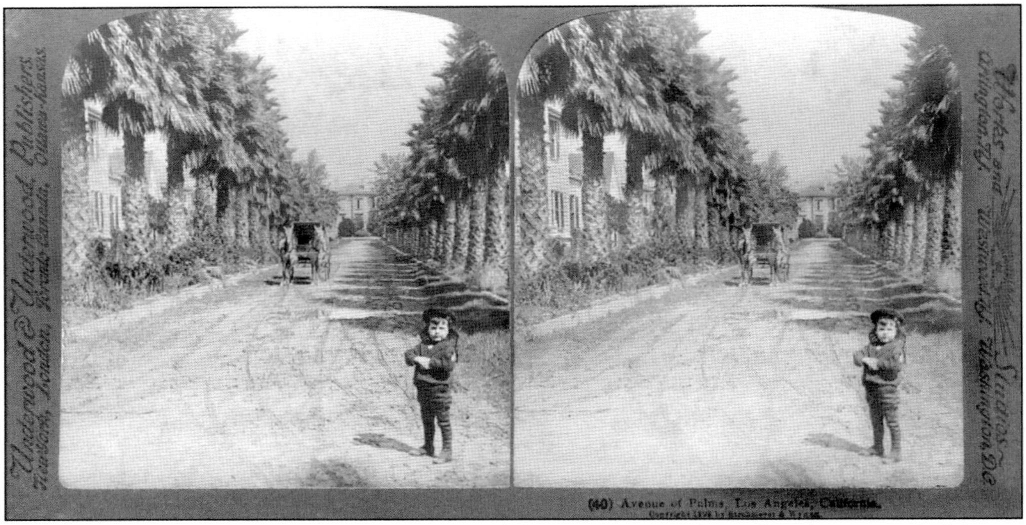

AVENUE OF PALMS (1894). When the rest of the country was buried under snow, California enticed visitors with visions of palm trees and bright midwinter flowers. The Avenue of Palms that led to the Longstreet mansion appeared in countless pictures and postcards around the end of the 19th century. Stereographs, two nearly identical photographs that appear three-dimensional when properly viewed, were nearly as ubiquitous as televisions are today.

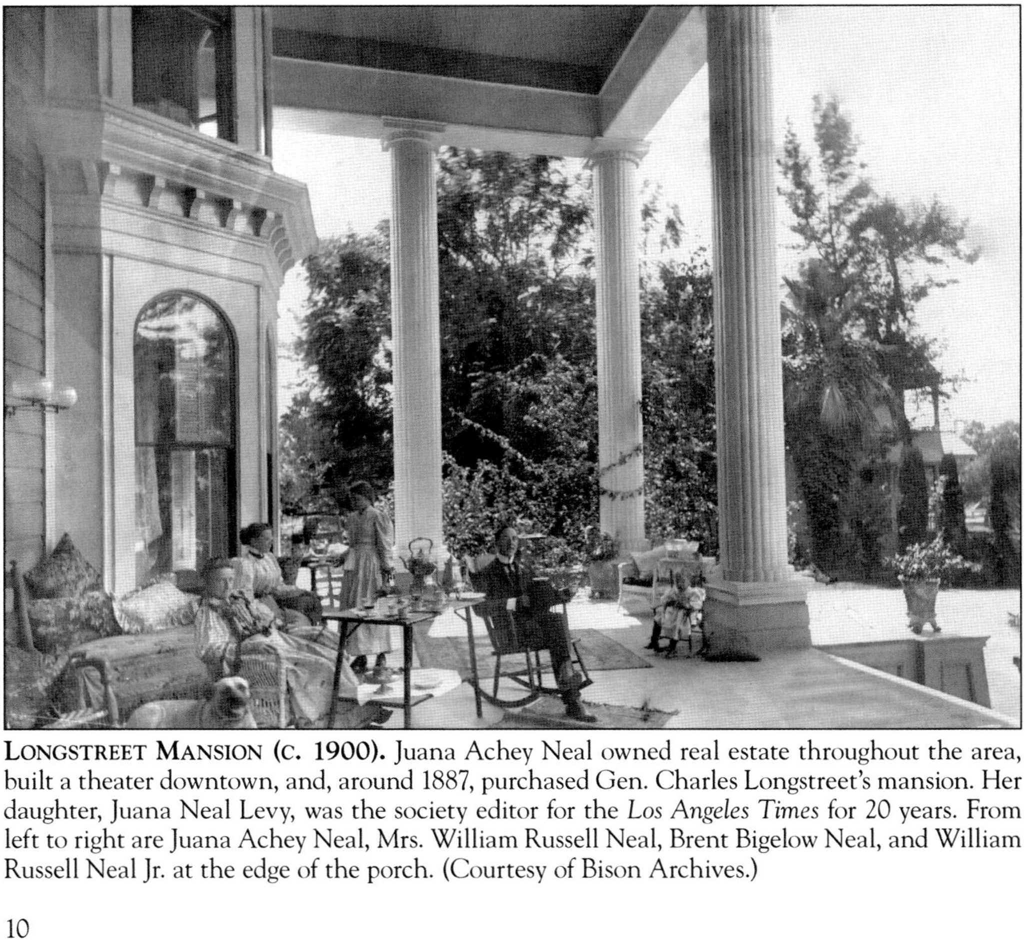

LONGSTREET MANSION (C. 1900). Juana Achey Neal owned real estate throughout the area, built a theater downtown, and, around 1887, purchased Gen. Charles Longstreet's mansion. Her daughter, Juana Neal Levy, was the society editor for the *Los Angeles Times* for 20 years. From left to right are Juana Achey Neal, Mrs. William Russell Neal, Brent Bigelow Neal, and William Russell Neal Jr. at the edge of the porch. (Courtesy of Bison Archives.)

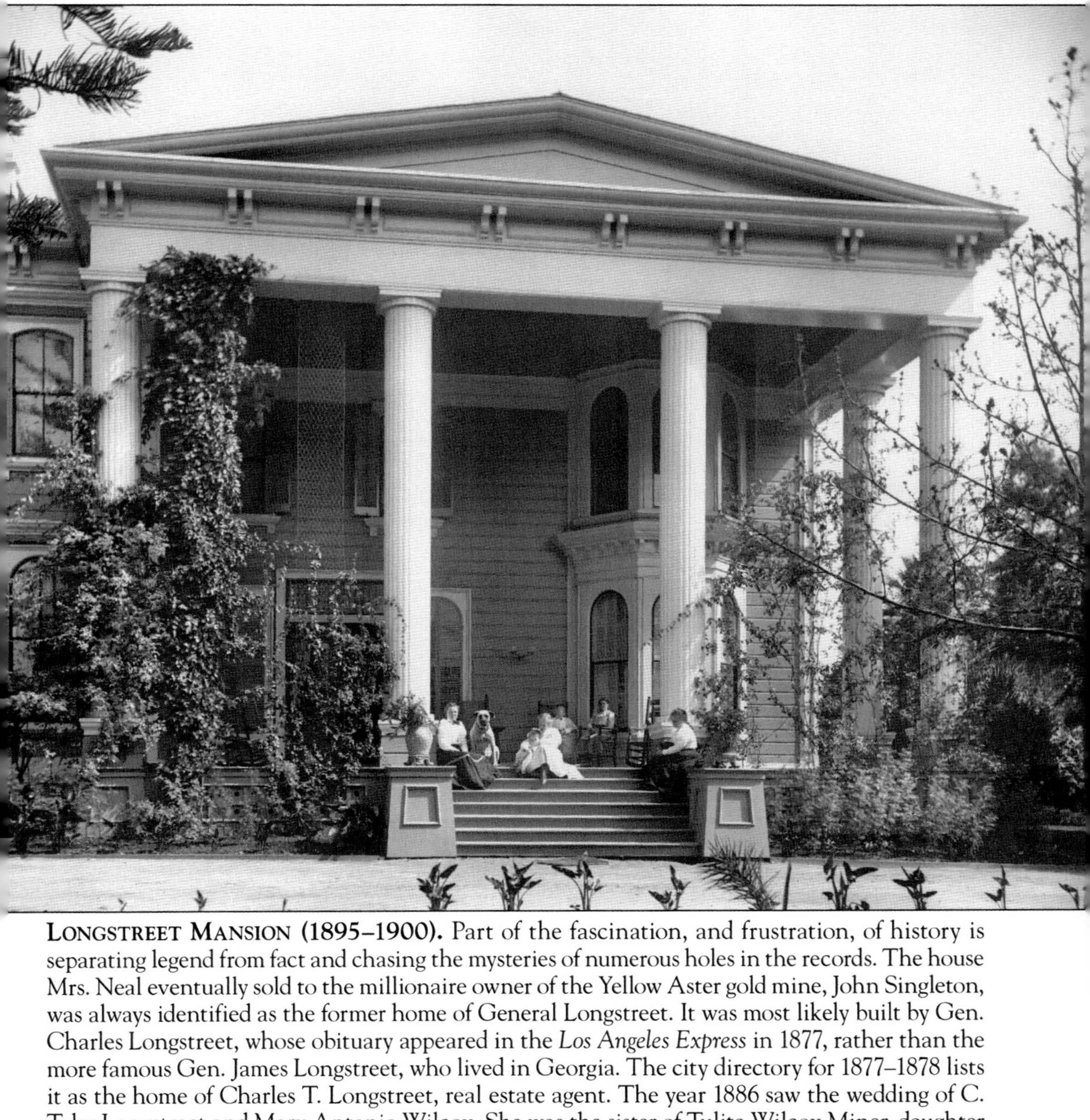

LONGSTREET MANSION (1895–1900). Part of the fascination, and frustration, of history is separating legend from fact and chasing the mysteries of numerous holes in the records. The house Mrs. Neal eventually sold to the millionaire owner of the Yellow Aster gold mine, John Singleton, was always identified as the former home of General Longstreet. It was most likely built by Gen. Charles Longstreet, whose obituary appeared in the *Los Angeles Express* in 1877, rather than the more famous Gen. James Longstreet, who lived in Georgia. The city directory for 1877–1878 lists it as the home of Charles T. Longstreet, real estate agent. The year 1886 saw the wedding of C. Tyler Longstreet and Mary Antonio Wilcox. She was the sister of Tulita Wilcox Miner, daughter of California's first steamship line operator and great-granddaughter of an early Spanish governor. In 1898, her divorce from Longstreet set a speed record for settlement. (Courtesy of University of Southern California, on behalf of the USC Specialized Libraries and Archival Collections.)

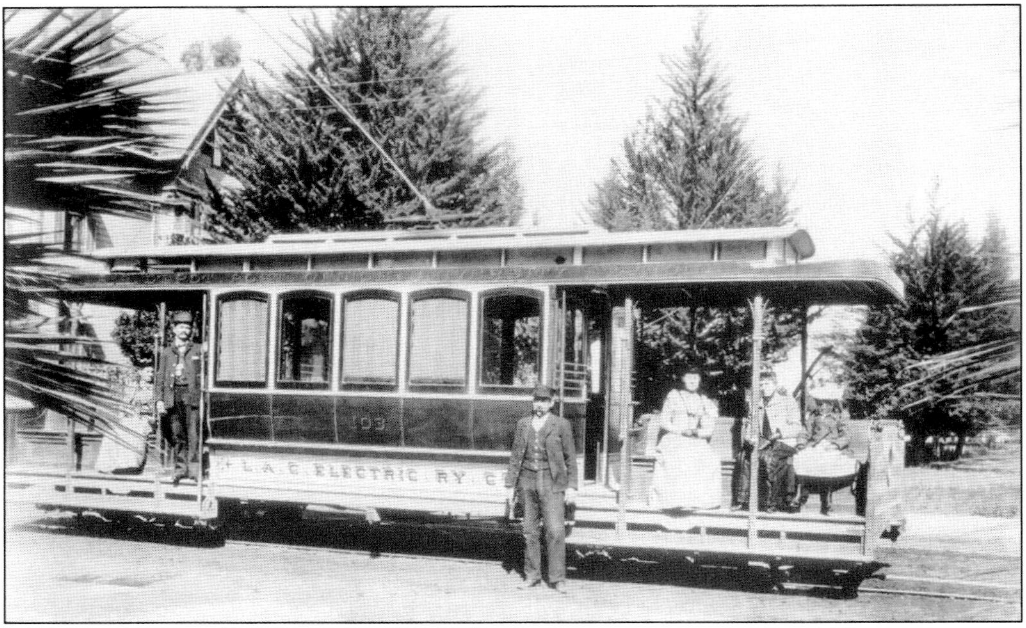

Electric Streetcar (c. 1894). West Adams has often been referred to as a "streetcar suburb." The convenient commute on electric streetcar lines running down Adams and Washington Boulevards was a selling point for those with businesses downtown. This early photograph was taken near Twenty-third and Scarff Streets, very near St. James Park. (Courtesy of the University of Southern California, on behalf of the USC Specialized Libraries and Archival Collections.)

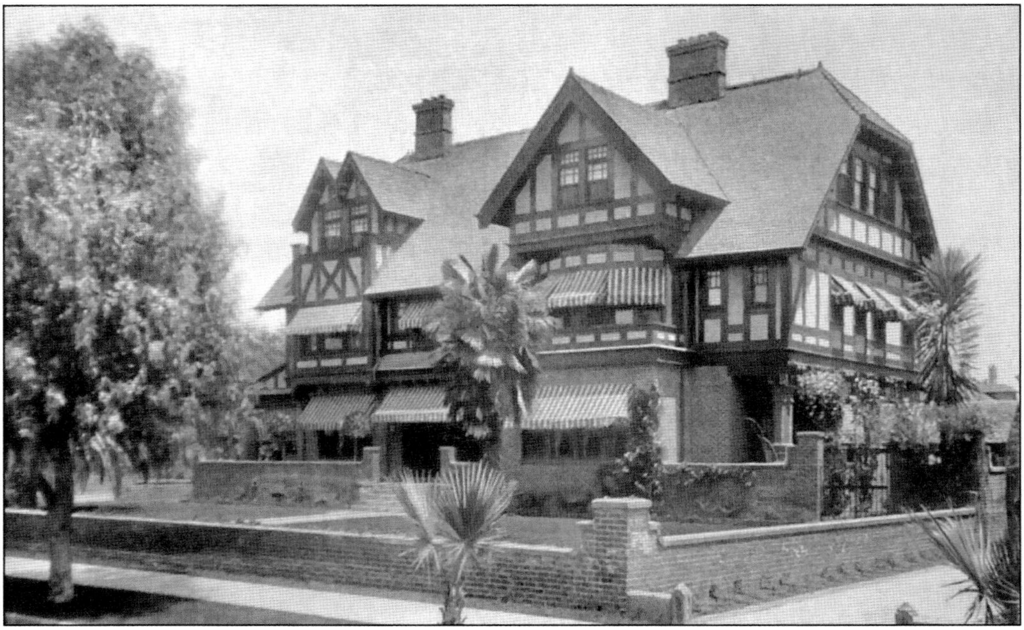

Solano Residence. Alfred Solano, a civil engineer, oversaw the subdivision of his family's 1866 land grant in Elysian Park. He and his wife, Ella, entertained frequently at their various Figueroa Street addresses, where horses were housed more elaborately than some middle-class families, and at their summer home, El Descanso. When Los Angeles organized a cavalry troop, Solano was among the first to join, attaining the rank of captain.

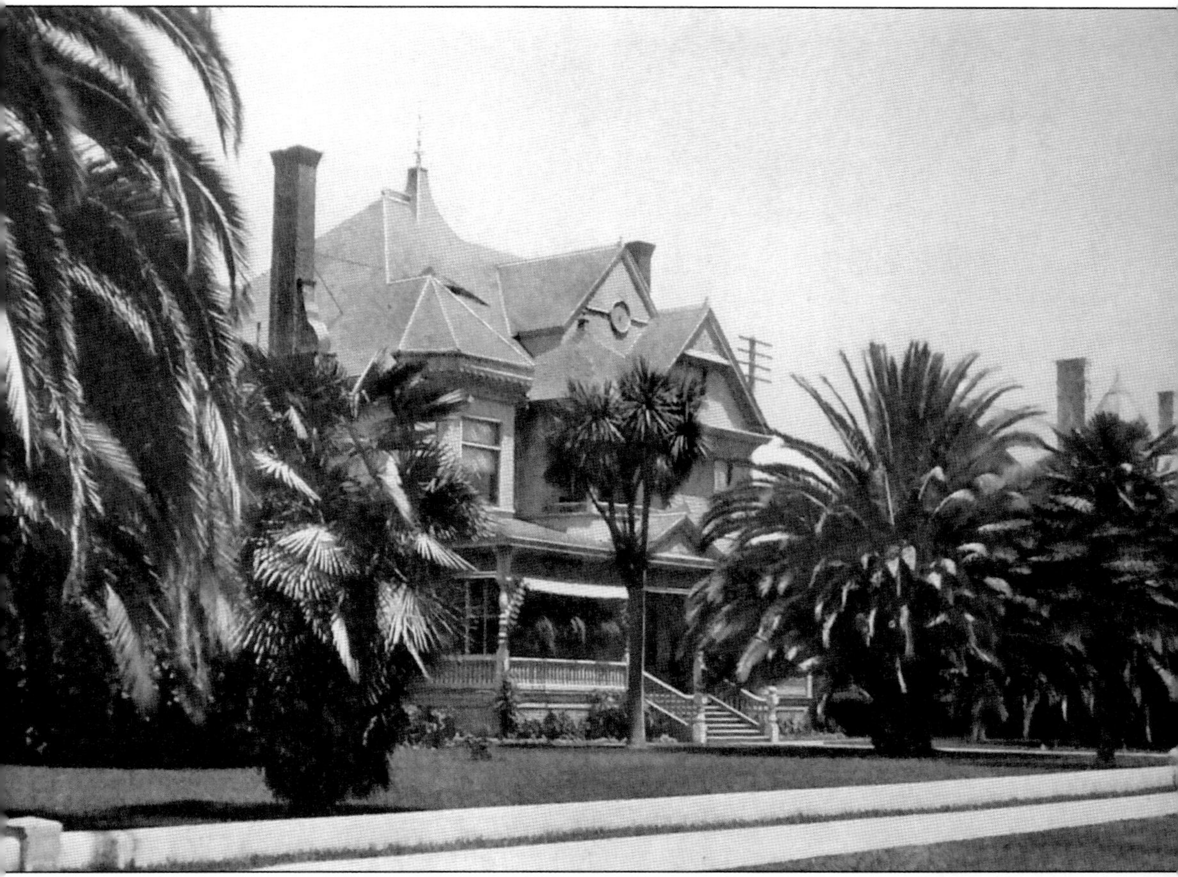

KLOKKE RESIDENCE. Maj. E. F. C. Klokke, an immigrant from Holland, was a veteran of the Civil War who was running a store in Chicago when that city's great fire destroyed his business. Perhaps to prevent such an event from happening again, he took the office of fire commissioner, later becoming police commissioner. In 1888, he brought his family to Los Angeles and built this home at the corner of Twenty-first Street and Figueroa Street. Klokke established himself as an orange grower and became a director of the chamber of commerce. He was such a promoter of California citrus that when he was held up outside his home in January 1902, with a gun held to his head, he offered the robbers some oranges. They declined the fruit, choosing to take $23 and a gold watch instead.

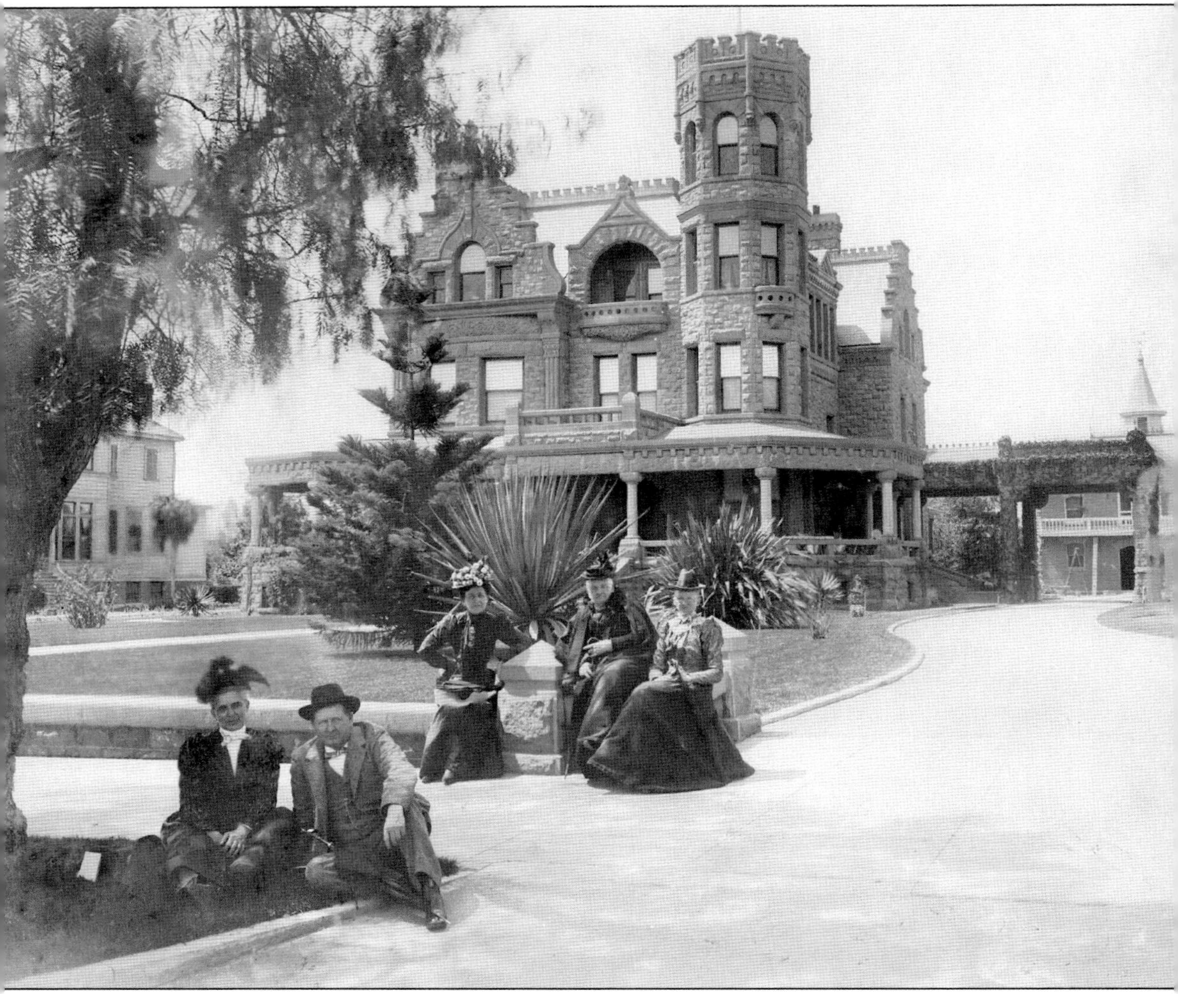

Stimson Residence (1908). When self-made lumber millionaire Thomas Stimson retired to Los Angeles in 1890, his first real estate investment was his home at 2421 South Figueroa Street, designed by Carrol A. Brown. In 1896, a blast awakened the neighborhood. An attempt had been made to blow up the Stimson mansion. The explosion did virtually no damage to the thick, red sandstone walls, so with the neighborhood abuzz, Stimson went back to bed. Frank Sabichi, returning from an evening out, spotted an intruder when he glanced out the window of the house next door. Although the explosion nearly knocked them off their feet, he and his brother took up the chase but lost the man when he hopped on a streetcar. A bit later, Harry Coyne, a private detective Stimson had hired to accompany his son to Mexico, came to see Stimson with a story of a notorious crook from Mexico who had come north with a burning desire to murder the family. Coyne was convicted in what seemed to be a bizarre attempt to extort money. (Courtesy of Bison Archives.)

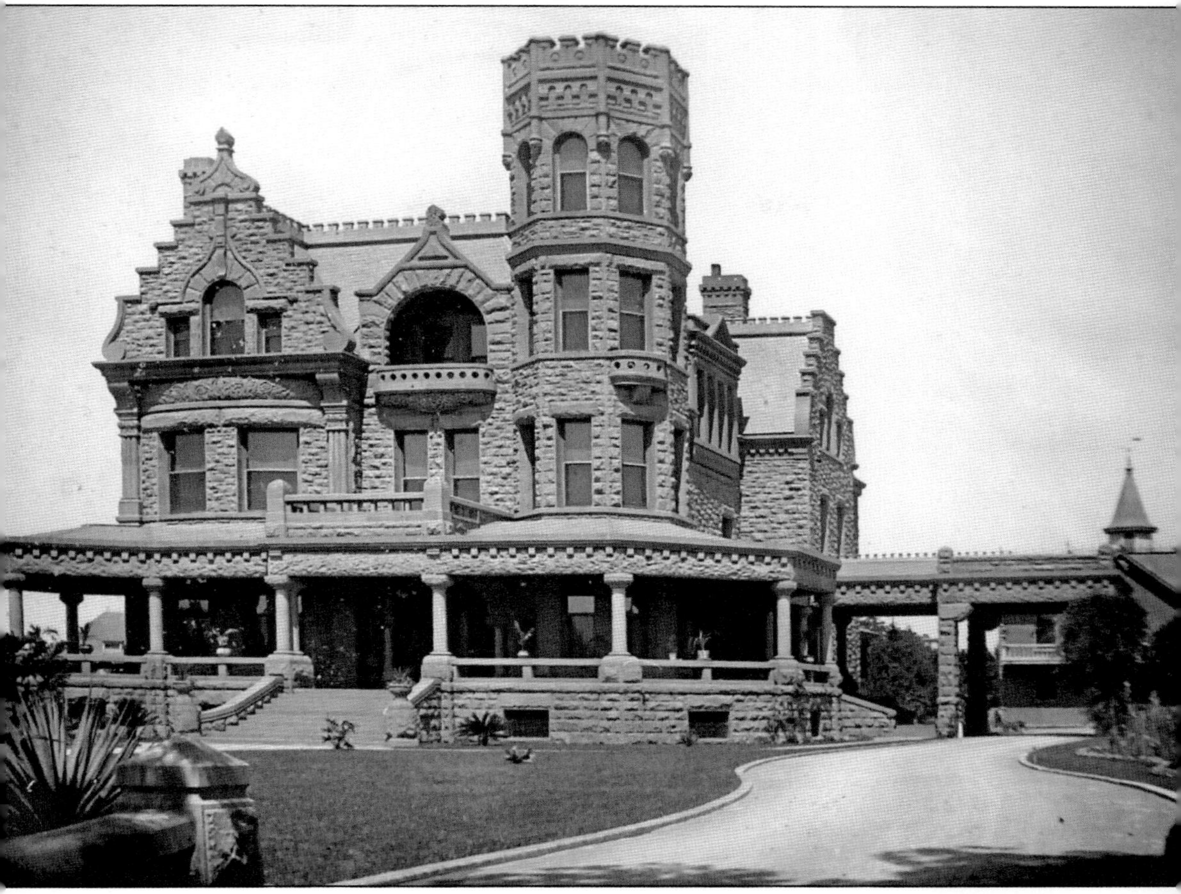

FINEST HOME IN LOS ANGELES. Stimson continued to invest heavily in real estate downtown, as well as in Seattle. By the time of his death in 1898, he had transferred much of his property in the Northwest to his sons, but his estate was still valued at $2.5 million. At a cost of $150,000, the Stimson house was considered the most expensive and the finest home in all of Los Angeles. It was certainly one of the most photographed. Postcards abound, and this glass slide was designed to be projected on a wall with a magic lantern. The Stimsons sold the house to Alfred Solano in 1907, and it was later purchased by Edward R. Maier. Following his death, it was a fraternity house until 1948. The Stimsons' parlor then became a chapel, and the boys of USC were replaced by nuns, when Estelle Doheny purchased the house for the use of the Sisters of St. Joseph of Carondelet.

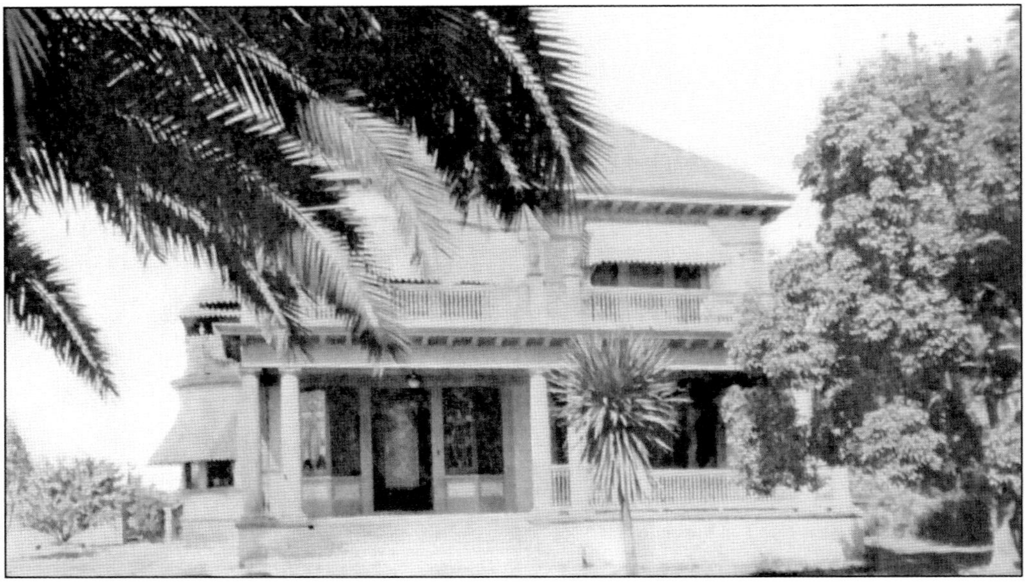

OFF RESIDENCE. J. W. A. Off lived a life so varied there should have been at least three of him. At his New Year's 1891 wedding to Blanche Bonebrake, the daughter of Maj. George H. Bonebrake, who founded a number of California banks, Off was identified as a popular druggist. By the time he died in 1946, his obituary read, "banker and pioneer real estate developer . . . one of the subdividers of Huntington Beach."

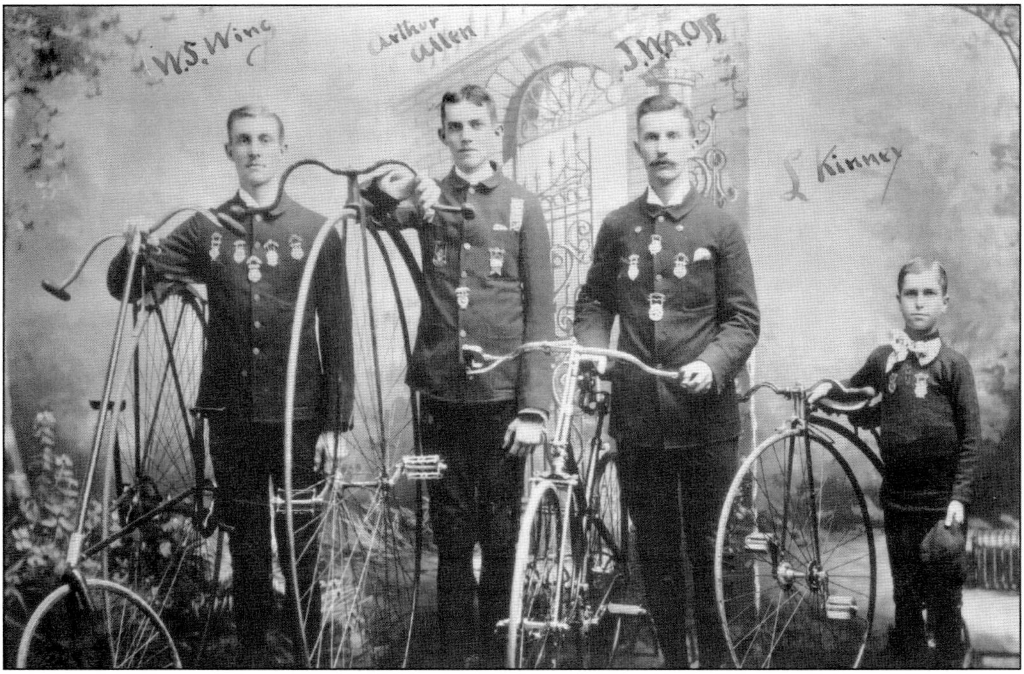

LOS ANGELES BICYCLE CHAMPIONS (C. 1888). It would appear that in his youth, John W. A. Off (third from the left) was also a cyclist and member of the Los Angeles Wheelmen. W. S. Wing (left) consistently won bicycle races, while Ledru B. Kinney (right) gained fame for fancy trick riding at the age of 11. (Courtesy of University of Southern California, on behalf of the USC Specialized Libraries and Archival Collections.)

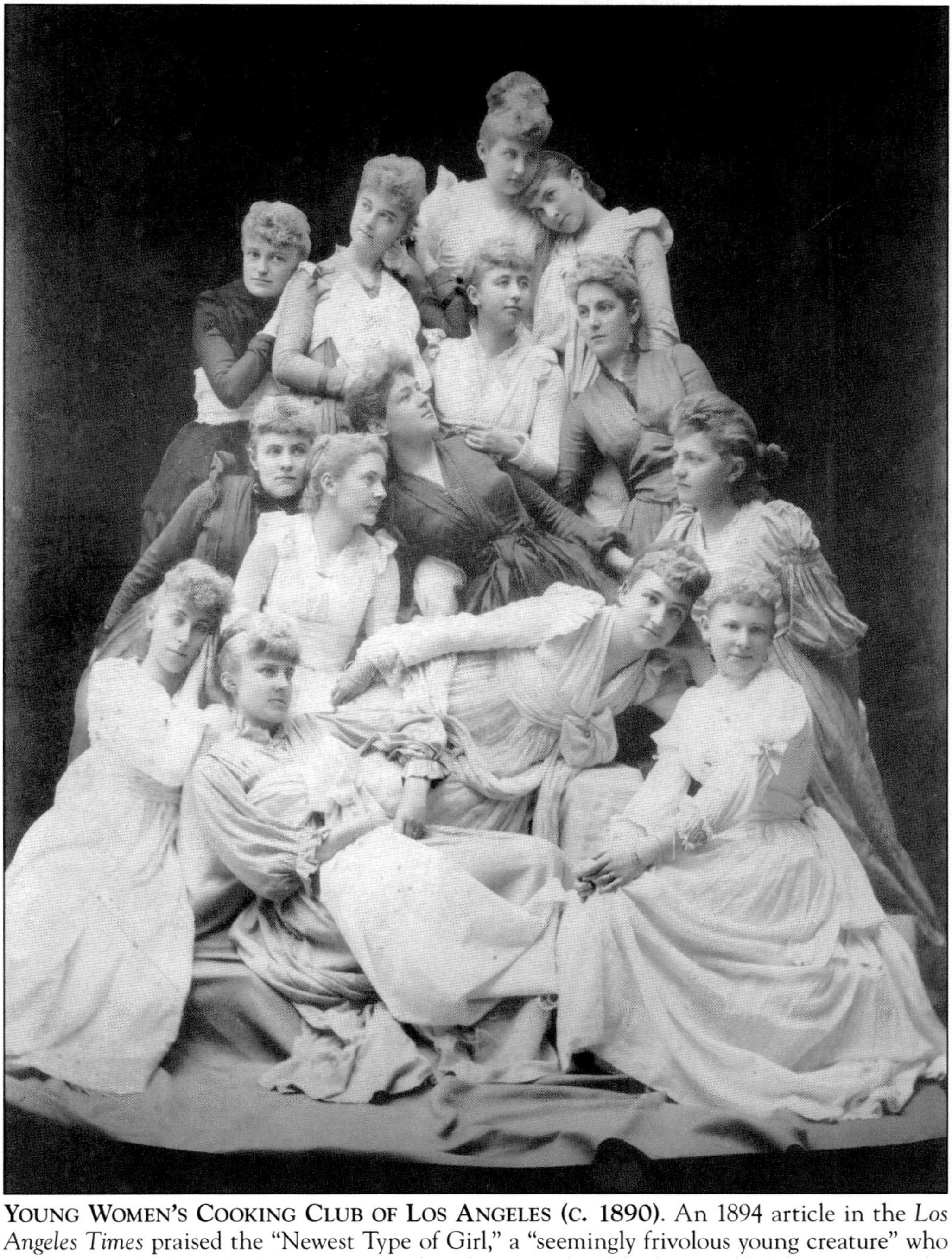

YOUNG WOMEN'S COOKING CLUB OF LOS ANGELES (C. 1890). An 1894 article in the *Los Angeles Times* praised the "Newest Type of Girl," a "seemingly frivolous young creature" who was beautifully dressed when encountered at the opera, but "the best and brightest among the rosebud garland of girls is the 'girl who does things'." Blanche Bonebrake Off and her friends were members of a cooking club, a very useful pursuit indeed. Parties at her home on Figueroa Street were inevitably described as delightful, whether the guests were her friends or playmates of her children, Georgia and John. The Offs' house was most likely designed by Carroll H. Brown, but the city has no building permit on file. (Courtesy of University of Southern California, on behalf of the USC Specialized Libraries and Archival Collections.)

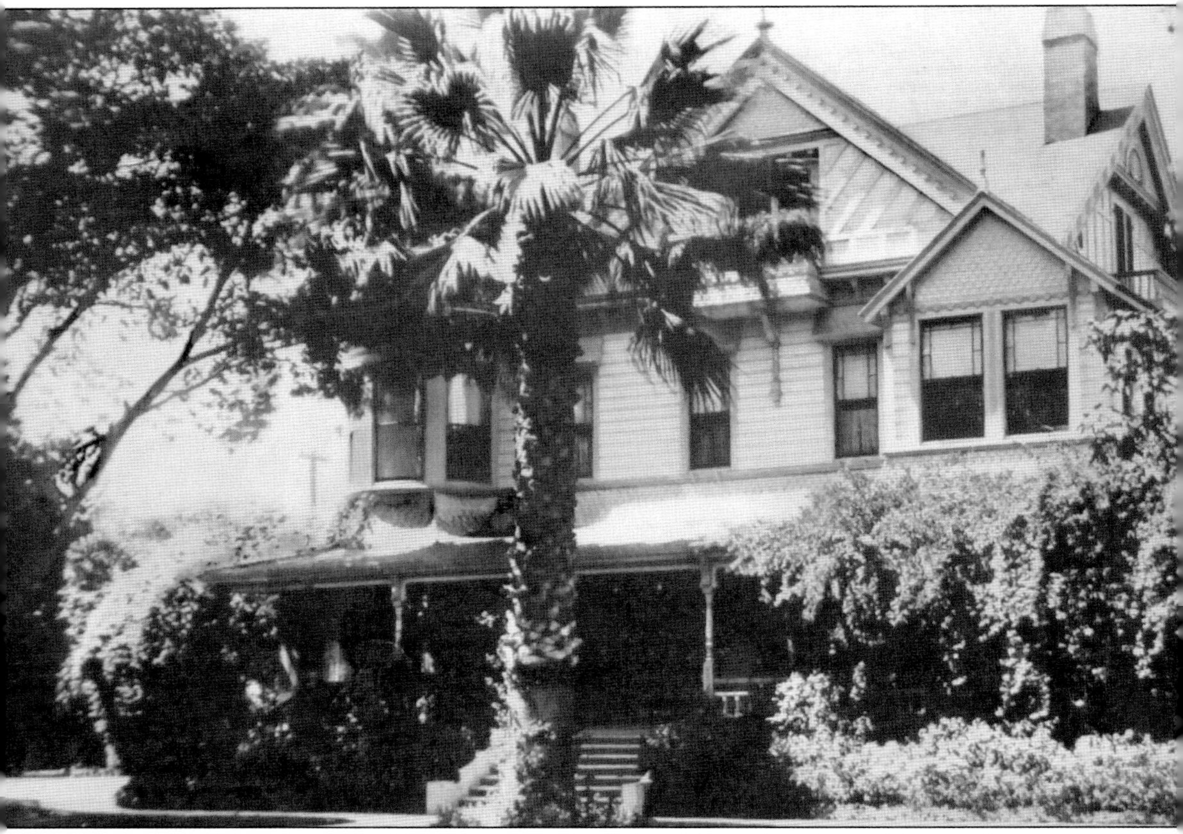

DORSEY RESIDENCE. Should one be tempted to believe that political scandals, sexual or monetary, are a modern phenomenon, consider the life of Stephen W. Dorsey. In 1881, the Star Route trials, based on a lucrative scheme for awarding postal routes by bribing postal officials, hit the courts, and the Republican senator from Arkansas was indicted. Dorsey was defended by noted orator Robert Ingersoll, who won acquittal for him. Later problems included lawsuits over various land deals. And sex? Within days of his wedding to his second wife, Laura Bigelow, he was sued by his private secretary. Mrs. Joralemon claimed she gave him "wifely love" and that he, in turn, gave her a house on Twenty-second Street. His friends insisted that the title to the house was in Dorsey's son's name and that Mrs. Joralemon was allowed to live there because he kindly felt she was in need of assistance. Somehow her name disappeared from the newspapers before the case came to trial, one of those mysteries that sometimes transpires in the vicinity of wealthy and powerful men.

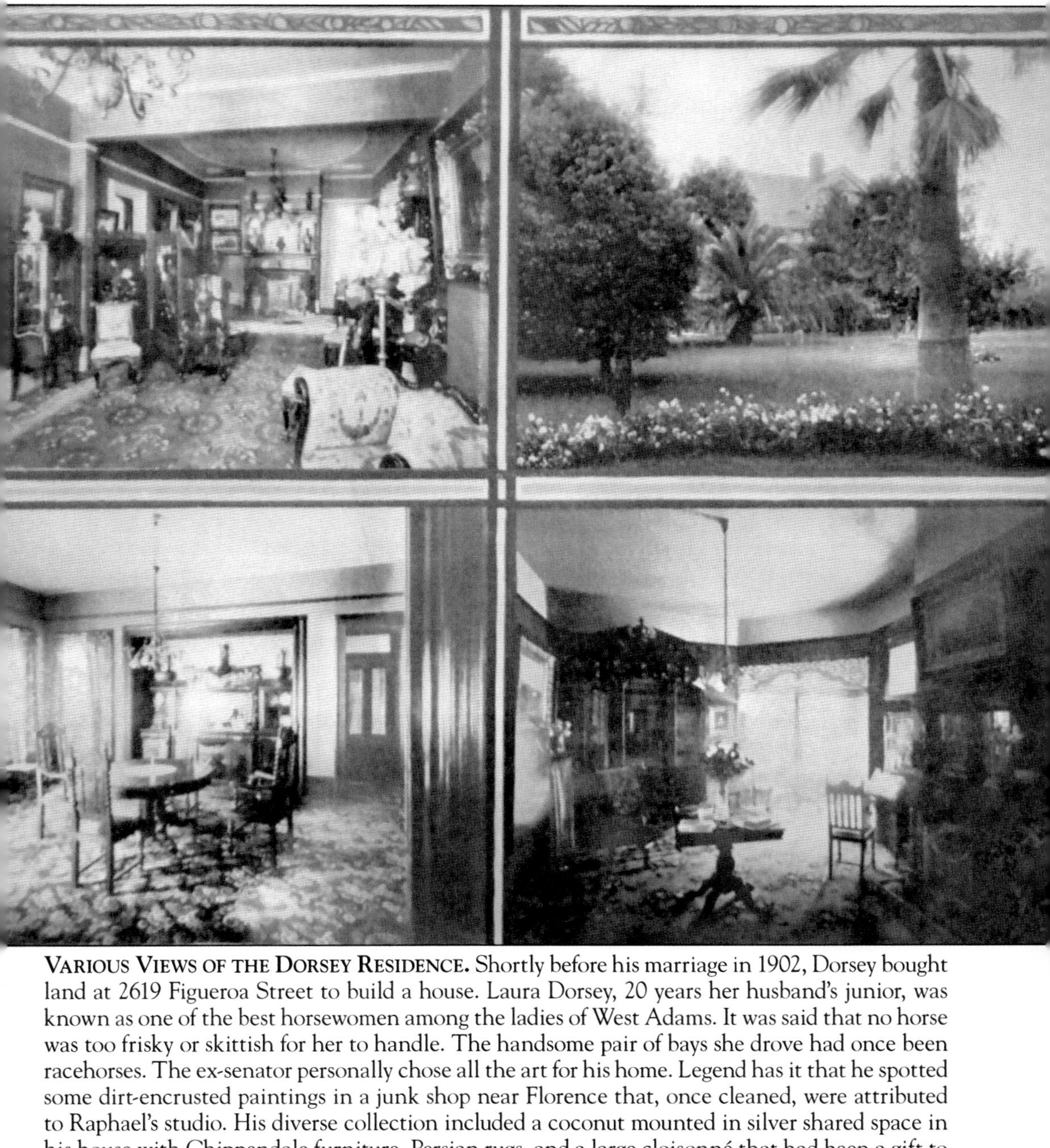

VARIOUS VIEWS OF THE DORSEY RESIDENCE. Shortly before his marriage in 1902, Dorsey bought land at 2619 Figueroa Street to build a house. Laura Dorsey, 20 years her husband's junior, was known as one of the best horsewomen among the ladies of West Adams. It was said that no horse was too frisky or skittish for her to handle. The handsome pair of bays she drove had once been racehorses. The ex-senator personally chose all the art for his home. Legend has it that he spotted some dirt-encrusted paintings in a junk shop near Florence that, once cleaned, were attributed to Raphael's studio. His diverse collection included a coconut mounted in silver shared space in his house with Chippendale furniture, Persian rugs, and a large cloisonné that had been a gift to Admiral Perry from the Emperor of Japan.

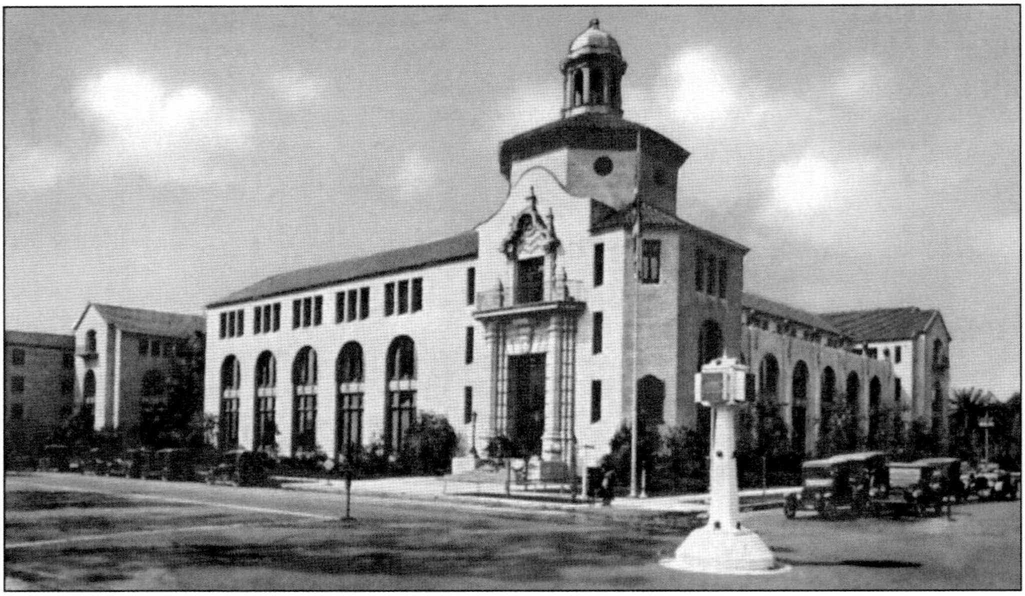

AUTO CLUB. The Automobile Club of Southern California was founded in 1900, shortly after the first car arrived in the city. By 1921, when Hunt and Burns designed their building, it was the largest auto club in the country. Traffic problems began about the same time. The *Los Angeles Times* claimed the "electric traffic lighthouse," installed at Adams Boulevard and Figueroa Street in 1924, did "everything but hand out tickets."

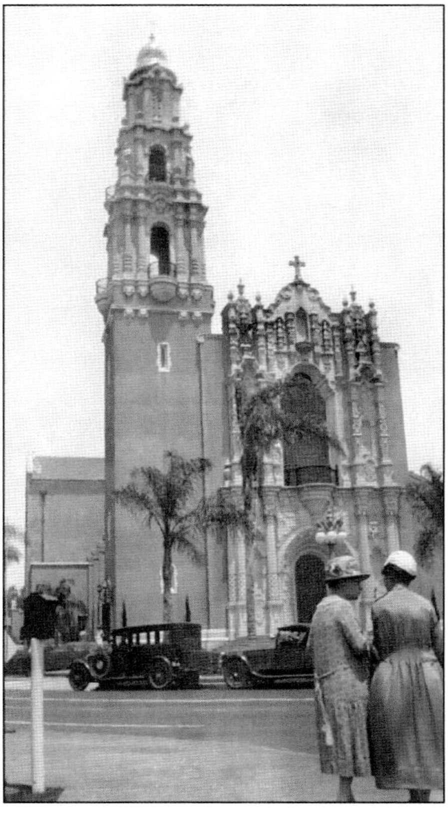

ST. VINCENT DE PAUL CATHOLIC CHURCH FROM FIGUEROA STREETS. Although architect Albert C. Martin described his design as Spanish in style, St. Vincent's Church looks more like a frothy wedding cake for a bride hoping for happily ever after. Built in 1925 with money from the Doheny family, the church is sited at a 45-degree angle to the corner of Adams Boulevard and Figueroa Street.

ST. VINCENT DE PAUL CATHOLIC CHURCH FROM ADAMS BOULEVARD. On October 24, 1930, the *Los Angeles Times* rhapsodized, "While dew-drenched doves rested on the beams of the towering crosses and fluttered about the head and feet of the stone-carved Christ in the hush of yesterday's dawn, magnificent St. Vincent's Church received its consecration." A procession blessed every part of the building before five simultaneous masses were celebrated in each of the chapels.

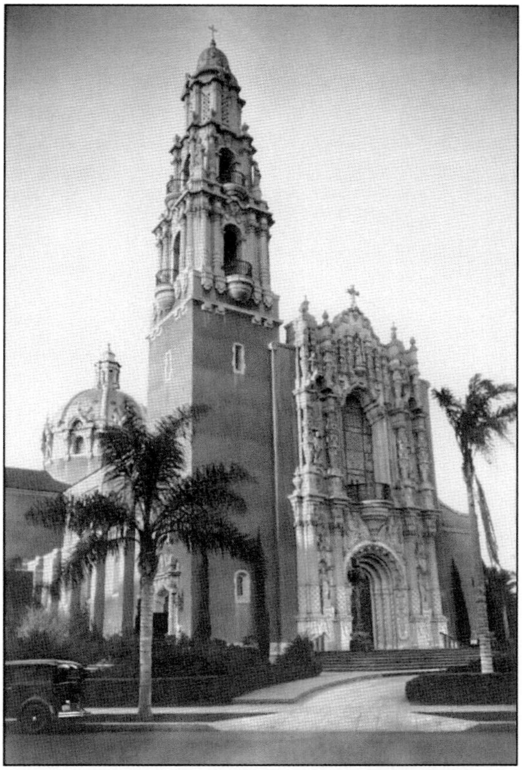

ST. VINCENT DE PAUL CATHOLIC CHURCH ALTAR. The elaborate Spanish-style high altar by Angelo Lualdi, a gift from Mr. and Mrs. Doheny in memory of his son, Edward L. Doheny Jr., was shipped from Boston in several sections. The building was most likely based on a historic church in Mexico, although interior designer Ralph A. Cram claimed, "The church was copied from no existing structure . . . in any respect."

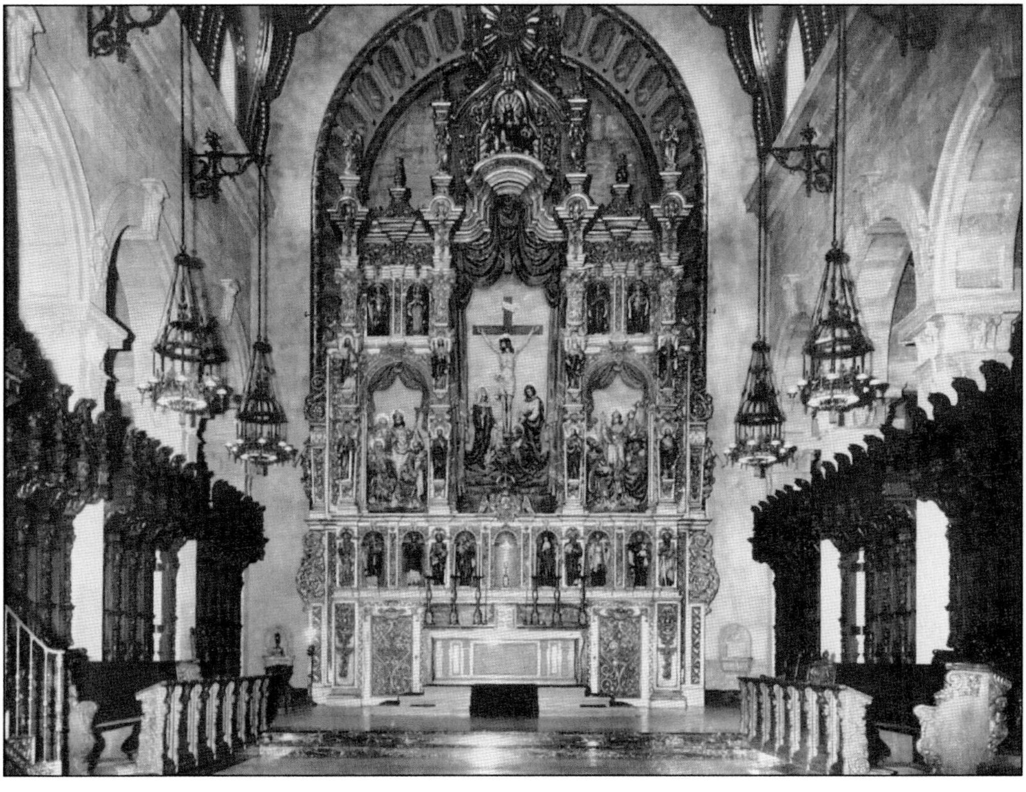

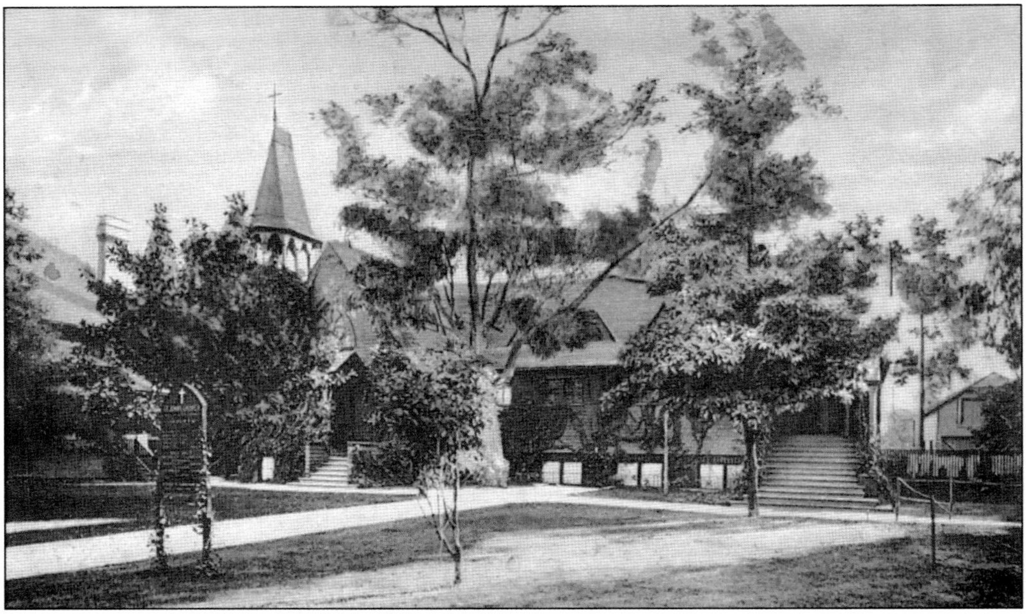

St. John's Episcopal Church (1896). The Episcopal parish that served West Adams grew so rapidly from the time it was organized in 1890 that by 1896 worshippers had to be turned away for lack of space. W. H. Willcox drew up plans for a frame structure that would seat 800, but by 1923, it, too, was outgrown and replaced by a larger sanctuary at the corner of Adams Boulevard and Figueroa Street.

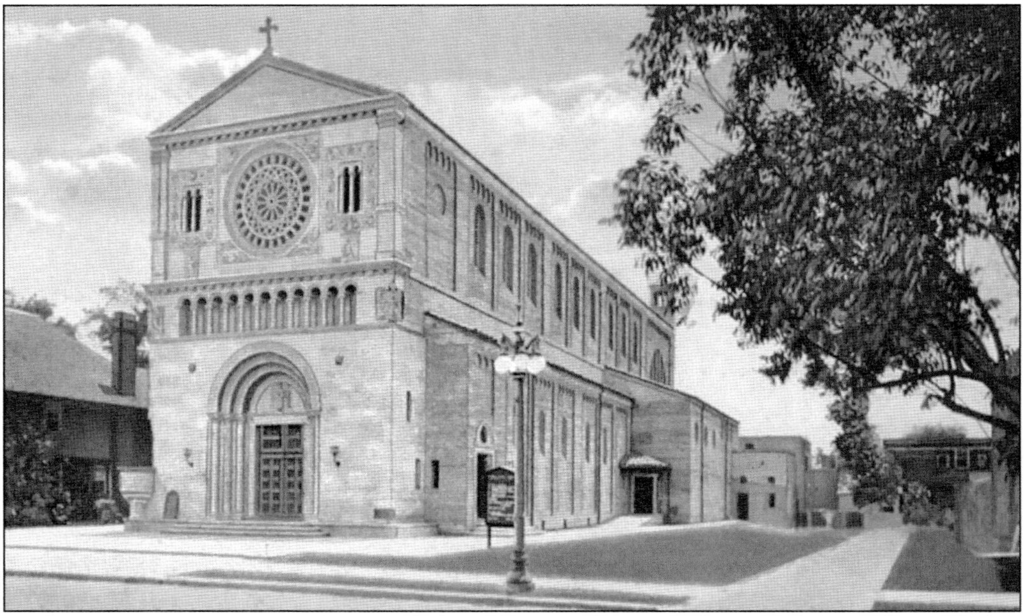

St. John's Episcopal Church. Architects Pierpont and Walter S. Davis were selected by a jury of architects, and in 1923, two cornerstones were laid for the Italian Romanesque building. Bringing together the old and the new, one stone was taken from the structure that the congregation had outgrown, while the new symbolized the future. The building, which seats 1,100, has recently become a procathedral for the Diocese of Los Angeles.

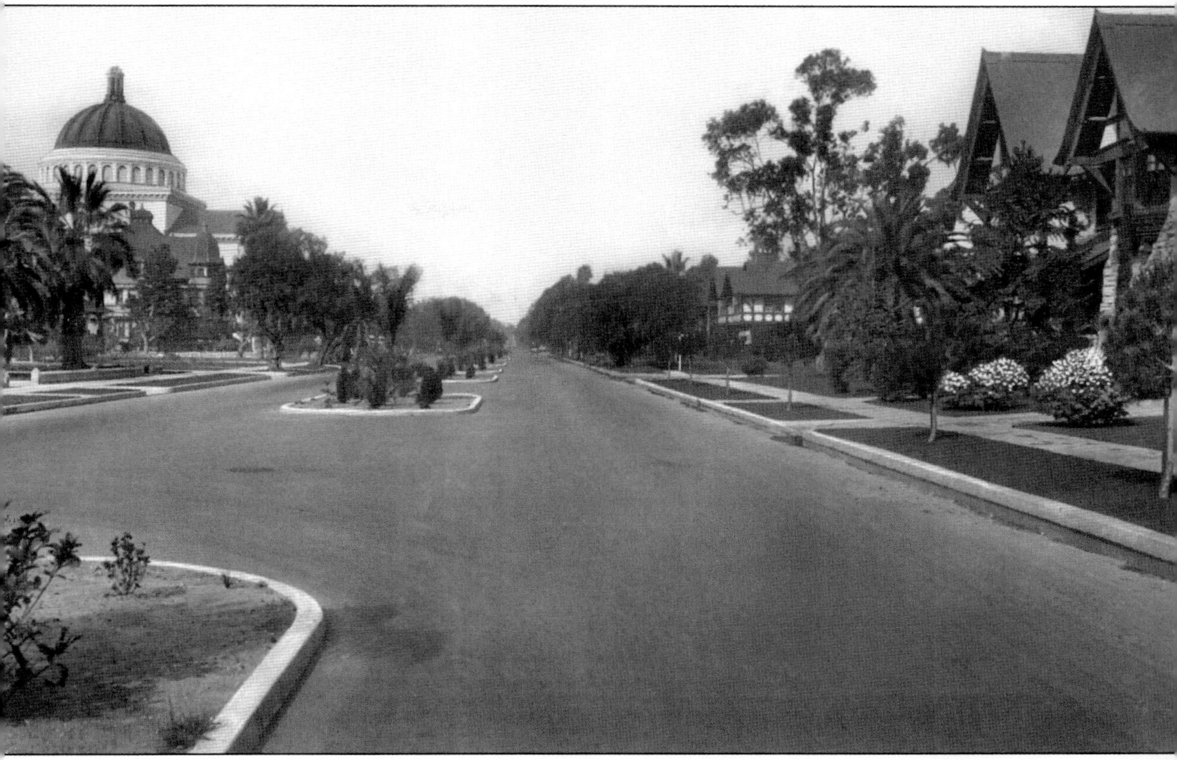

ADAMS STREET WEST OF FIGUEROA. This photograph is of Adams Boulevard in its prime. There is virtually no traffic, and a wide landscaped median runs down the center. On the right is the Ezra Stimson mansion, and rising above the trees only a short distance away is the Second Church of Christ, Scientist, one of many large religious structures throughout the neighborhood. Ezra Stimson was a son of lumber millionaire Thomas Stimson, whose castle stood on nearby Figueroa Street. The Ezra Stimsons endured one of the most sensational divorce cases in Los Angeles when Annie Stimson caught her husband having an affair with a "plump" nurse, Virginia Gay. To protect herself financially, Annie Stimson removed nearly $1 million worth of securities from her husband's safe deposit box and filed for divorce. The marriage was dissolved. Annie Stimson got to keep most of the securities, and Ezra Stimson got to keep Virginia Gay, whom he later married. (Courtesy of Rory Cunningham.)

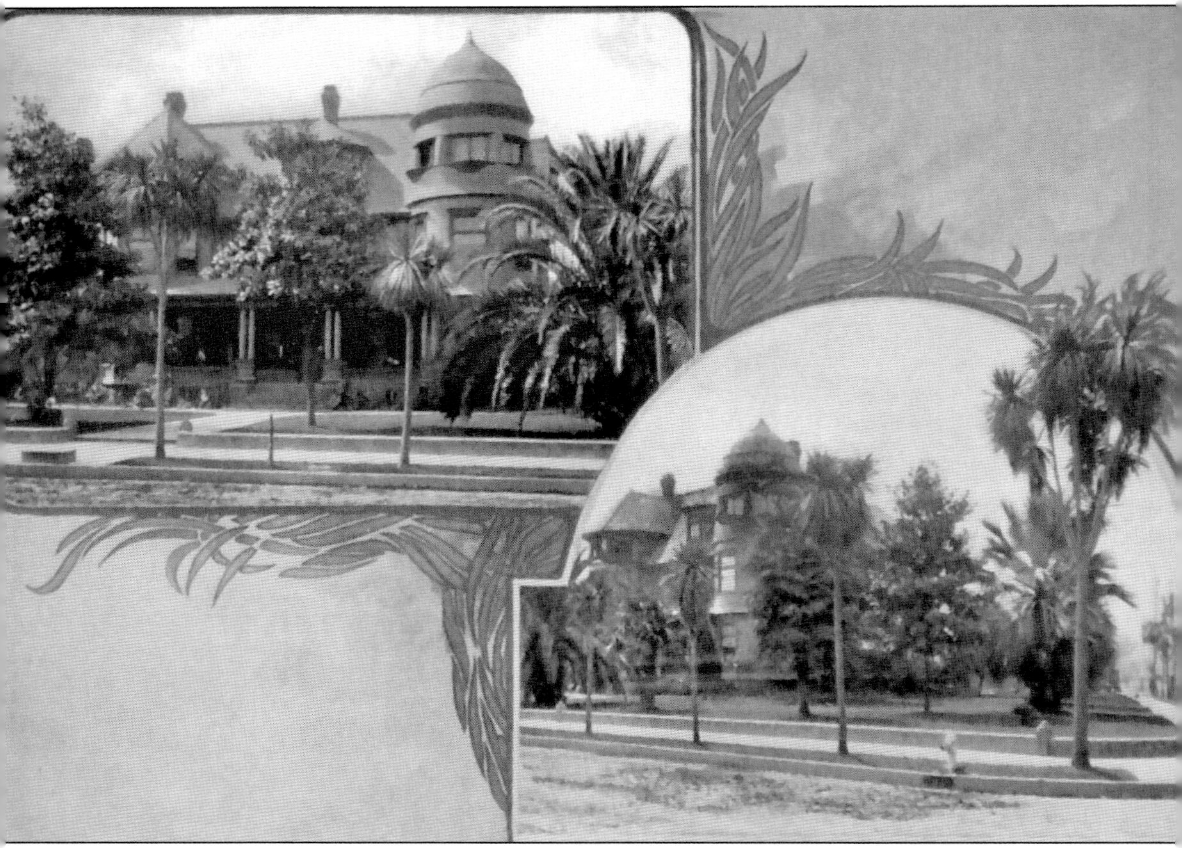

BURKHARD (GRADY) RESIDENCE. Joseph Burkhard made a fortune in Oregon shipping pork to Alaska and the Orient. In 1890, upon reaching New York after touring Europe with his family, Burkhard tossed a coin to decide whether to return to Portland or settle his family in Los Angeles. Five times in a row the coin landed the same, so the family headed for California. During the financial panic of 1893, he built this impressive mansion for only $12,000 at 938 West Twenty-eighth Street, then known as "Banker's Row." The living room alone extended 42 feet, and the house was full of expensive woodwork. After only seven years, Burkhard more than doubled his money when he sold it to Dr. James B. Grady of Maine, who used the home only in the winter. Eventually the house became a fraternity for nearby USC. In 1929, it was nearly destroyed by fire, and 20 years later, it finally succumbed to the wrecking ball so that the Phi Sigma Kappas could build a new home for themselves.

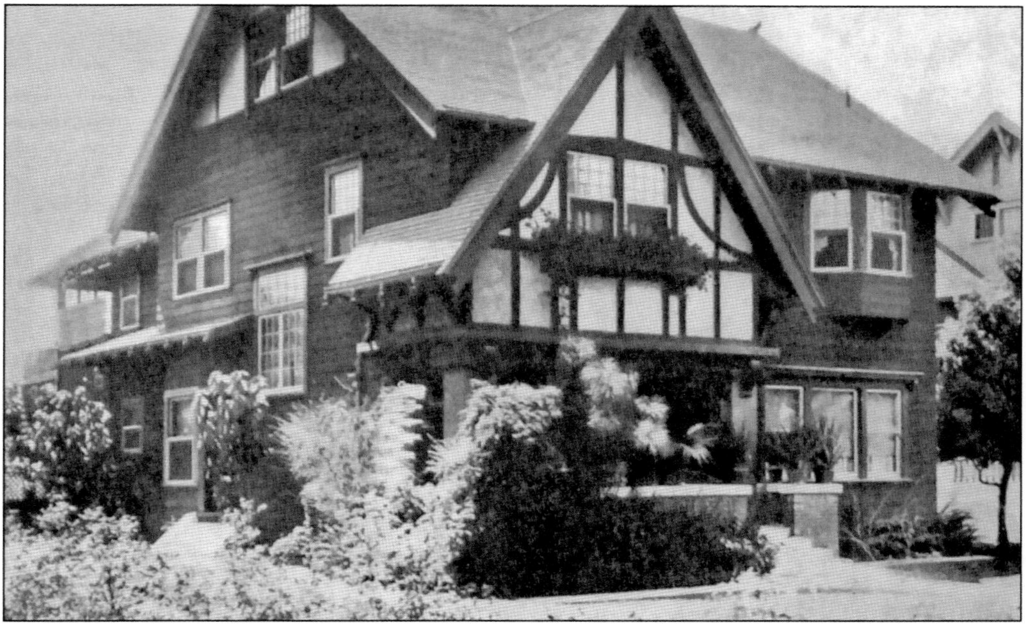

Byrne Residence. This striking home, at 630 West Twenty-eighth Street, belonged to John Joseph Byrne, assistant passenger traffic manager for the Santa Fe Railroad. A self-made man, Byrne started as an office boy for the Great Western Railway in 1873 and through the decades worked for many major railroads. The large front porch of his English arts and crafts–style home functions as an outdoor room, ideal for beautiful California weather.

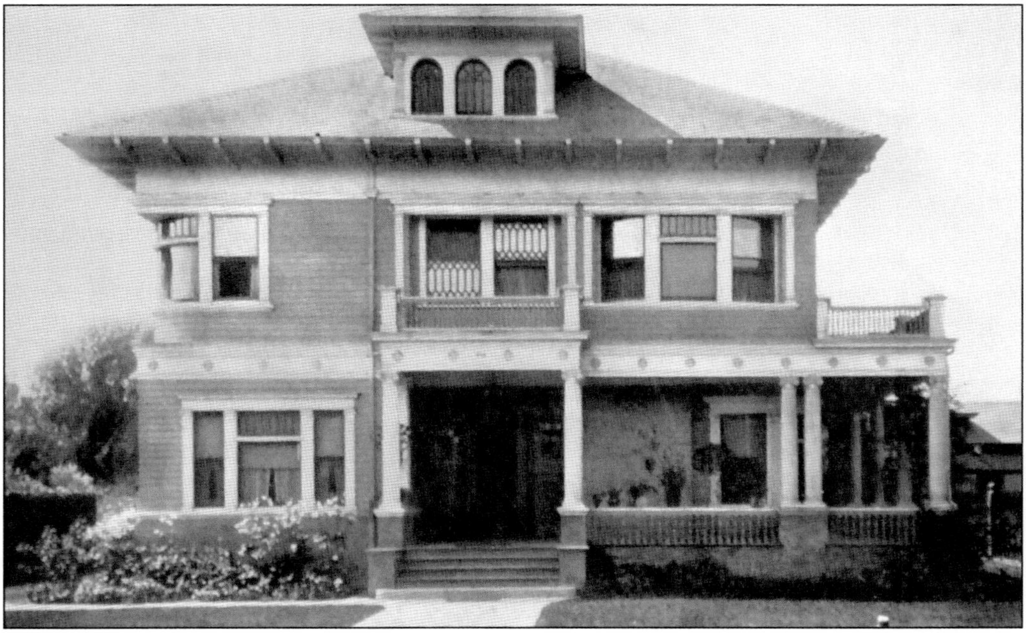

Elliott Residence. This home at 914 West Twenty-eighth Street is modest, considering it was the home of the president of First National Bank, John M. Elliott. A native of South Carolina, Elliott served in the Confederate army before coming to Los Angeles, where he founded the first fruit cannery in the city. His wife, Alice, was credited as a founder of Good Samaritan Hospital before her death in 1902.

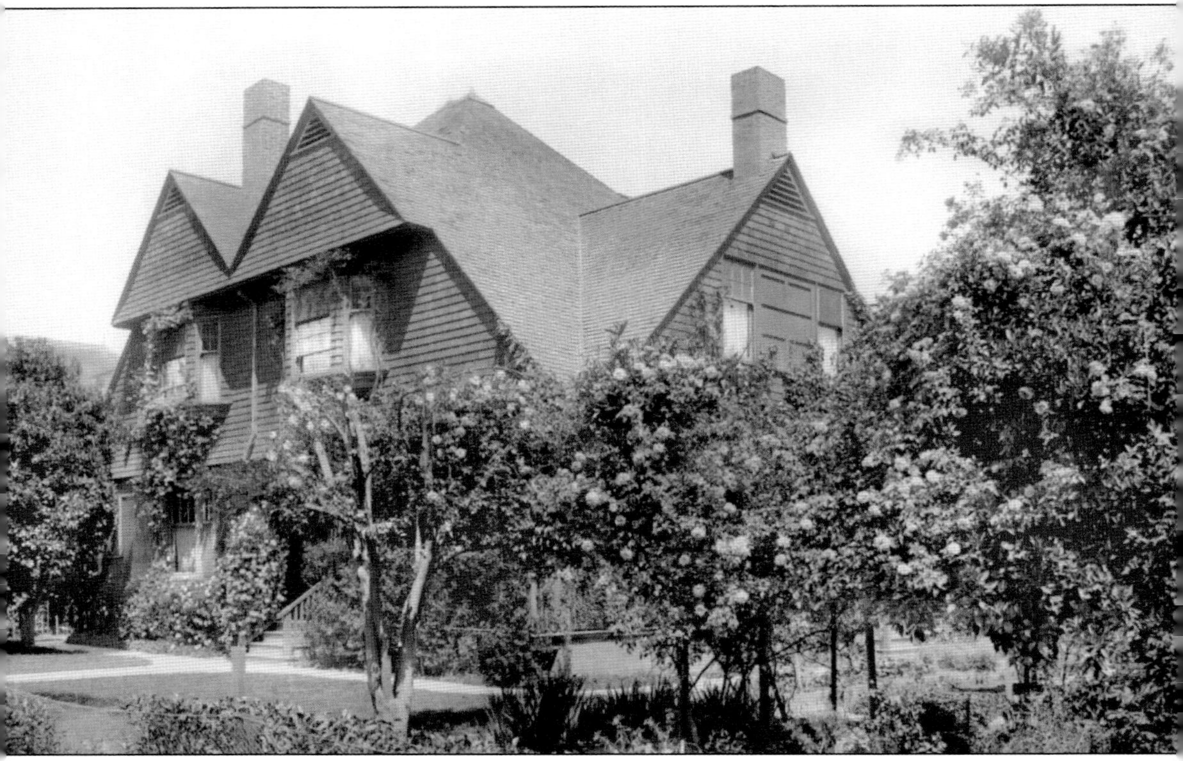

FREMONT RESIDENCE (C. 1896). This rose-embowered cottage at 1107 West Twenty-eighth Street was built from funds raised by the women of Los Angeles so that Jessie Benton Fremont might have a retirement home. The widow of the first Republican presidential candidate had been left destitute. Her father, Sen. Thomas Hart Benton, disapproved of her choice of husband, but the beautiful 16 year old eventually persuaded him to accept John Charles Fremont. In 1842, her husband led an expedition to the Rocky Mountains and later to Oregon. Her writing skills made his topographical reports into something that fascinated readers. When Fremont lost to James Buchanan in 1856, she believed that, had he been elected, there would have been no Civil War. She claimed, "My father and my husband had the intellect and purpose, and I have gone along in the wake of their big ships," but by the time she was buried in Rosedale Cemetery, she had her own place in the heart of the country. (Courtesy of the University of Southern California, on behalf of the USC Specialized Libraries and Archival Collections.)

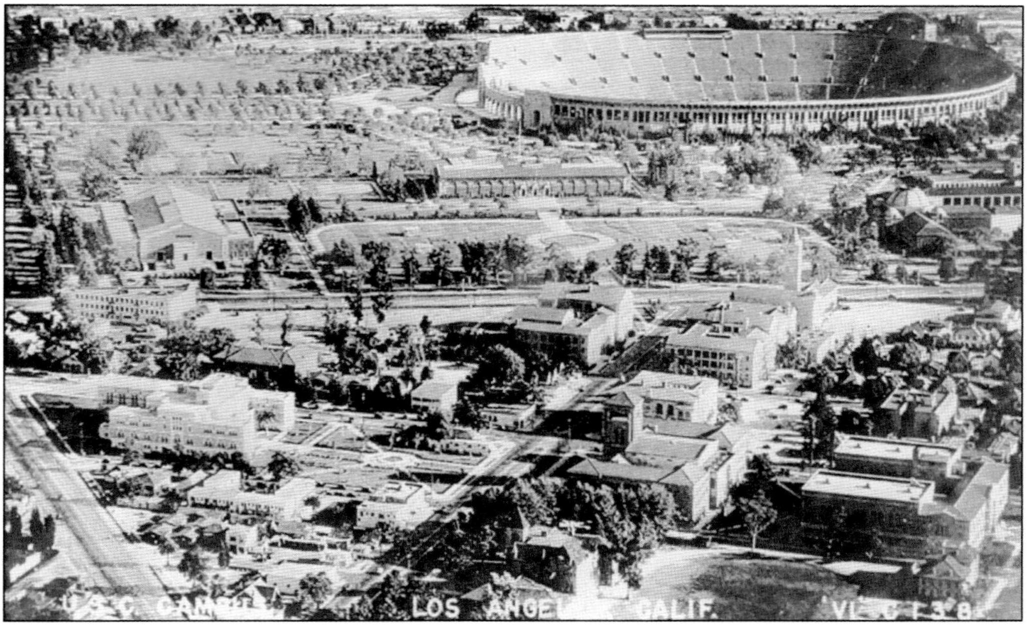

COLISEUM. In 1921, a convenient gravel pit provided an already excavated location for the Los Angeles Memorial Coliseum (named to honor the dead of World War I) designed by John Parkinson. For the X Olympiad in 1932–1933, Parkinson and Parkinson enlarged the stadium and added the Olympic Arch to honor athletes marching behind 39 flags. The torch was relit in 1984, when Los Angeles again hosted the Olympic Games.

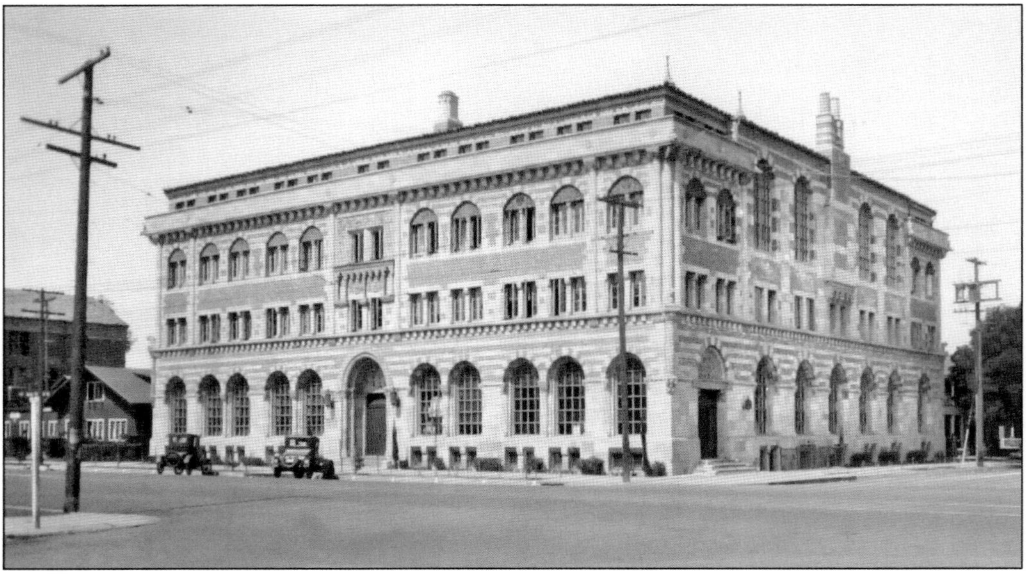

USC STUDENT UNION. As the University of Southern California expanded, a Student Union building was needed. Designed by John Parkinson and Donald B. Parkinson, it was built in an Italian-Romanesque style, in brick with terra-cotta decorations. The four stories, with full basement, included the student store, barbershop and hair salon, offices for the student body elected officials, coffee shop, and the offices of the campus newspaper, the *Daily Trojan*.

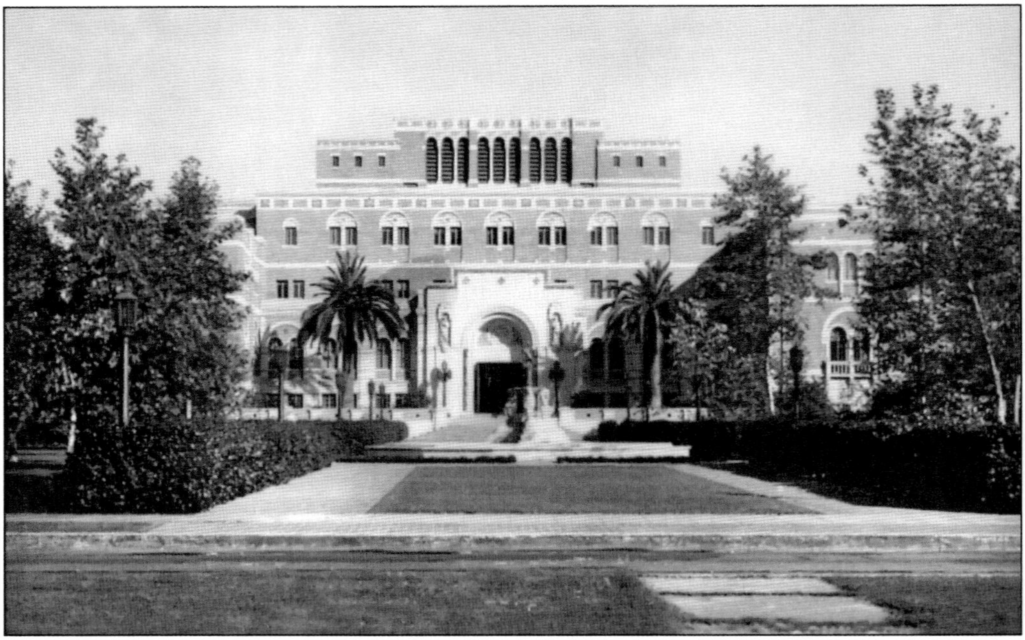

E. L. DOHENY MEMORIAL LIBRARY. In a fast-growing city, there were ample opportunities for the wealthy to be charitable benefactors. Edward L. Doheny Sr. erected the E. L. Doheny Memorial Library at the University of Southern California to honor his late son, a graduate and a trustee of the university. Designed by the Boston firm Cram and Ferguson, it was completed in 1932 after less than two years of construction.

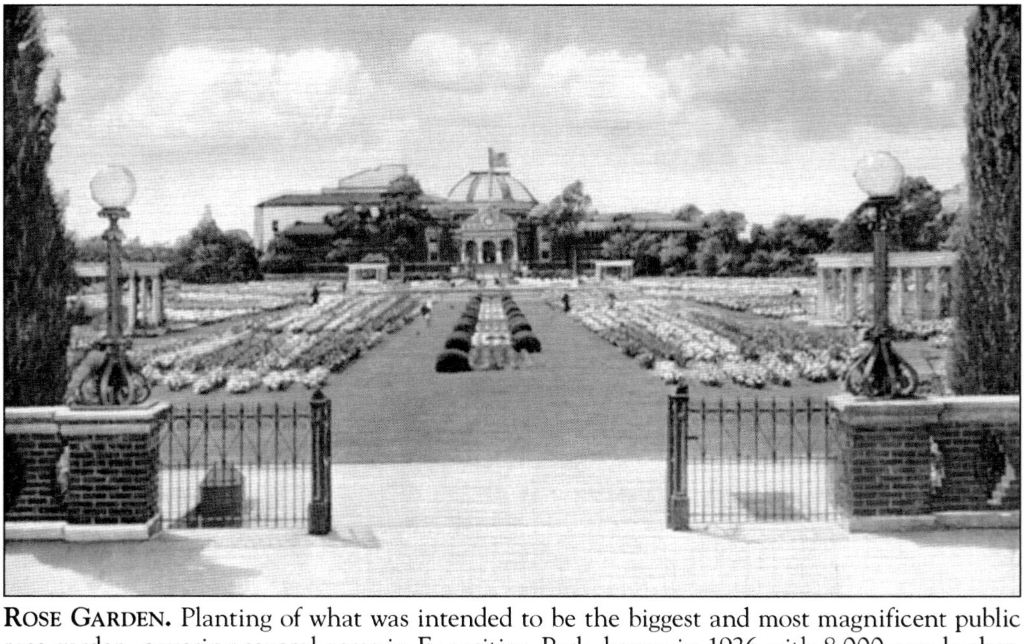

ROSE GARDEN. Planting of what was intended to be the biggest and most magnificent public rose garden, covering several acres in Exposition Park, began in 1926 with 8,000 rose bushes. The flowers still bloom profusely in the sunken garden. In the background is the Natural History Museum, designed by Hudson and Munsell in 1910.

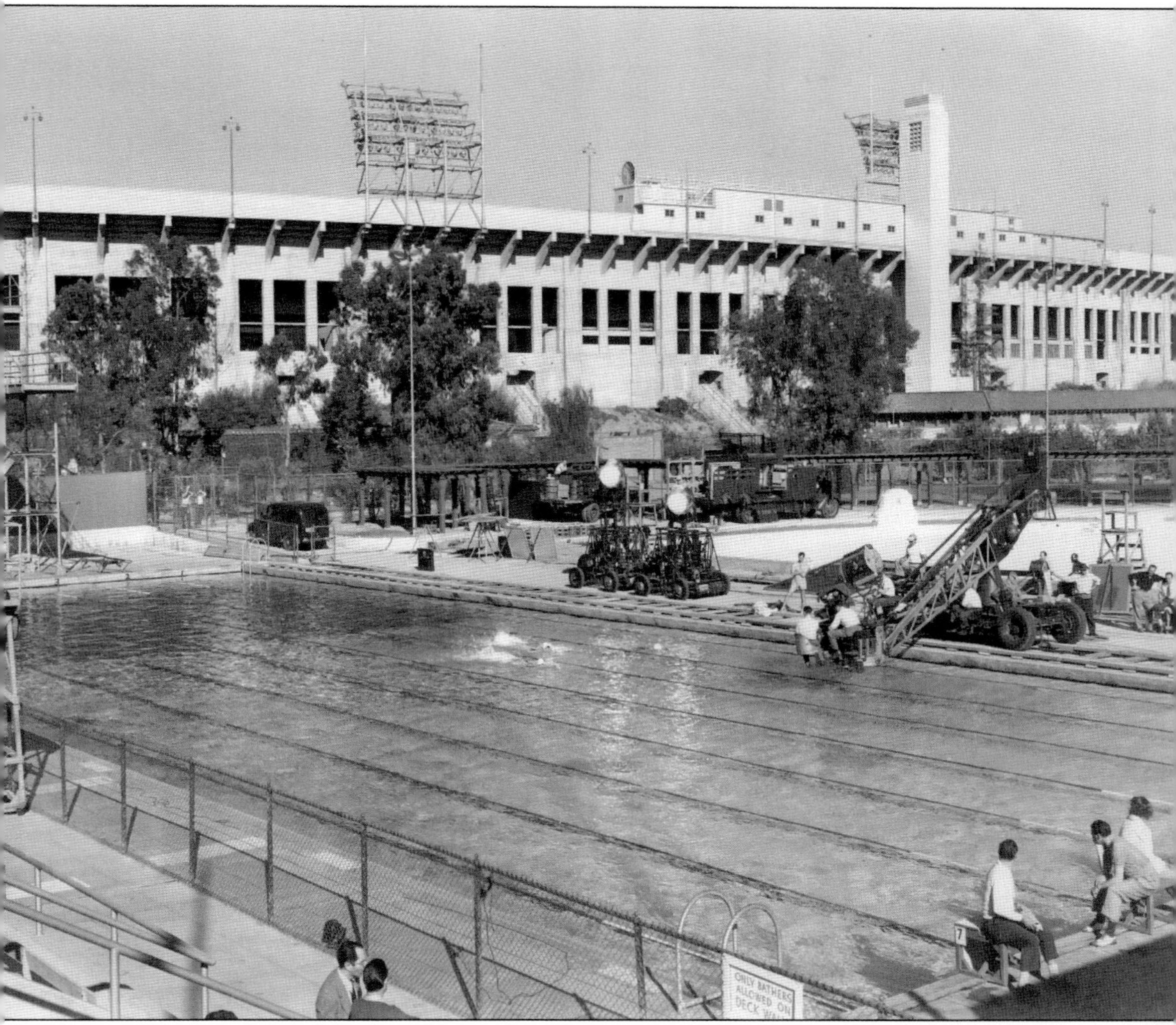

SWIM STADIUM (C. 1949). "This is where I came in," said Esther Williams of the Coliseum pool while filming *Neptune's Daughter* in 1949. "Hollywood's Mermaid" was too young to compete in the 1933 Olympics when the swim stadium made its debut, but other participants swam to stardom. During the games, a young athlete named Buster Crabbe broke the swimming record set by Johnny Weissmuller; later Crabbe replaced him as Hollywood's Tarzan. Moviemakers may have missed another sure thing by not signing several female divers who caused a minor scandal in their low-cut bathing suits. Olympic officials insisted they change into something more modest before being allowed to compete. It did not seem to deter them, as all three women won medals.

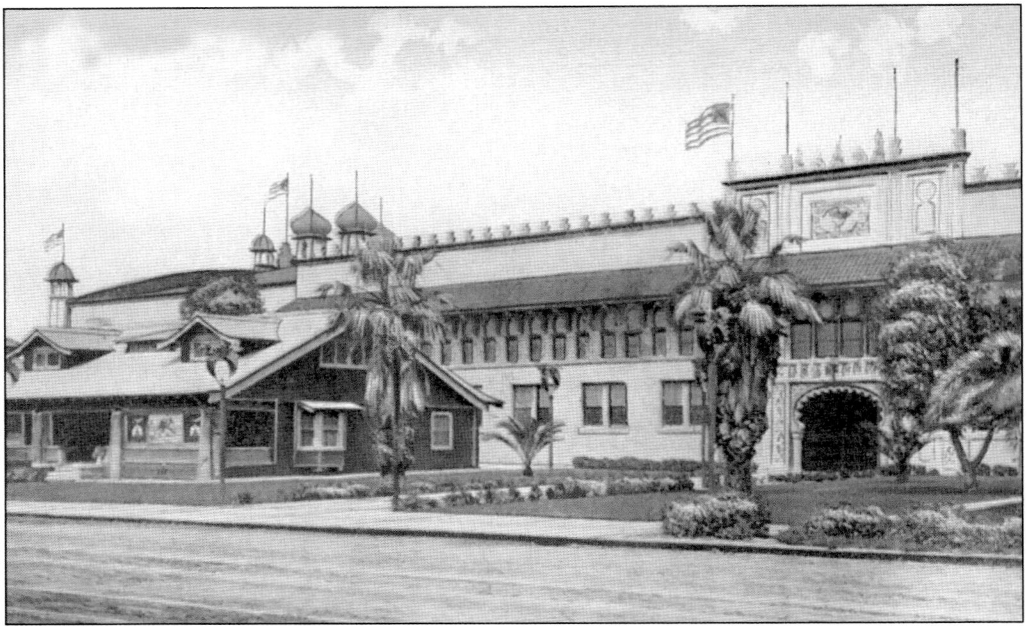

Shrine Auditorium. In 1907, the press raved that the new Shrine Auditorium was larger than Madison Square Garden. It was said that when the Boston Shriners saw the skeleton rising, they scrapped their original plans and adopted the Los Angeles design. The theater was enthusiastically described as Moorish and absolutely fireproof. Unfortunately, the last claim proved false. Twelve years later, it burned to the ground. (Courtesy of Rory Cunningham.)

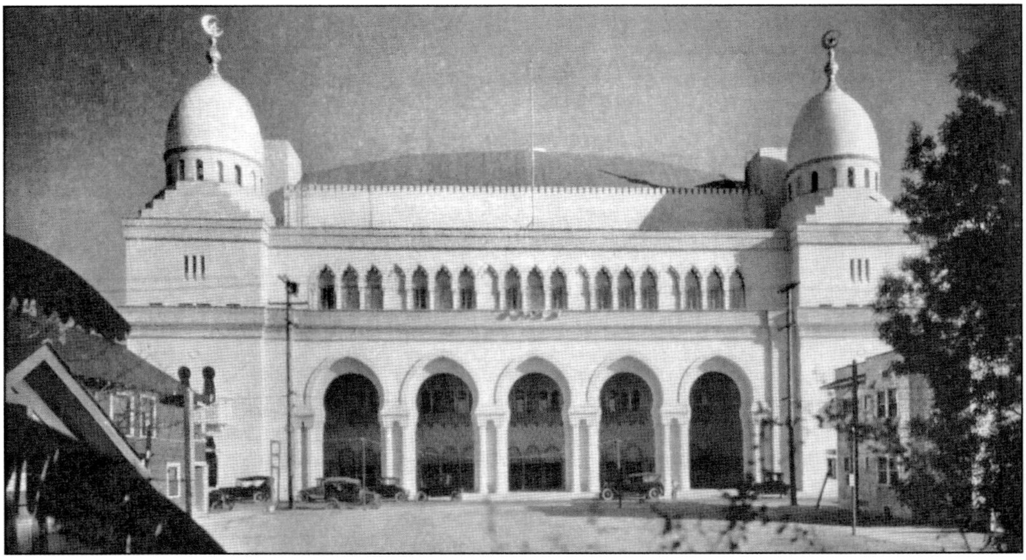

Bigger Shrine Auditorium. The ashes had not even cooled when plans got underway to build a bigger, more elaborate theater at the same site on West Jefferson Boulevard and Royal Street. The Al Malaikah Auditorium Association chose John C. Austin and A. M. Edelman as architects, with G. Albert Landsbaugh as collaborating architect. A draftsman, working one of his first jobs, went on to fame of his own. His name was Paul Williams.

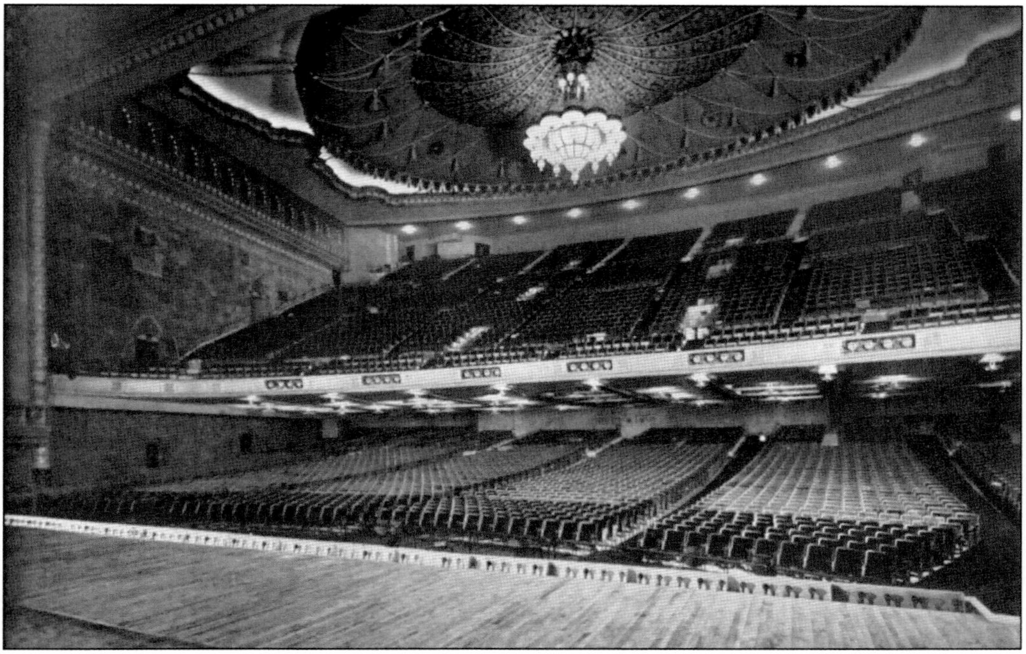

SHRINE OF "RARE BEAUTY." The *Los Angeles Times* particularly noted the "rare beauty" of the ceiling "with its jeweled tapestry-suspended canopy, reflecting the blue of an Arabian sky, and in the center a magnificent chandelier" glowing with "virtually every tint and color known to man." The 22-foot-high chandelier weighs approximately 5 tons.

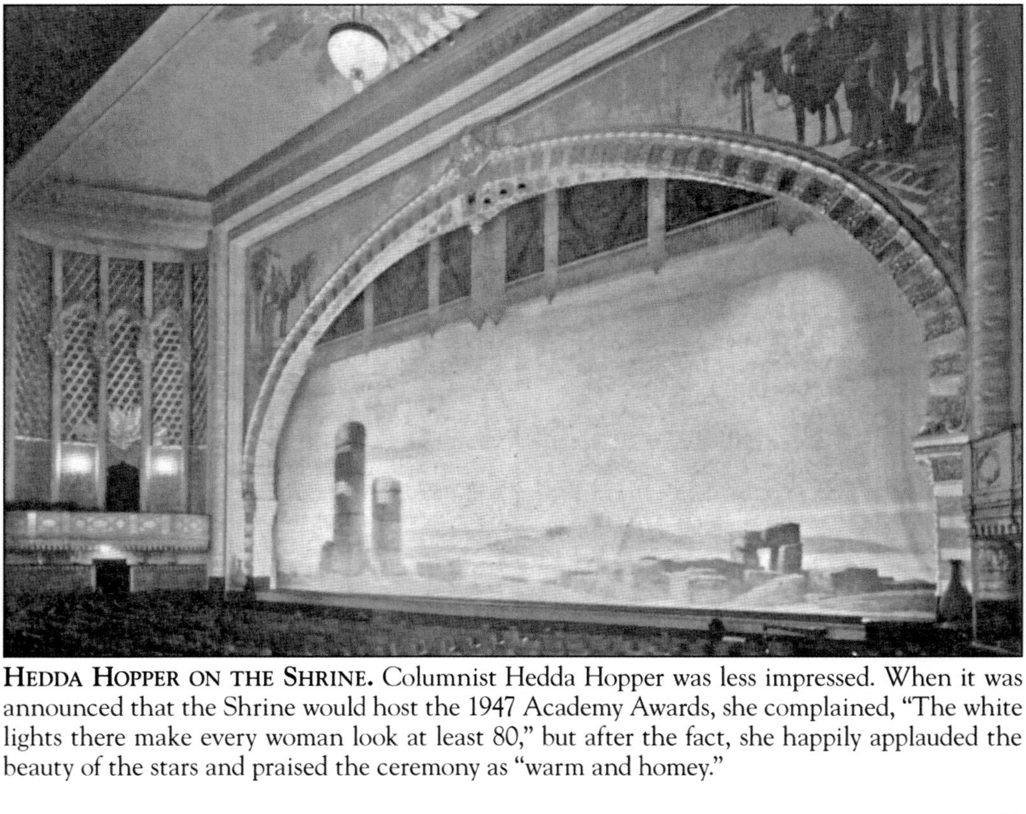

HEDDA HOPPER ON THE SHRINE. Columnist Hedda Hopper was less impressed. When it was announced that the Shrine would host the 1947 Academy Awards, she complained, "The white lights there make every woman look at least 80," but after the fact, she happily applauded the beauty of the stars and praised the ceremony as "warm and homey."

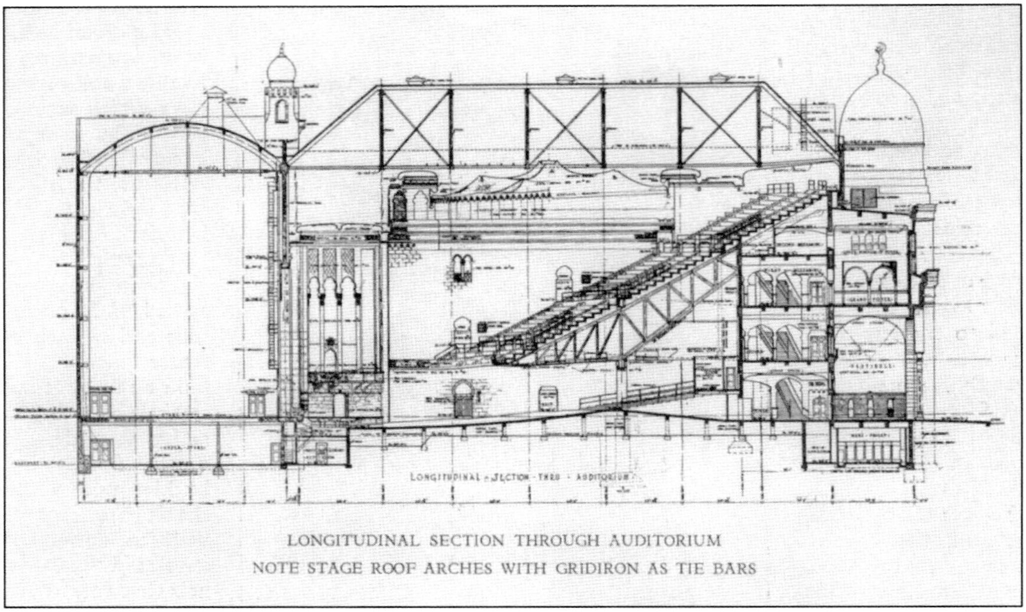

MORE SHRINE COMMENTARY. "Outer ends of the balcony cantilever trusses were supported by cables from roof trusses before riveting," said the *American Architect* in 1928. The balcony was tested with metal barrels filled with water. After it was proved that it could hold a sufficient amount of weight to keep the audience safe, the water was siphoned from the barrels.

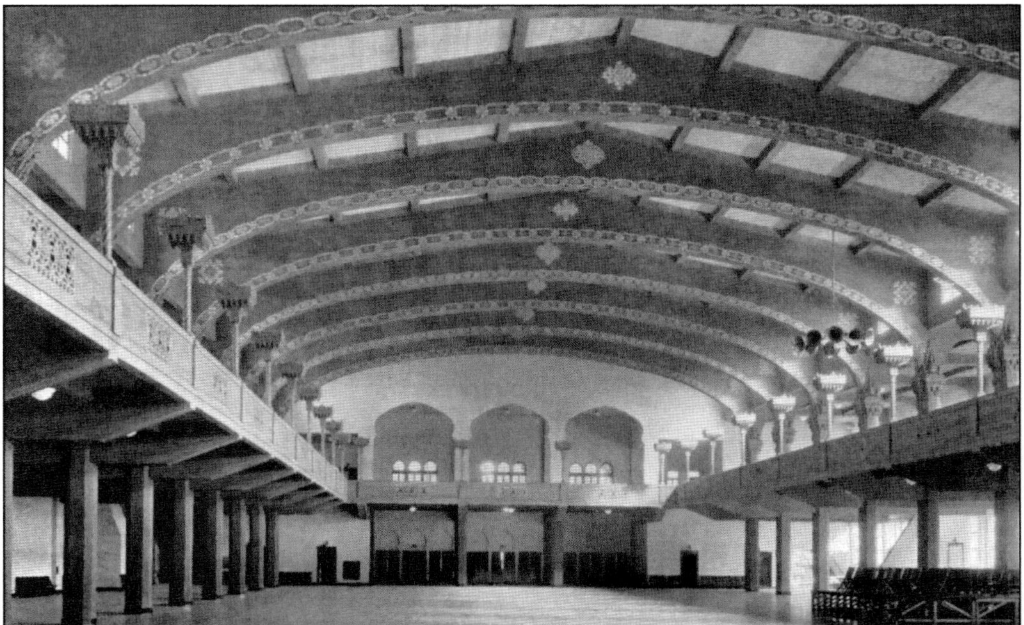

SHRINE AUDITORIUM BANQUET HALL. Hollywood has always had a love-hate relationship with the Shrine. The Oscar ceremonies have been held there numerous times, but in 1935, costume designer Max Ree complained that there was no where to make an entrance, no graceful staircase in the theater or banquet hall where "spectacularly well-dressed women can insure (sic) being the cynosure of all eyes." Thus, he continued, "they leave their best jewels at homes."

Two

Down Adams Boulevard

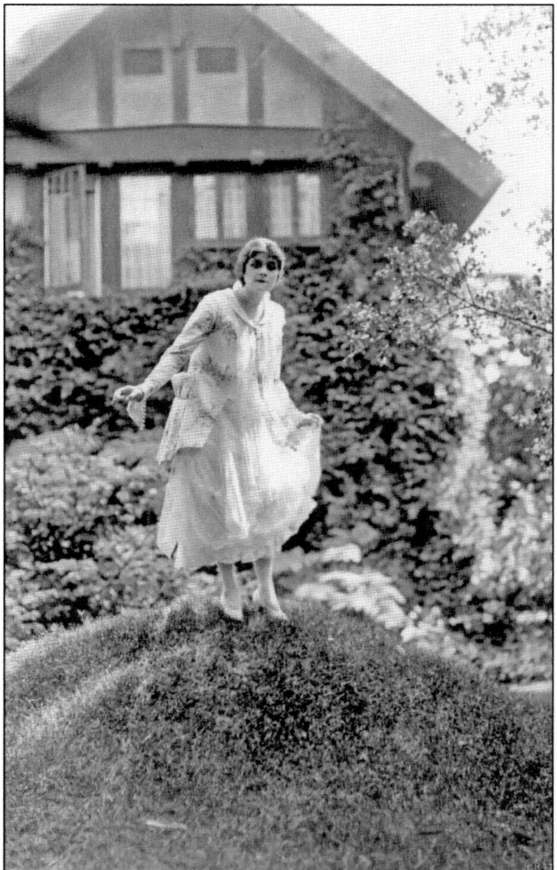

Theda Bara. "Houses must have a tremendous influence on people," wrote Alma Whitaker in 1918. "For instance, since the world's pet film vampire, Theda Bara, assumed the chatelaineship of Mrs. Randolph Huntington Miner's West Adams-street mansion . . . Theda will vamp no more." She went on to say, "Mrs. Miner has long stood for solid exclusiveness, cultured decorum, general uplift and Navy League devotion," as was proper for the society wife of a naval captain. Theda Bara, on the other hand, was famed for leading men astray "in two breast plates and a wisp of chiffon." No doubt her friends believed that the former Theodosia Goodman of Cincinnati was considerably less scandalous than her on-screen incarnation, but to the public she was always the sultry, tempestuous home wrecker. And her erstwhile landlady? In 1933, Tulita Wilcox Miner reminisced about her own youth, "The world was ours. And, oh, dear, we felt so advanced, so naughty, doing things that would be the pink of old-fashioned propriety today. . . . We thought ourselves so daring, but oh, how good we really were!" (Courtesy of Bison Archives.)

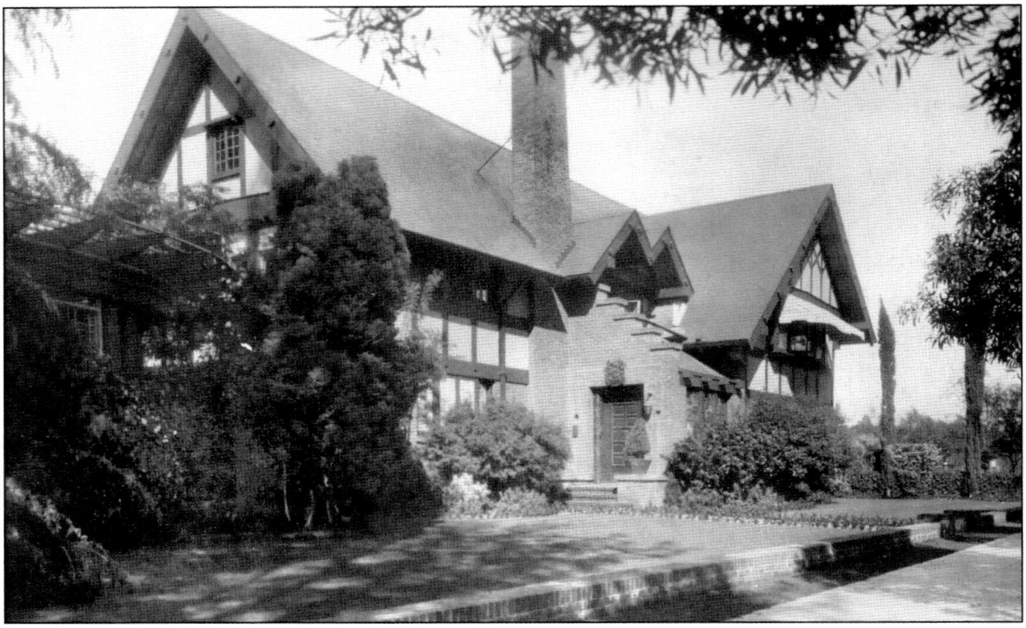

MINER RESIDENCE. Tulita Wilcox Miner was the daughter of Alfred Henry Wilcox, a sea captain said to have brought the first lighthouse to California, and the great-granddaughter of the last Spanish governor of the California Territory under Spanish rule. Her linguistic skills, honed by her husband's naval career, enabled her to translate correspondence for the Red Cross during World War II. (Courtesy of Bison Archives.)

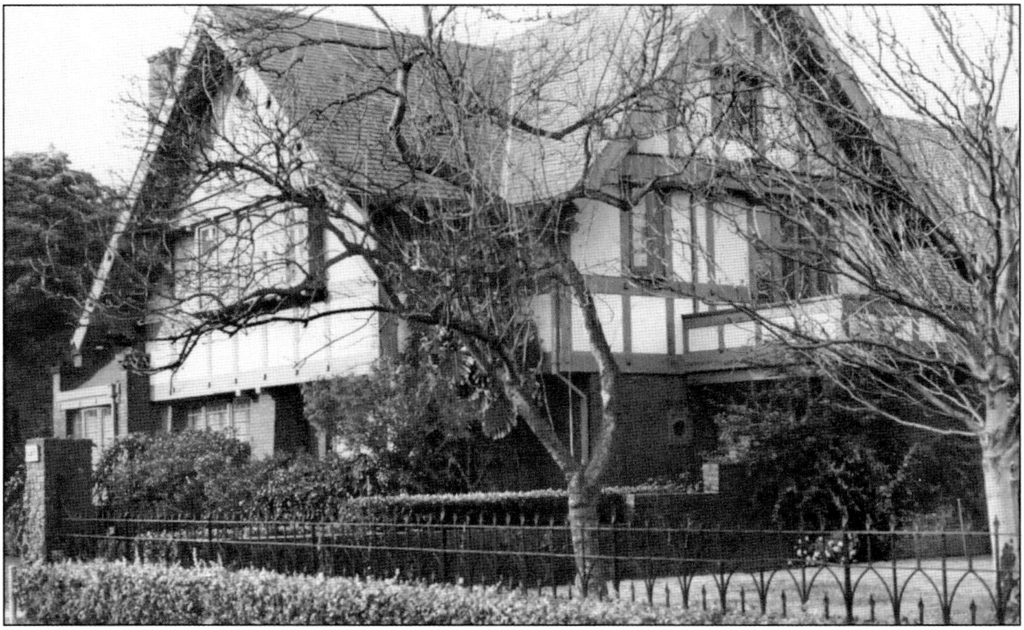

MINERS' ASIAN TREASURES. The Miners' house had a splendid room filled with treasures from their years in Asia. In Japan, Tulita took music lessons from a famous geisha as her only non-Japanese pupil. After her instructor died, Miner was surprised when the woman's husband arrived with a legacy wrapped in silk—a 200-year-old gaikan, a stringed instrument decorated with dragons and plum blossoms. (Courtesy of Bison Archives.)

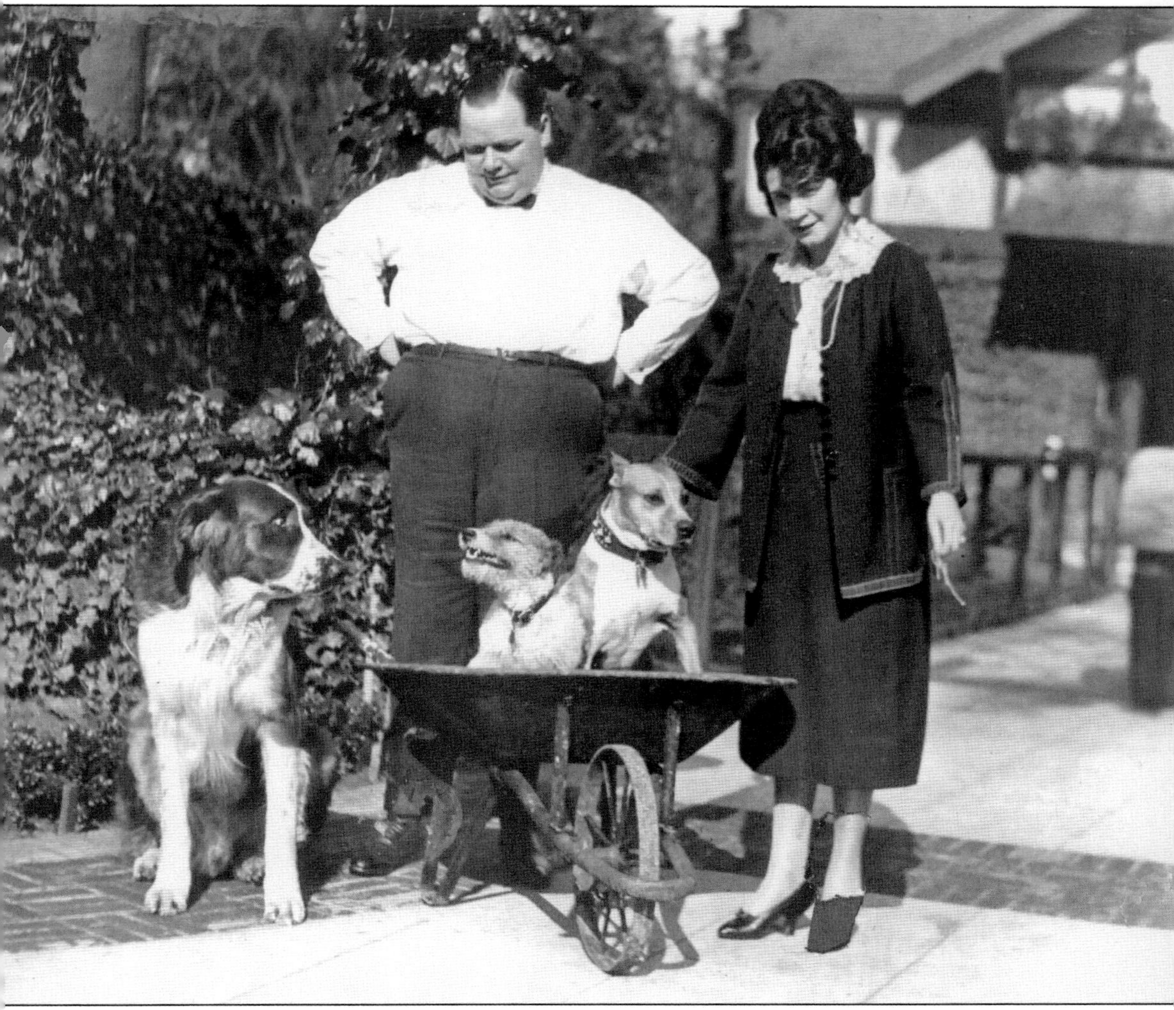

FATTY ARBUCKLE. When comedian Roscoe "Fatty" Arbuckle took up residence at 649 West Adams Boulevard in 1919, Grace Kingsley also decried the house's civilizing effect, claiming, "Fatty is slowly but surely sinking from . . . a rude, two-fisted guy . . . to a cultured state just too darned refined for anything. . . . Oh, dear, Mrs. Miner, how strong is your refining influence." Or perhaps, she thought, "the vulgar dross is all being refined out of the lad through the influence of Theda Bara's astral mind," (adding that "she believes she can just sling her astral body around any old place she wants to!"), but neither lady's influence could save him from scandal. Two years later, accusations surfaced claiming he had raped and killed a starlet during a wild party in San Francisco. Although acquitted in three separate trials, his film career never recovered. (Courtesy of Bison Archives.)

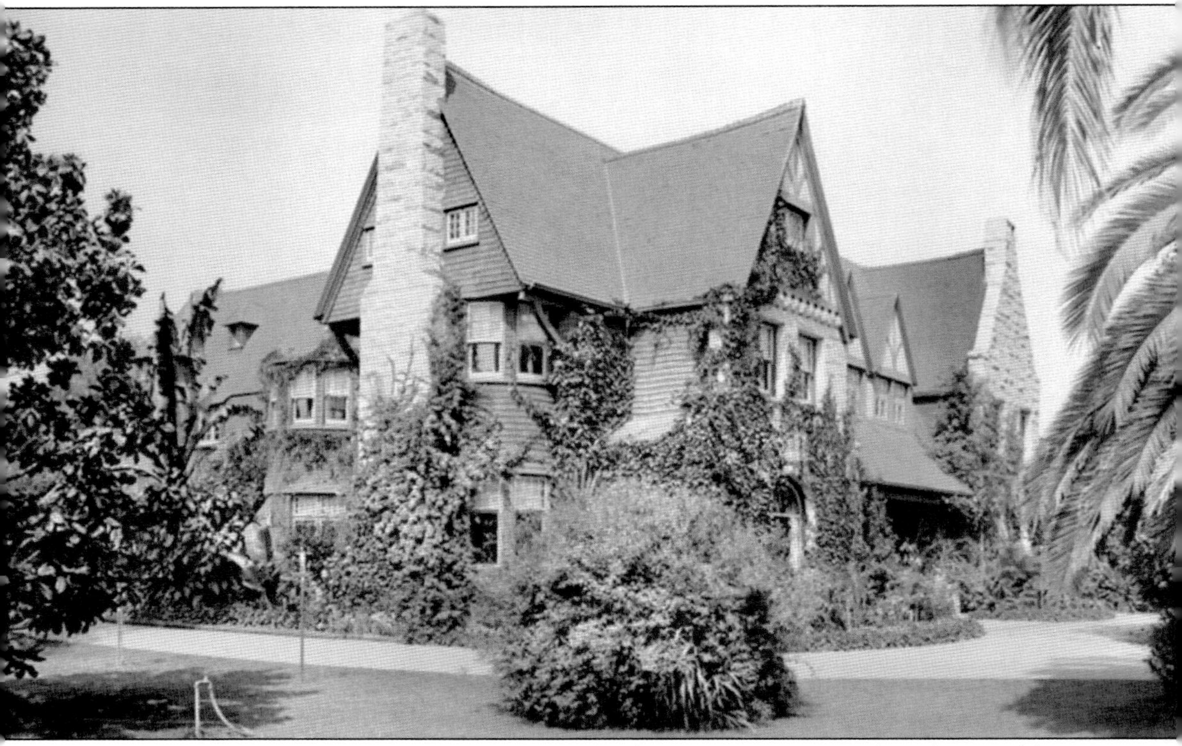

LAUGHLIN RESIDENCE (C. 1900). Among the first guests entertained in the Laughlins' new house at 666 West Adams Street were President McKinley and his wife, Ida. For the president's visit, Japanese lanterns and colored globes led guests through picture-postcard perfect gardens to a house riotous with flowers. A local barber and an anonymous boy were brave enough to ask a policeman if they could see the grounds. The president was strolling, cigar in hand, when their paths crossed. The barber remembered, "That big man, President of 75,000,000 people, was politer than we were, for as soon as he saw us he extended his right hand, and took off his hat—took it off to me, the barber, an' to him, the kid." (Courtesy of University of Southern California, on behalf of the USC Specialized Libraries and Archival Collections.)

HOMER LAUGHLIN. Homer Laughlin was an entrepreneur from Ohio who founded the china company bearing his name and built Los Angeles's first fireproofed and steel-enforced building on Hill Street. Homer Laughlin China is most famous today for Fiestaware, brightly colored, highly collectible dishes.

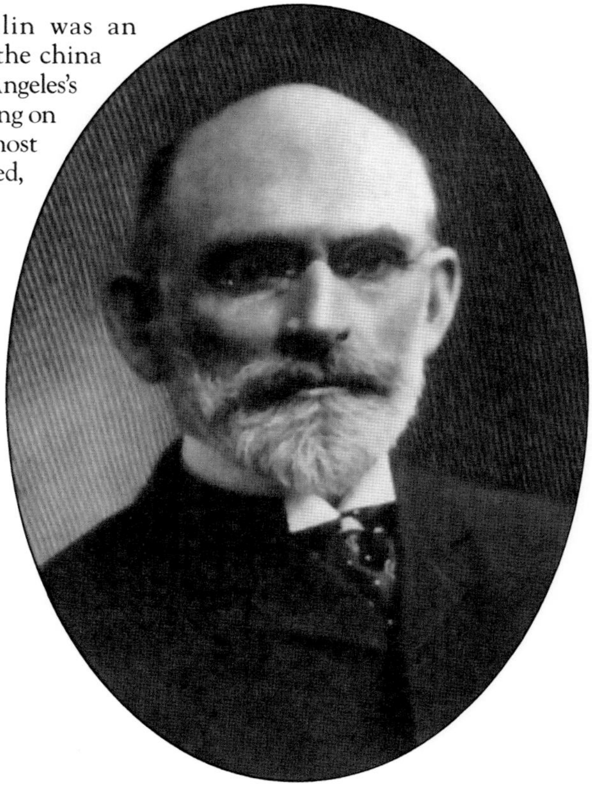

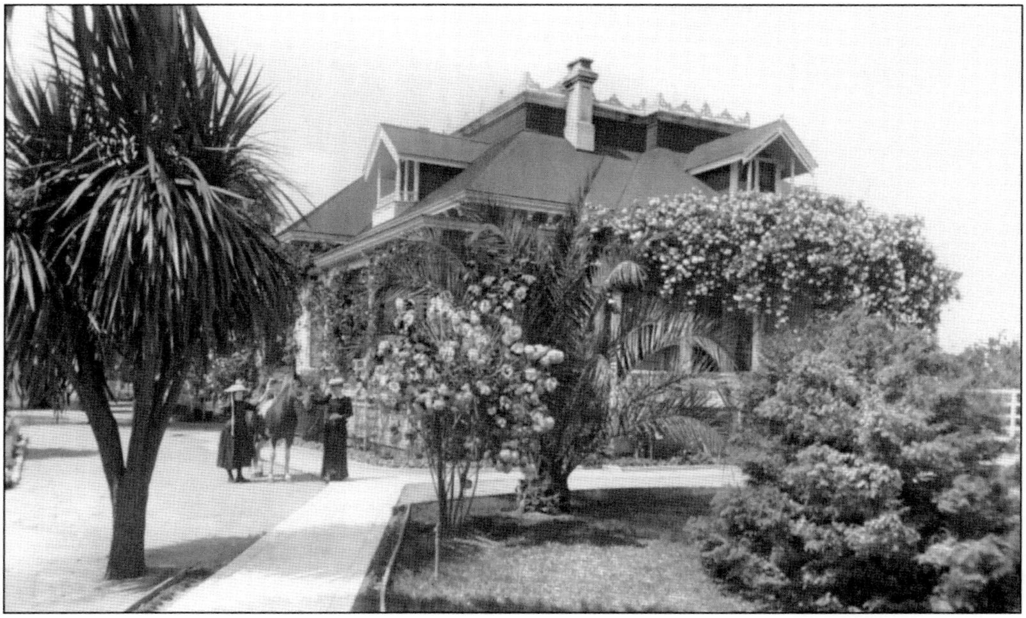

LEWIS RESIDENCE (1900). After a neighbor's house burned, S. B. Lewis solicited a new fire station for West Adams, saying, "Horses cannot run a mile in two, three or five minutes dragging a heavy engine." In 1902, he hired Hudson and Munsell to design a 12-room residence across from Chester Place, possibly never built, as J. Ross Clark's house occupied this site scant years later. (Courtesy of Bison Archives.)

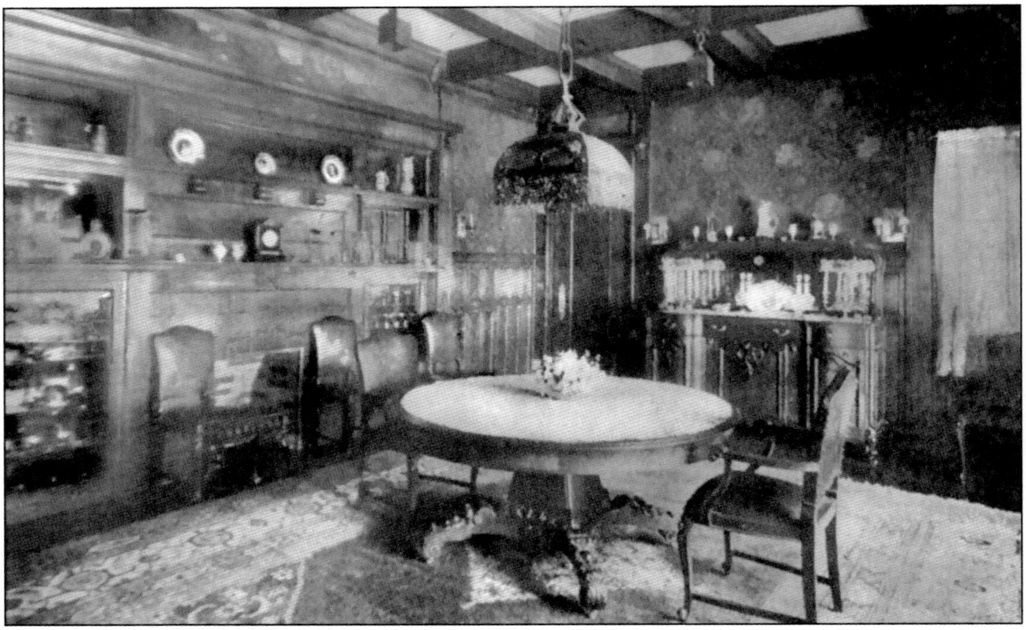

CLARK RESIDENCE. Meals could sometimes be strained in the J. Ross Clark home. His wife, Miriam, never used the back of a chair and pointedly expected the same of her family. The Clarks appeared regularly in the society columns and entertained frequently in their home. One of their largest parties was in 1910, when they hosted 75 debutantes and guests for dancing in the third-floor ballroom.

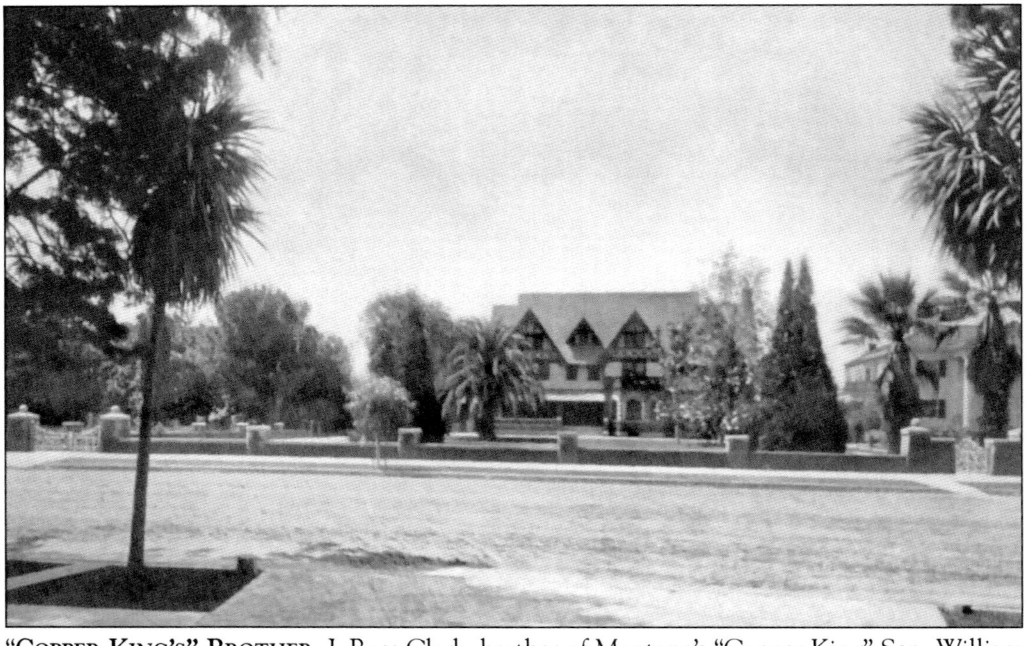

"COPPER KING'S" BROTHER. J. Ross Clark, brother of Montana's "Copper King" Sen. William Andrews Clark, was vice president of the Citizen's National Bank, the Salt Lake Railroad, and the Los Alamitos Sugar Factory. In 1903, Hunt and Eager designed his mansion at 710 West Adams Boulevard. Set far back on its lot, it distanced itself from the street, not only creating an air of privacy but accentuating the grandeur of the home.

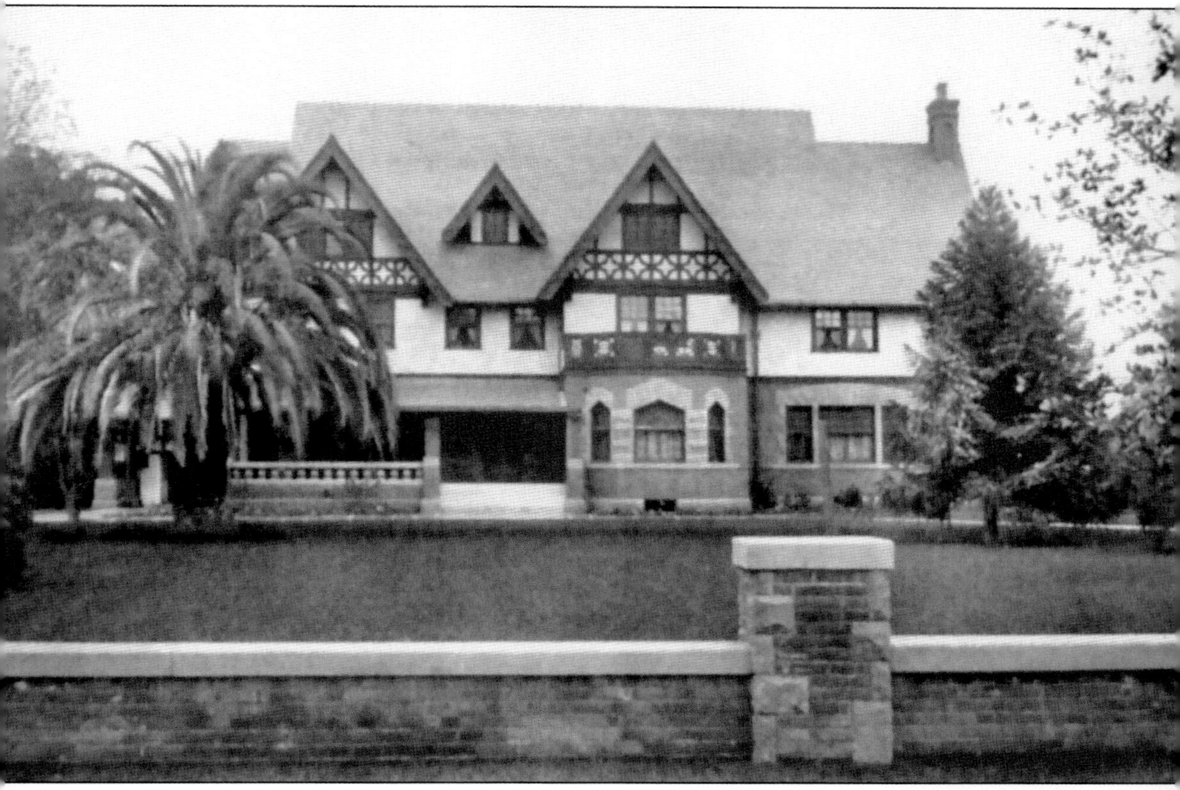

***Titanic* Connection.** The J. Ross Clark home had its share of sadness over the years. Mr. and Mrs. Clark outlived all four of their children, the most tragic death being that of their son, Walter, also a resident of West Adams Boulevard, in the sinking of the *Titanic*. The Clarks were not enamored of his wife, Virginia McDowell Clark, and her remarriage in less than six months did not help. While she was on her honeymoon, they took their only grandchild from Virginia's mother and filed child abandonment charges against their former daughter-in-law. Virginia raced home from Europe in a record 12 days to reclaim her son. As an ugly court battle loomed, the two parties finally agreed to share custody of the infant, and Virginia reportedly never entered their home again. Miriam lived on in the mansion, outliving even more relatives and gradually withdrawing until she lived out of virtually one room. After her death in 1951, the house was taken over by the USC School of Music until it was eventually replaced by a modern apartment building.

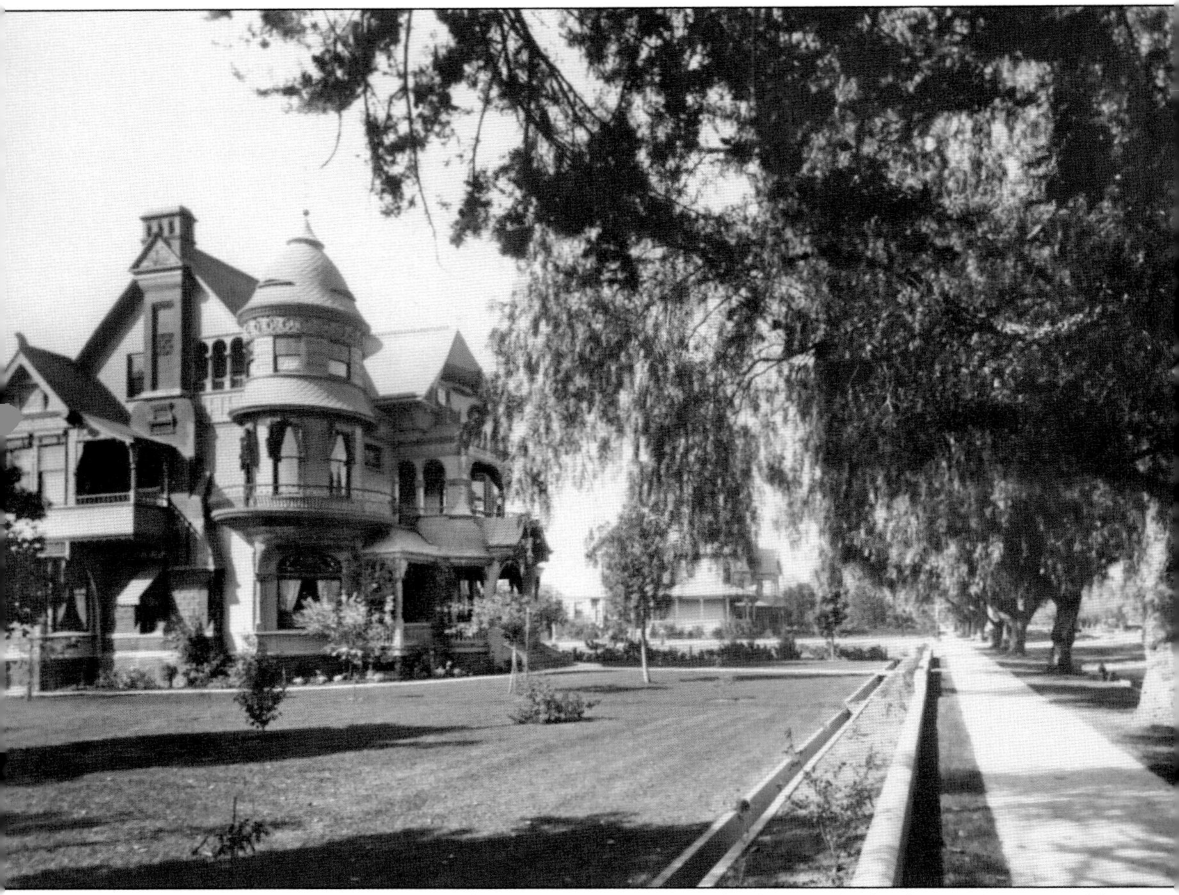

CAPEN RESIDENCE (1900). This lovely house was once the home of Charles H. Capen and his family (although various sources spell the name as Copen or Capan). Mrs. Capen was impressed enough with the Schiffman Dental Method Company on Spring Street to allow her name and address, 818 West Adams Street, to be used as a reference in several advertisements between 1897 and 1900. In the foreground is a zanja, the concrete ditch that brought water from the Los Angeles River. It followed the general direction of Broadway, crossed Olvera Street, and eventually dwindled away in West Adams. In the century before the mansions were built, much of the life of the Pueblo de Los Angeles centered on its water, but by 1898, homeowners were ready to get rid of it in favor of convenient modern plumbing. (Courtesy of Bison Archives.)

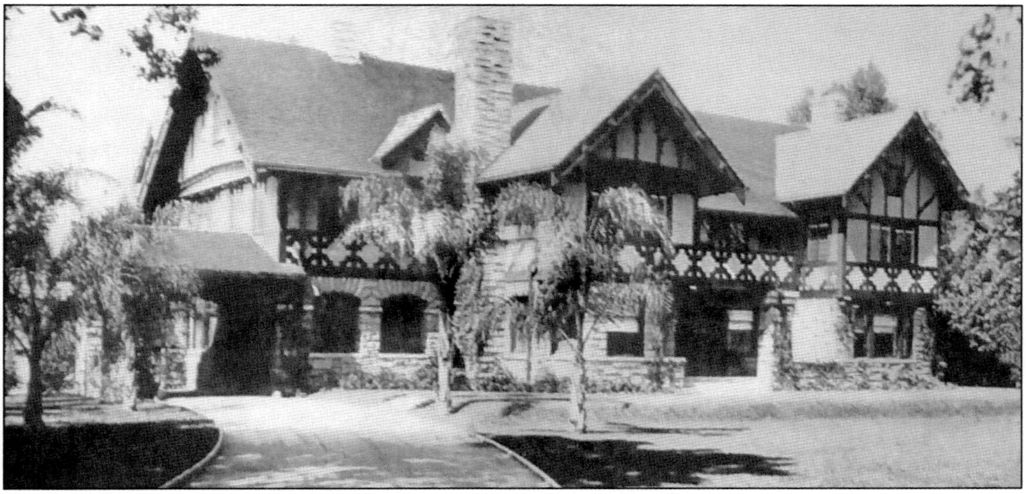

KERCKHOFF RESIDENCE. Louise Kerckhoff probably would not have allowed rodents in her home while she was alive, but after she willed 734 West Adams Boulevard to the USC Medical School, lab rats inhabited the wine cellar. It is now the Annenberg School for Communication. Among William Kerckhoff's many business ventures was regional development of hydroelectric power. The couple donated $1 million to Cal Tech and the Kerckhoff Union Building to UCLA.

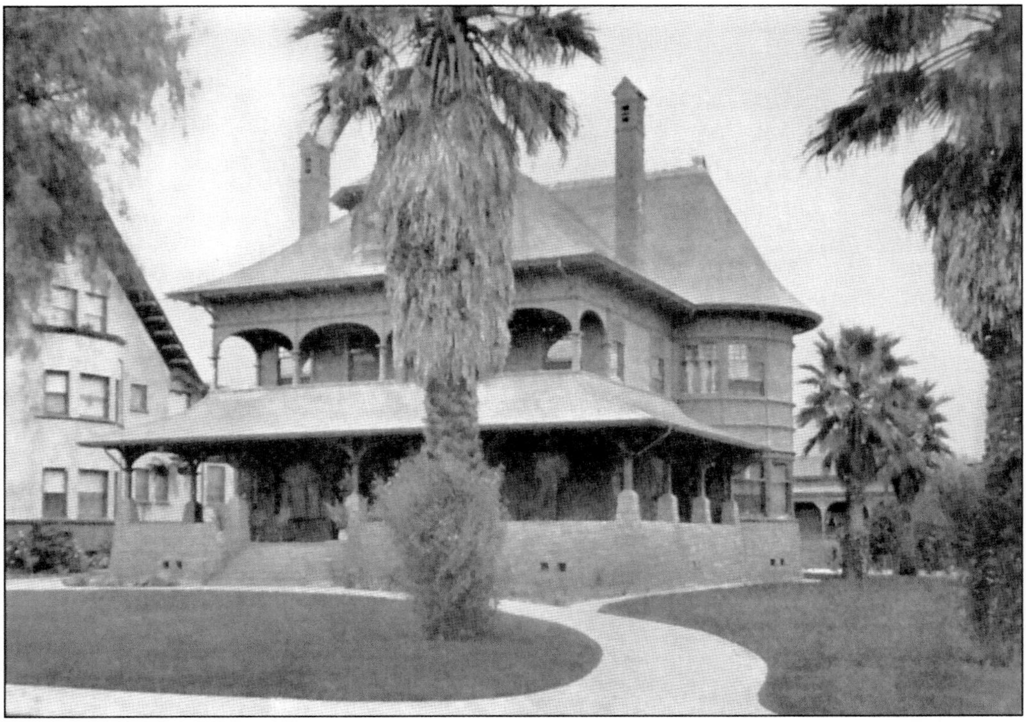

NEWMARK RESIDENCE. Maurice A. Newmark was president of a large wholesale grocery company and a pioneer in the canning industry. He and his wife, Harriet, showed up frequently in lists of charitable contributions, with Harriet particularly active in Jewish charities. Newmark was not as generous with the vote, however, and opposed women's suffrage. The Newmarks lived at 880 West Adams Boulevard from 1905 until their deaths.

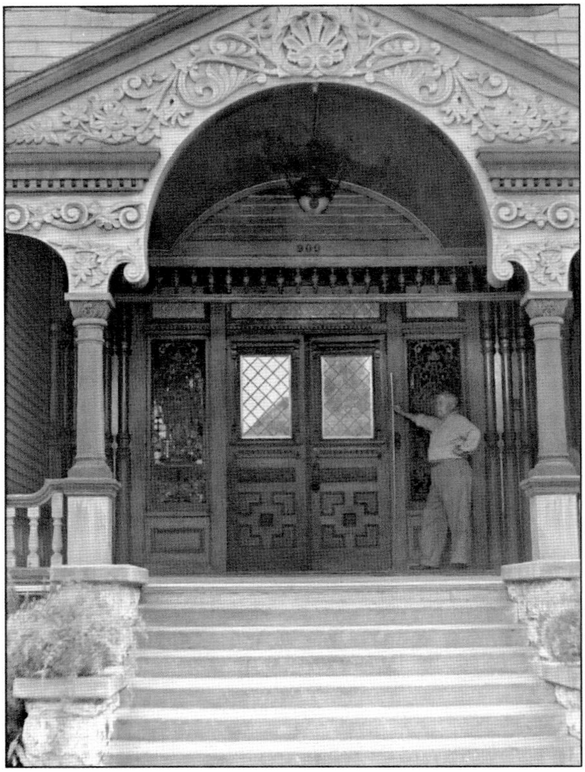

WATERS RESIDENCE (1940). Russell Judson Waters had a busy retirement, or as his obituary commented, his retirement "failed too brilliantly for him to repeat the experiment." In 1886, he was so enthused with his retirement location that he founded the city of Redlands. When he was ready to retire again, he settled at 900 West Adams Boulevard, but by 1897, he represented the area in Congress. (Courtesy of Bison Archives.)

WATERS HOME (1940). Trained as a blacksmith in his youth, Waters practiced law in Chicago. He was president of several banks, a husband and father, and his many friends agreed he was a good man who loved nature. In spare minutes, he wrote novels and poetry, although his many accomplishments seem to belie his lines, "Calm and restful, nothing wanted, we live today our simple life." (Courtesy of Bison Archives.)

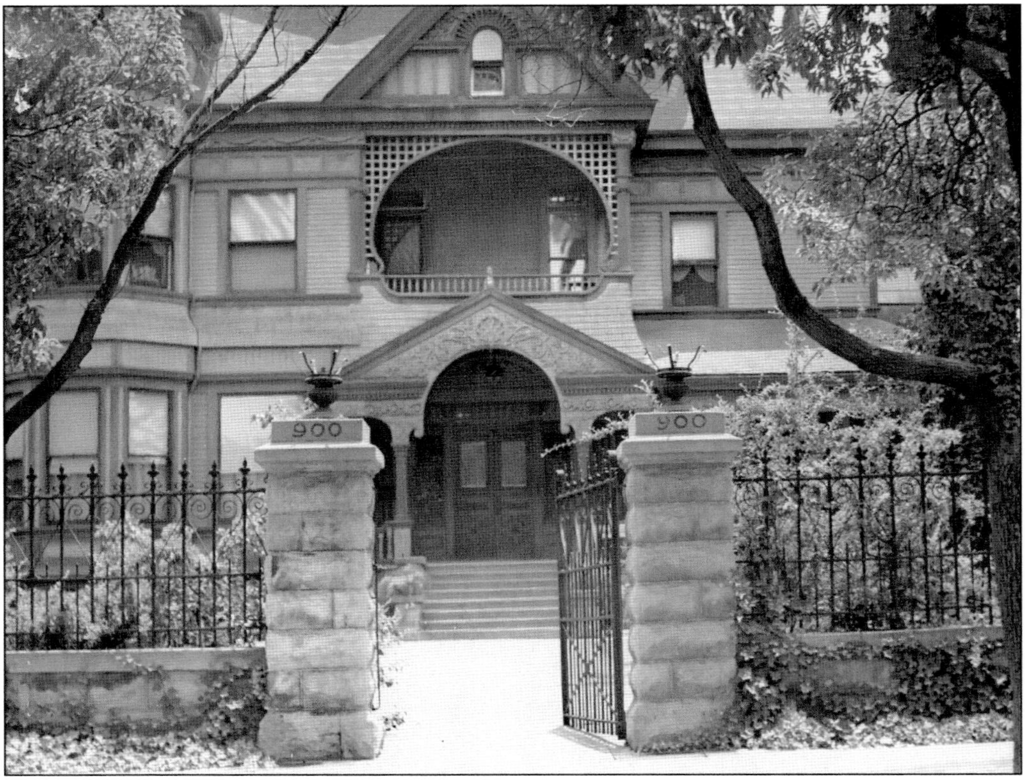

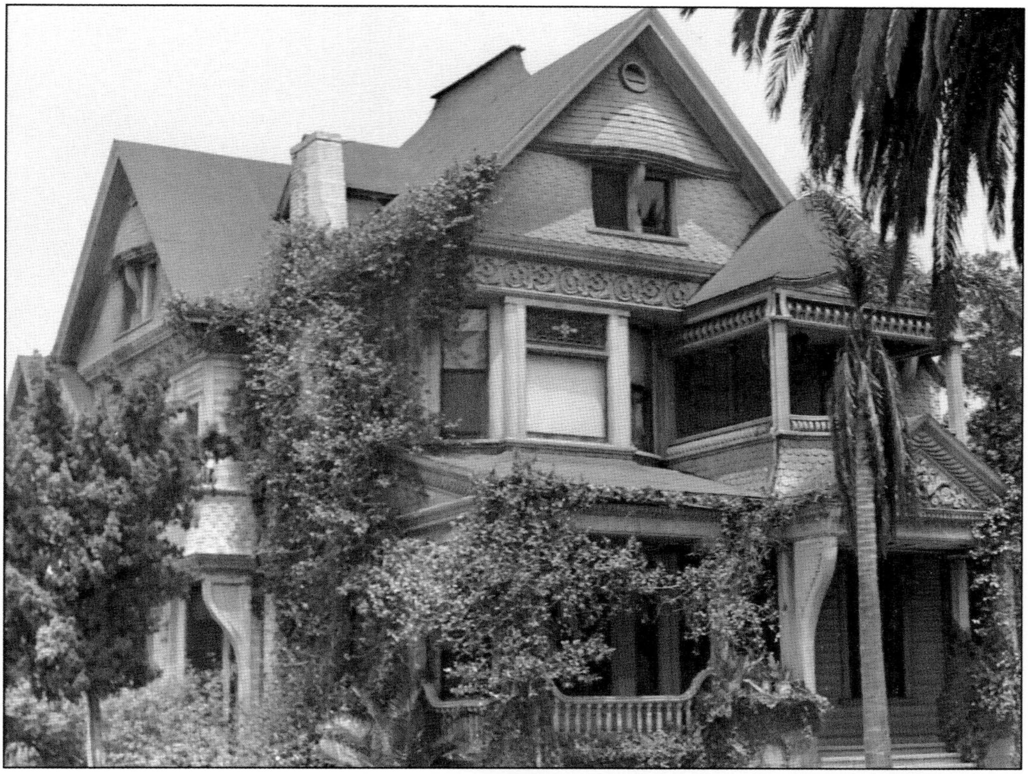

BARD RESIDENCE (1944). Sen. Thomas R. Bard is remembered as the man who founded Hueneme in 1881. He maintained addresses there, and at 957 West Adams Boulevard, for many years. As an amateur floriculturist, he developed two new roses, named Berylwood for his eldest daughter and Dr. Bard for his brother. He was known as an honest man and a conservative Republican who opposed saloons and too much legislation.

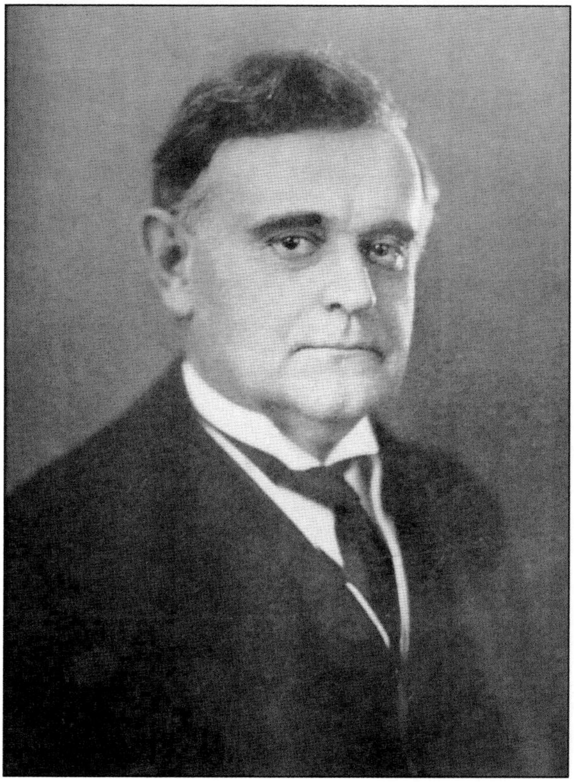

ISADORE B. DOCKWEILER. Born downtown at First Street and Broadway, Isadore Dockweiler was a lawyer, prominent Democrat, and father of 11 children. He and his wife, Gertrude, lived at 2321 South Figueroa Street. After his death, the man who served on the state board of parks and beaches was honored with a beach of his own when the name of Venice-Hyperion Beach was changed to Dockweiler Beach.

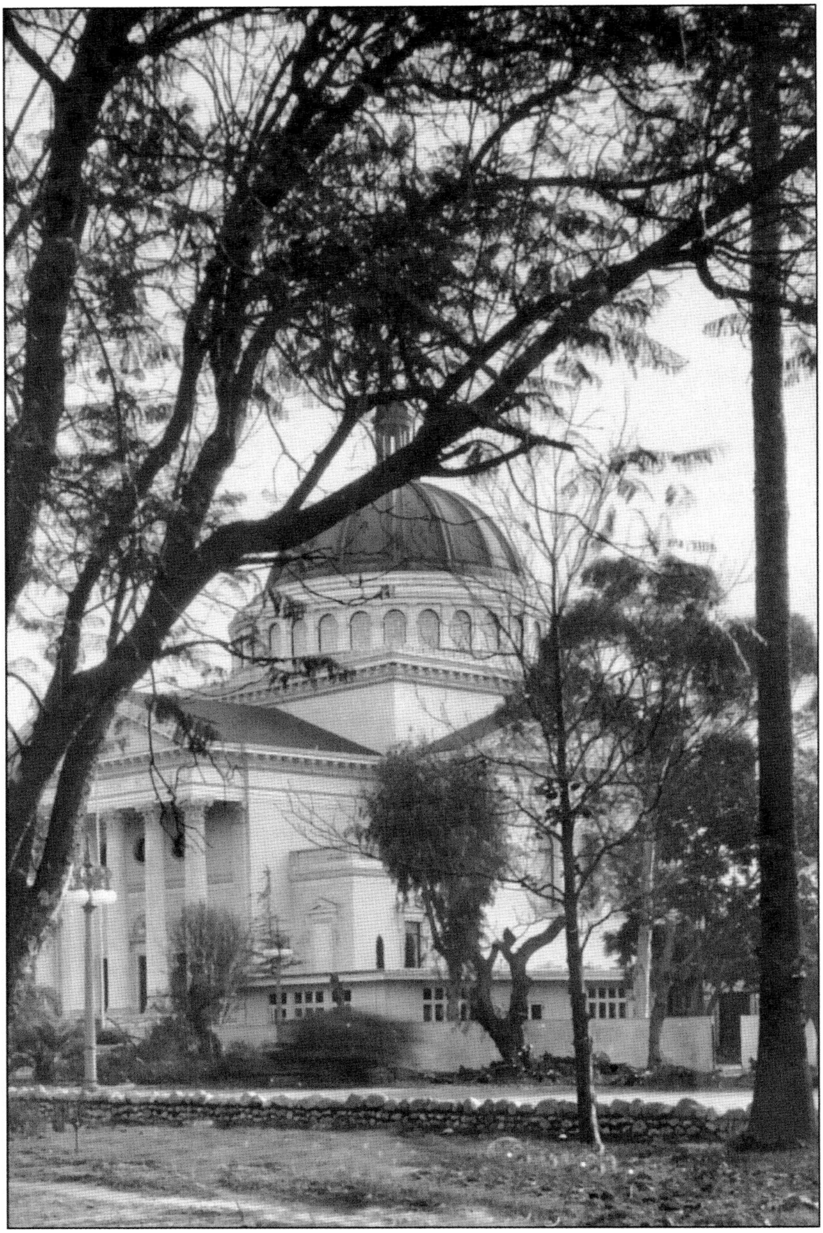

SECOND CHURCH OF CHRIST, SCIENTIST THROUGH TREES. The Christian Science philosophy begun by Mary Baker Eddy in the 1860s experienced phenomenal growth during the first part of the 20th century. By 1909, churches were outgrowing their simple meeting places in parlors and small halls and looking for grander accommodations. Paul Eli Ivey states in *Prayers in Stone*, his book on Christian Science architecture, "Christian Science congregations . . . were genuinely concerned about the rhetorical aspect of the architecture of their big city churches," and that "the Gothic style was viewed as traditional and antimodernist; the classical style was generally defended as progressive." By that standard, the classic beauty of the Second Church of Christ, Scientist reflects well on architect A. F. Rosenheim. Albert C. Martin was employed as engineer, an important job for a building that featured a 1,400-ton reinforced-concrete dome, at that time the largest in existence.

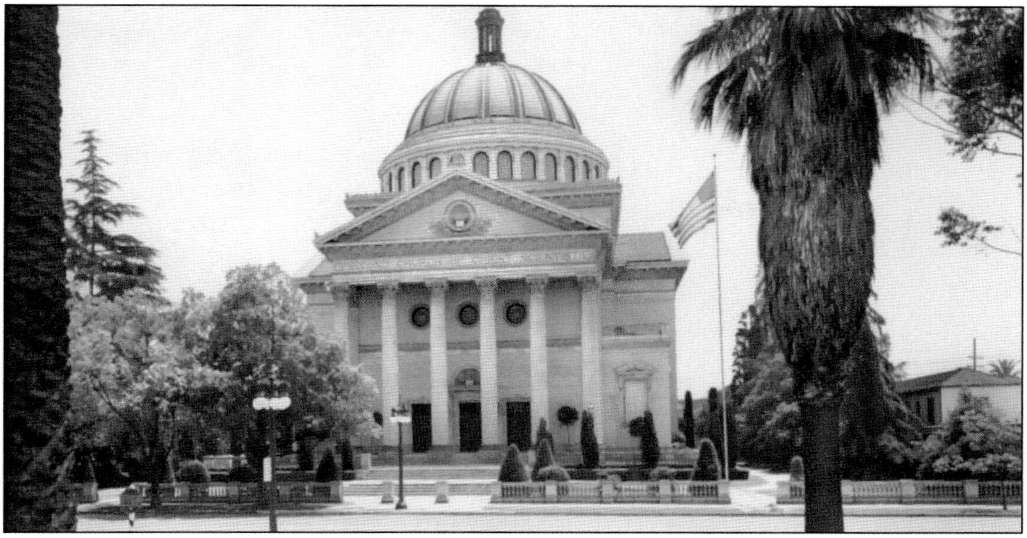

SECOND CHURCH OF CHRIST, SCIENTIST. The church was added to the National Register of Historic Places in 1987. The Christian Science philosophy has fallen out of fashion, and the still beautiful church is now closed. The 70-foot copper-sheathed dome has weathered to a soft green patina, but deferred maintenance and the difficulty of supporting such a large building threaten its existence.

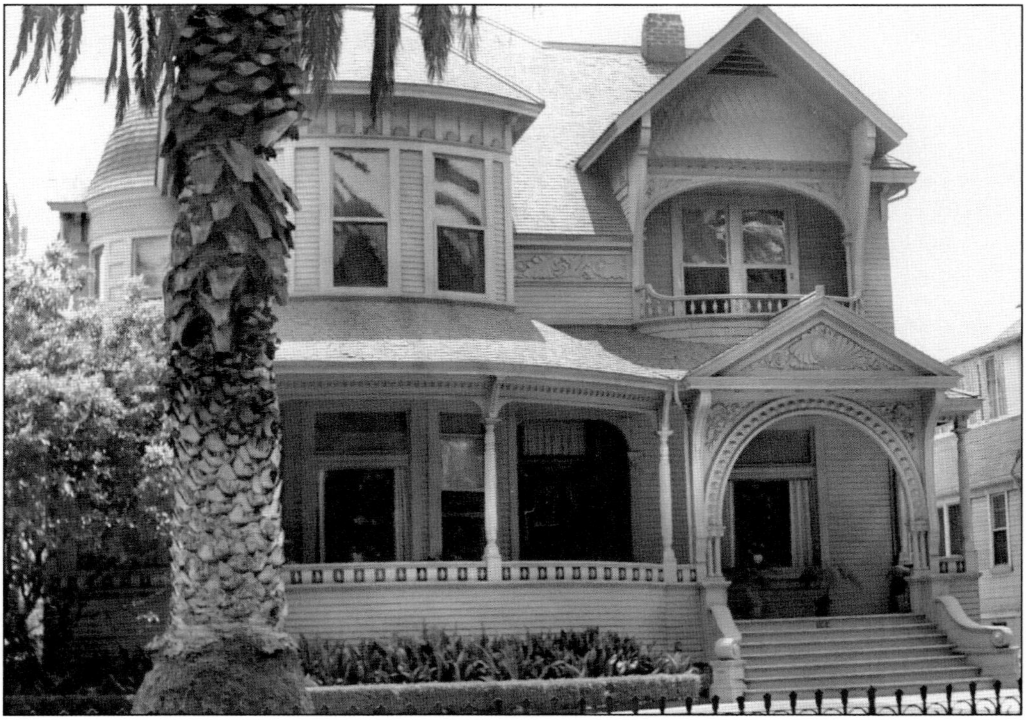

WIGMORE RESIDENCE (1944). John Wigmore founded a hardware firm called John Wigmore and Sons. A sensational bankruptcy in 1903 led to his collapse and eventual death, but his son, George, took the reins, and the company survived. George, like his father, lived at 949 West Adams Boulevard, but he, too, faced tragedy, including the death of his son, a naval aviator, in a 1919 plane crash. (Courtesy of Bison Archives.)

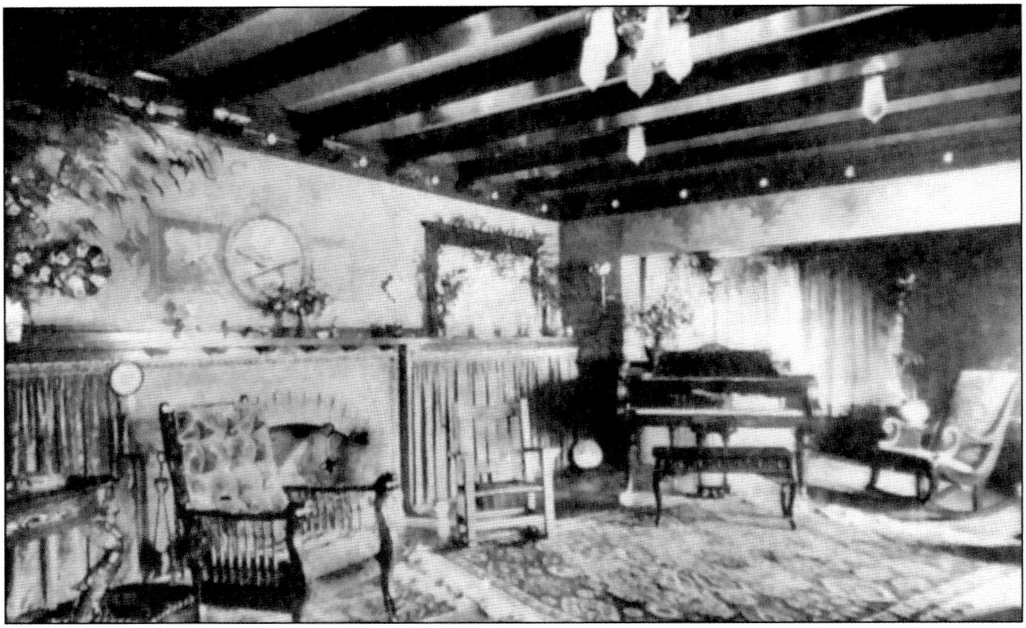

WILSON RESIDENCE INTERIOR. Yet another wealthy West Adams resident who made his money in Montana mining was Frank King Wilson. His home at 1200 West Adams Boulevard boasted a billiard room and a "Turkish" room. Mrs. Wilson was easily able to entertain 68 guests at a card party in 1903, "in rooms so elaborately decorated that they resembled grottoes of greenery and flowers," according to the *Los Angeles Times*.

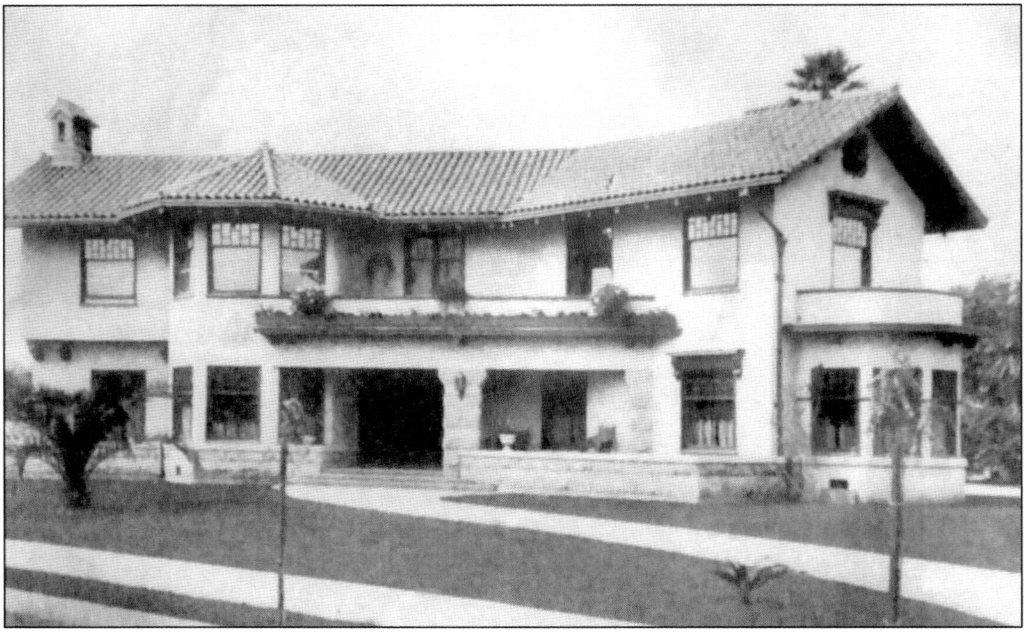

WILSON RESIDENCE. All was not bridesmaid roses and scarlet carnations within the walls of 1200 West Adams Boulevard. In 1909, Mrs. Frank Wilson was granted a divorce on grounds of physical cruelty and infidelity. She also claimed that her husband did not bathe often enough, while he maintained that she spent too much money. Mrs. Wilson was awarded the house and an undisclosed settlement.

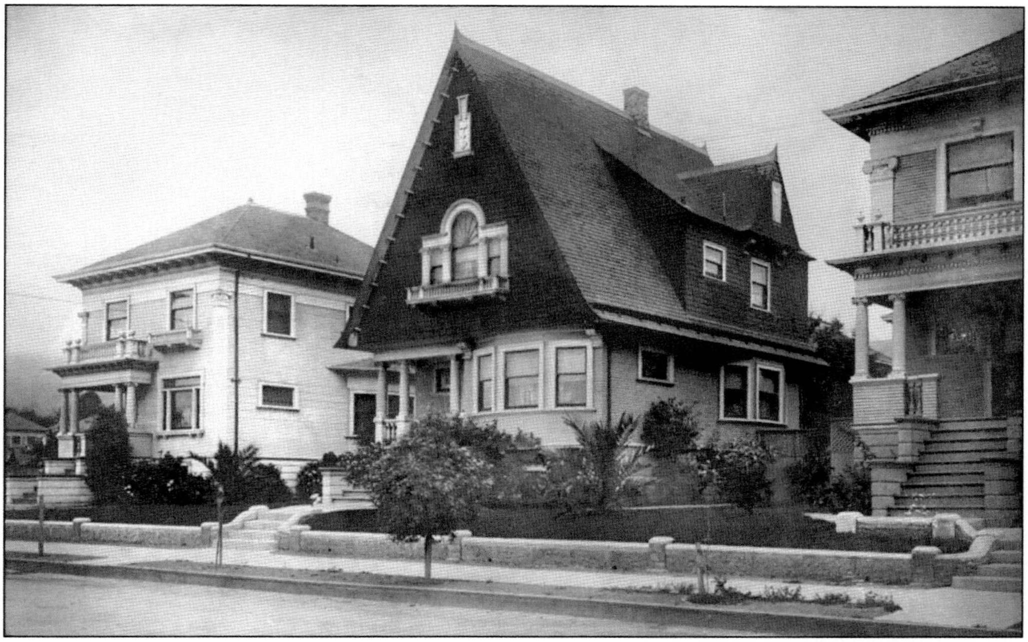

HOUSE IN UNIVERSITY PARK. Despite their proximity to the elaborate mansions on St. James Park and Chester Place, many middle-class homes were built in North University Park. Floor plans were frequently repeated by contractors, so several examples of this particular house appear in the neighborhood. With an unusually steep pitch to the roof and a small porch, it seems more suited for a snowy climate than comfortable West Adams.

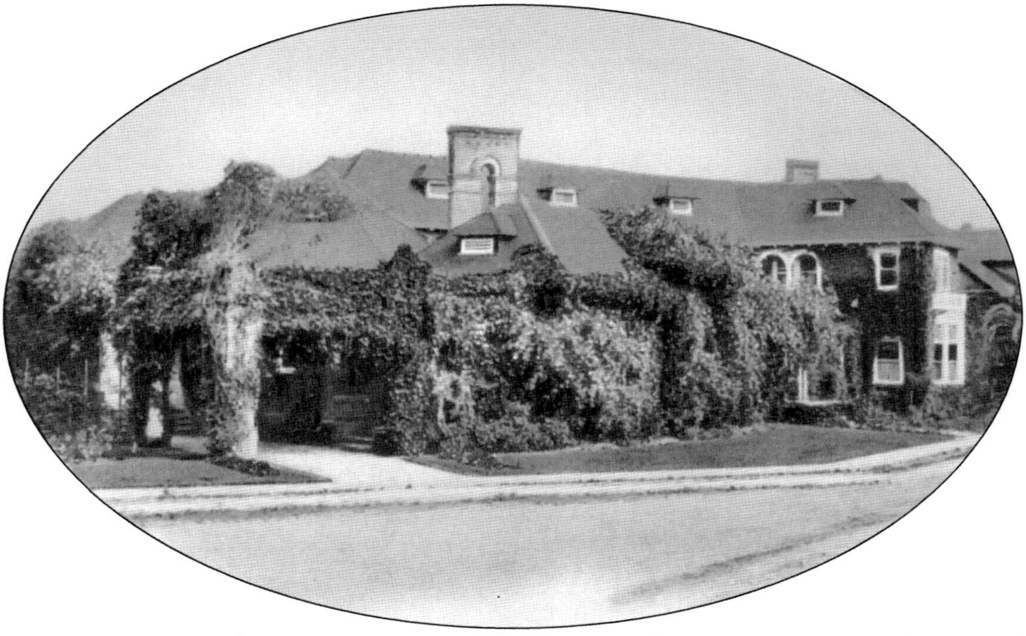

CASA DE ROSAS. Kindergarten was a new concept in 1893, when Caroline M. N. Alden opened the Froebel Institute at the corner of Adams and Hoover Streets. The building, by architect Sumner P. Hunt, featured a courtyard, walls of windows, a fountain, and sand gardens to please the children. Covered with flowers and vines, Casa de Rosas merited its name.

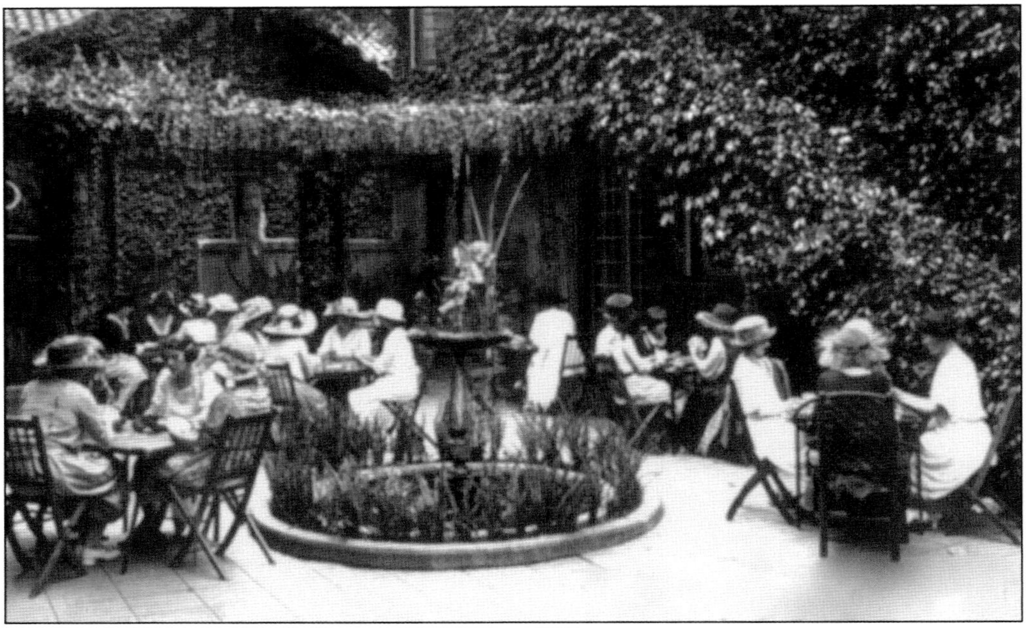

THE GIRLS COLLEGIATE SCHOOL. The school moved into Casa de Rosas around the turn of the 20th century. In addition to English, art, science, and language, young ladies were prepared for an easy entrance into the social life by means of well-arranged affairs at which the girls were instructed in the art of graceful entertaining. Bowling, golf, and fencing were also on the agenda. (Courtesy of Joe Ryan.)

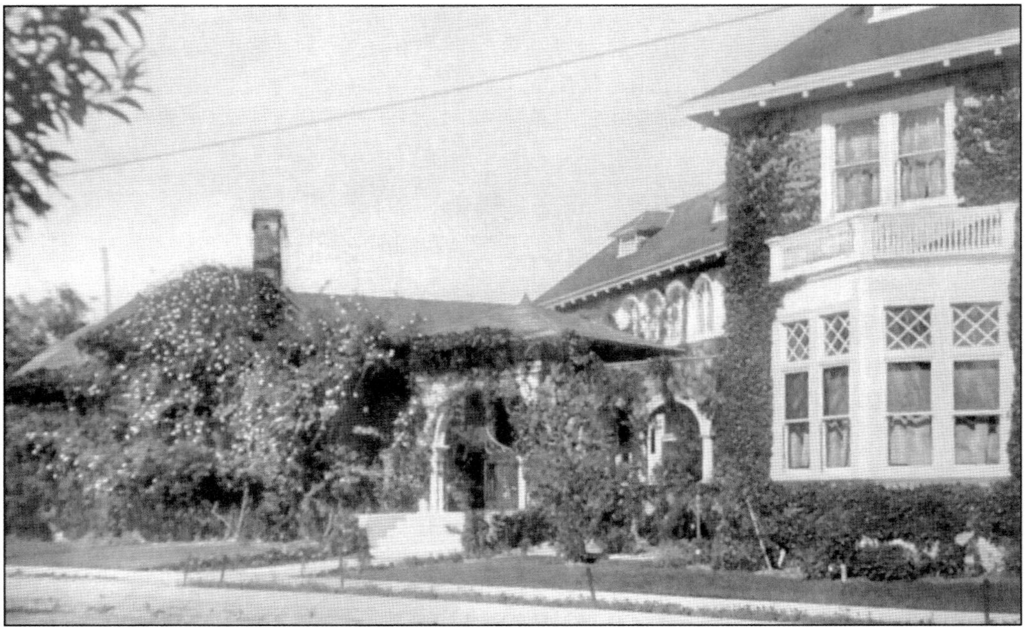

CASA DE ROSAS FIRE. In 1904, the school was gutted by fire when a janitor overturned a coal-oil lamp and ran to alert the fire department rather than extinguishing the blaze before it leapt out of control. The second floor was gutted, and the first sustained serious water damage. During repairs, a third story was added, enlarging the school, and the lot next door was purchased for tennis and basketball courts.

Three

CHESTER PLACE

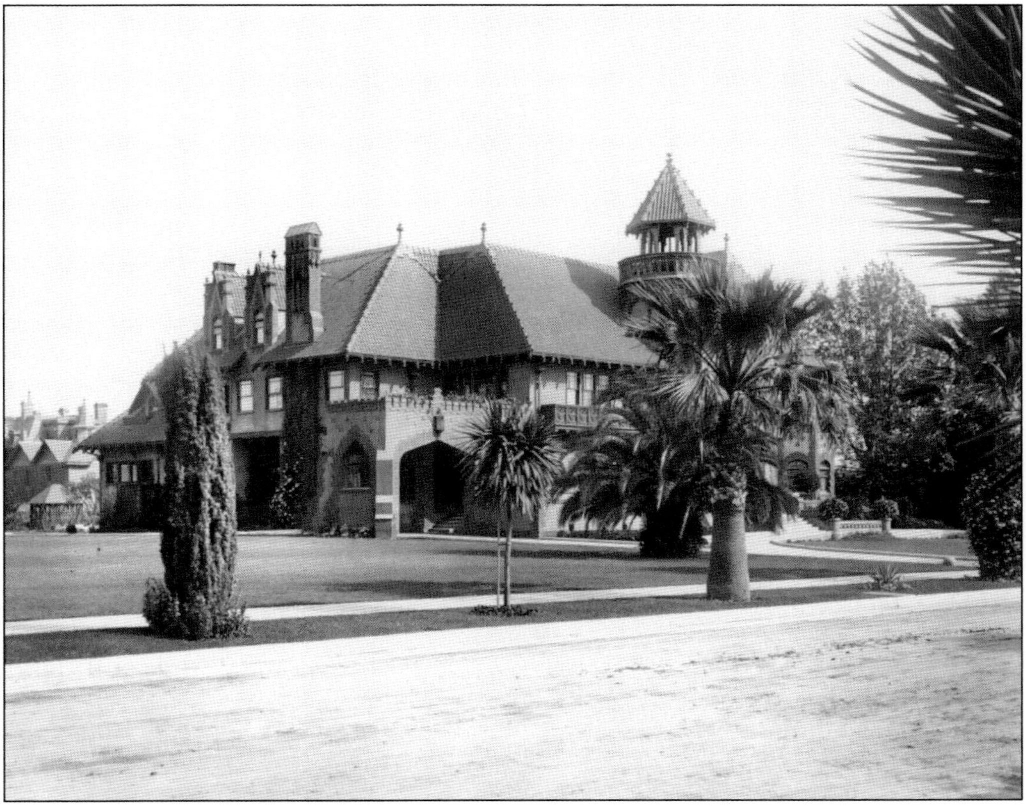

DOHENY RESIDENCE. "Yes, I believe I should hate to part with this beautiful home if I had to do so," said Mrs. Oliver Posey, discussing the sale of 8 Chester Place to Edward L. Doheny in 1901, but her plans for a larger, grander house left her "nothing to regret." Doheny had recently married his second wife, Carrie Estelle Betzold, a telephone operator who first intrigued him with the sound of her voice. The couple purchased nearly all of Mrs. Posey's furnishings, including a first-floor wigwam furnished with baskets and rugs. The house had been designed by Theodore Augustus Eisen and Sumner Hunt in 1898, but by the time Doheny finished with it, it included new rooms, a conservatory designed by Alfred F. Rosenheim, and an amazing collection of rare palms. The Dohenys also added the costliest piano in Los Angeles. The *Los Angeles Times* dryly commented that the $10,000 gilded instrument, with paintings by Edward Dowdall, was probably not a style that would "come into popularity at once, especially for children to practice on." (Courtesy of Bison Archives.)

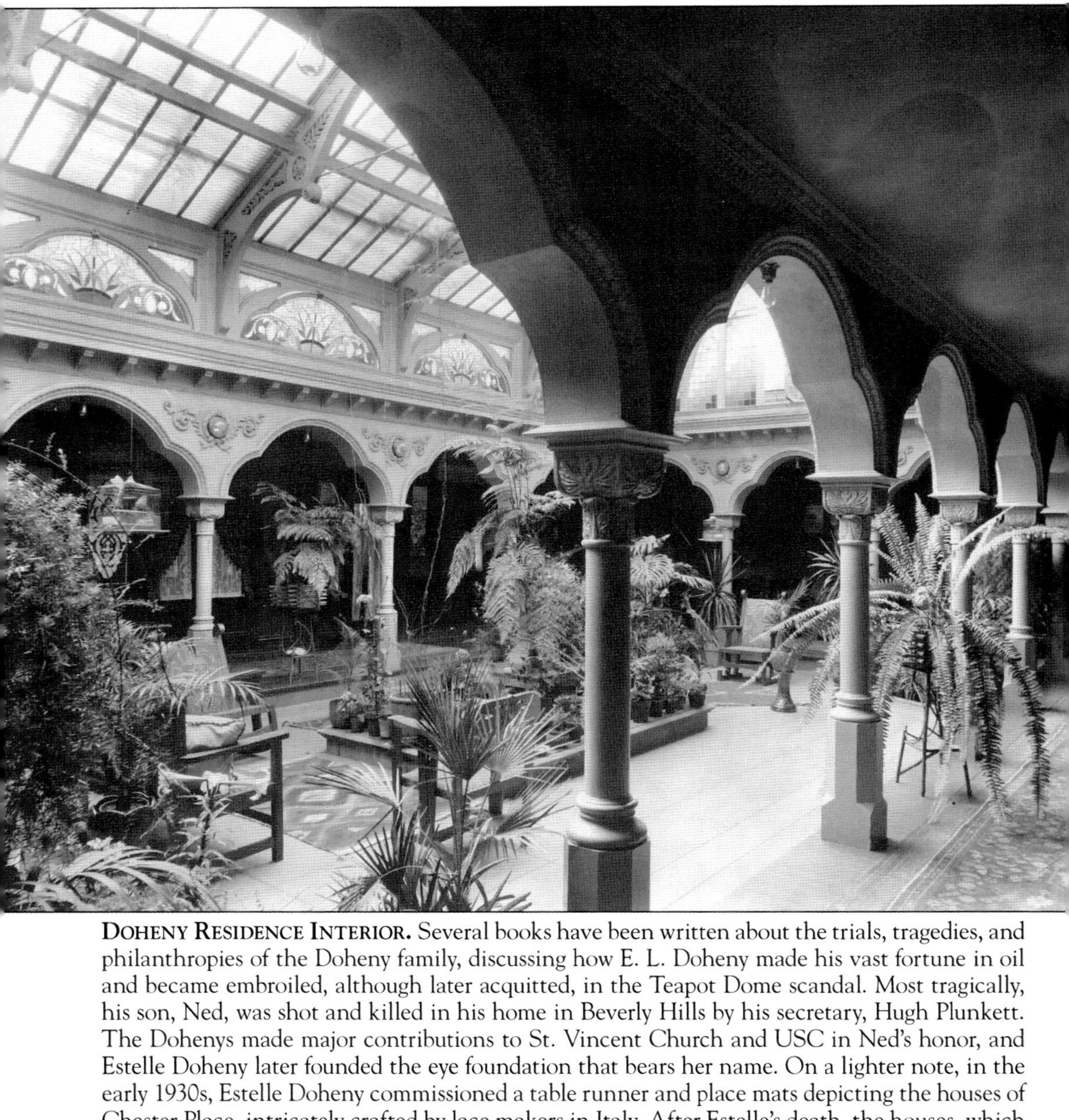

DOHENY RESIDENCE INTERIOR. Several books have been written about the trials, tragedies, and philanthropies of the Doheny family, discussing how E. L. Doheny made his vast fortune in oil and became embroiled, although later acquitted, in the Teapot Dome scandal. Most tragically, his son, Ned, was shot and killed in his home in Beverly Hills by his secretary, Hugh Plunkett. The Dohenys made major contributions to St. Vincent Church and USC in Ned's honor, and Estelle Doheny later founded the eye foundation that bears her name. On a lighter note, in the early 1930s, Estelle Doheny commissioned a table runner and place mats depicting the houses of Chester Place, intricately crafted by lace makers in Italy. After Estelle's death, the houses, which included not only the Doheny home, but also neighbors' homes that had been purchased by the family, became Mount St. Mary's Doheny Campus. (Courtesy of Bison Archives.)

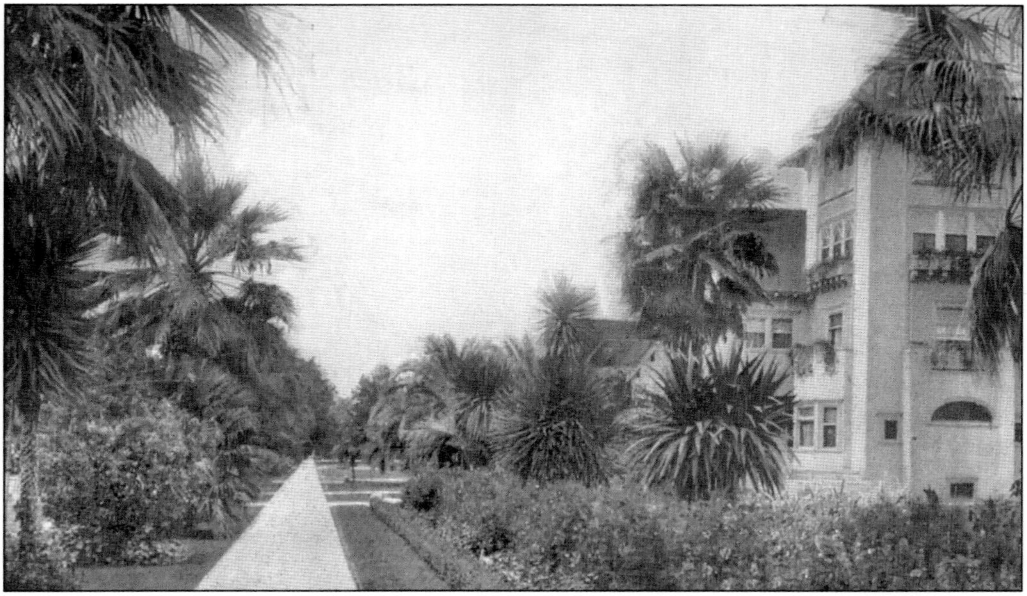

WILSON RESIDENCE. This view along Chester Place shows the impressive tower of the home at number 7, built by Erasmus Wilson. A Civil War veteran who participated in Sherman's march to the sea, Wilson made a fortune in cattle ranching in Texas before retiring to Los Angeles in 1902. When he moved from Chester Place, he did not go far, dying at 745 West Adams in 1928. (Courtesy of Rory Cunningham.)

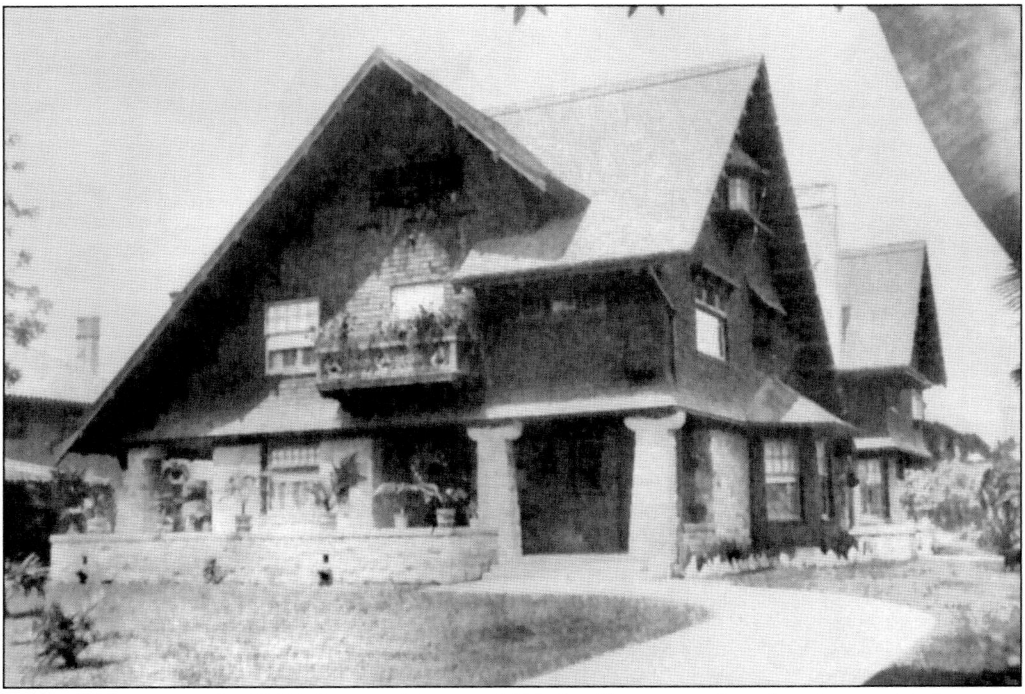

PERRY RESIDENCE. In 1907, Sumner Hunt and Wesley Eager were hired to design this home at 12 Chester Place, occupied by Charles F. Perry and his wife, Ada. Perry had inherited a good deal of lumber money from his father. Like so many of the Chester Place residents, he did not remain long and in 1913 built an Italian villa in the Hollywood Hills.

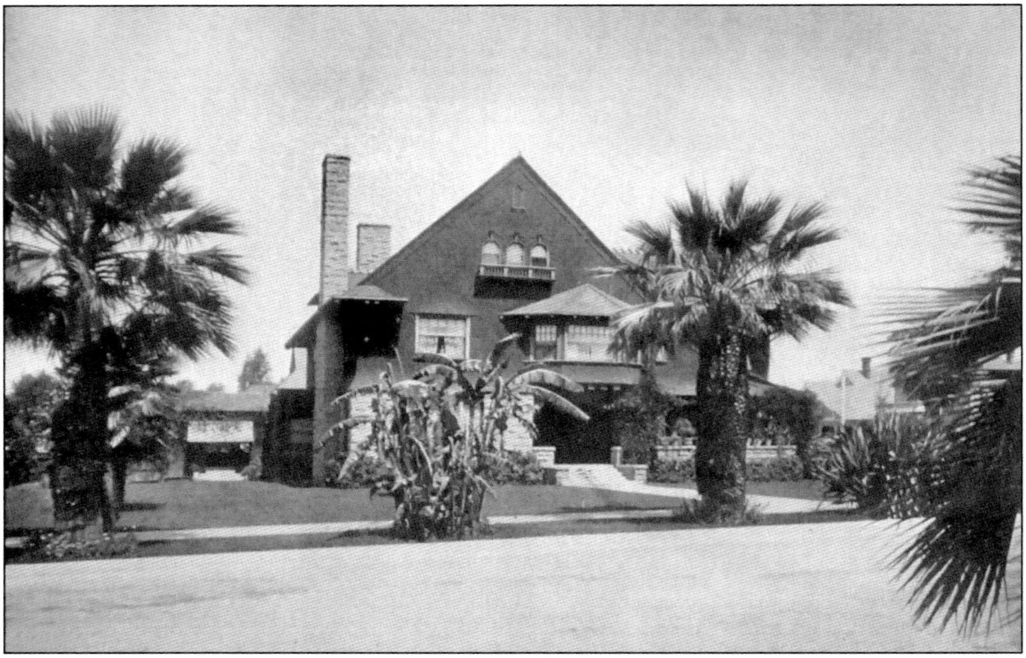

VON SCHMIDT RESIDENCE. Count Jaro von Schmidt was one of the very first to build a home on Chester Place, at the corner of Twenty-third Street. He and the countess were exceptionally popular in West Adams society, but after over a dozen years in the home, his health began to fail. He sold the property at a discount, fled to Europe to recuperate, and died in Prague in 1914.

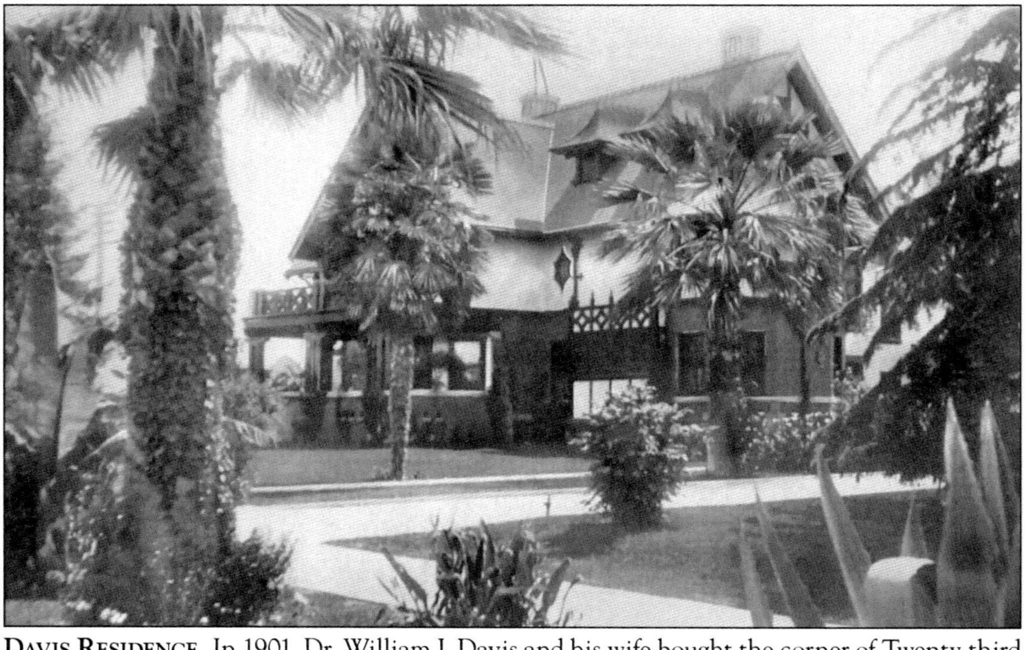

DAVIS RESIDENCE. In 1901, Dr. William J. Davis and his wife bought the corner of Twenty-third Street and Chester Place to build this English-style, 14-room residence. The cost reported in the newspapers ranged anywhere from $12,000 to $20,000. Davis, who made a fortune in Arizona mining, did not stay in the house very long. In April 1906, he sold the home for $45,000 and moved to the more suburban Westchester Place, still in the West Adams area.

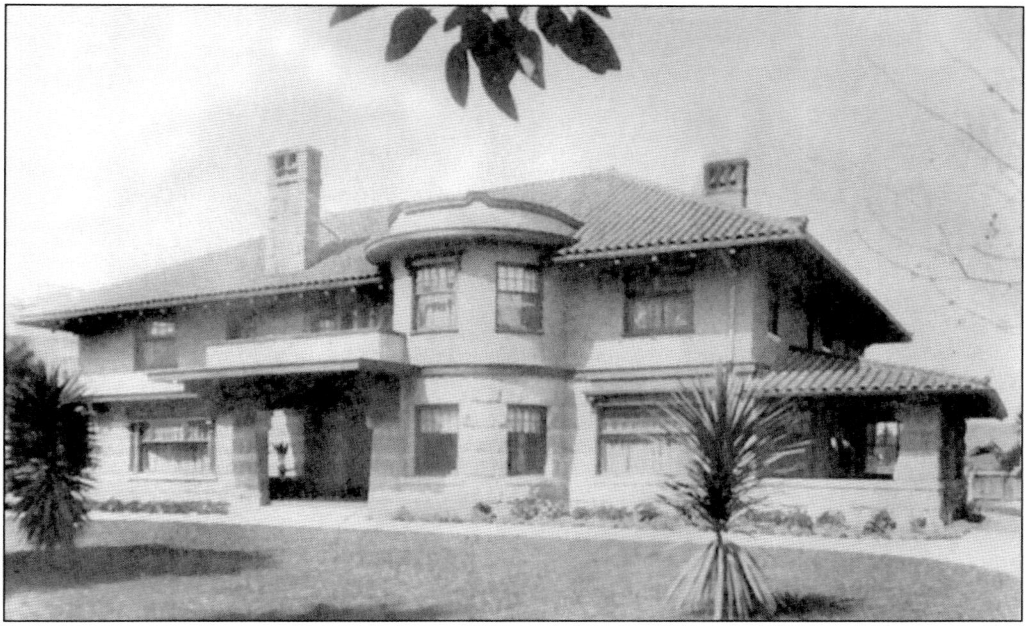

Foster Residence. Lee W. Foster had made a fortune in Montana mining before building this Italian Renaissance home at 17 Chester Place. The interior featured beamed ceilings, hardwood wainscoting, a Turkish smoking room and den, and a sophisticated heating and electrical system. Foster enjoyed it for only four years before his wife found him on the tiled floor of one of his wainscoted bathrooms, dead from a stroke.

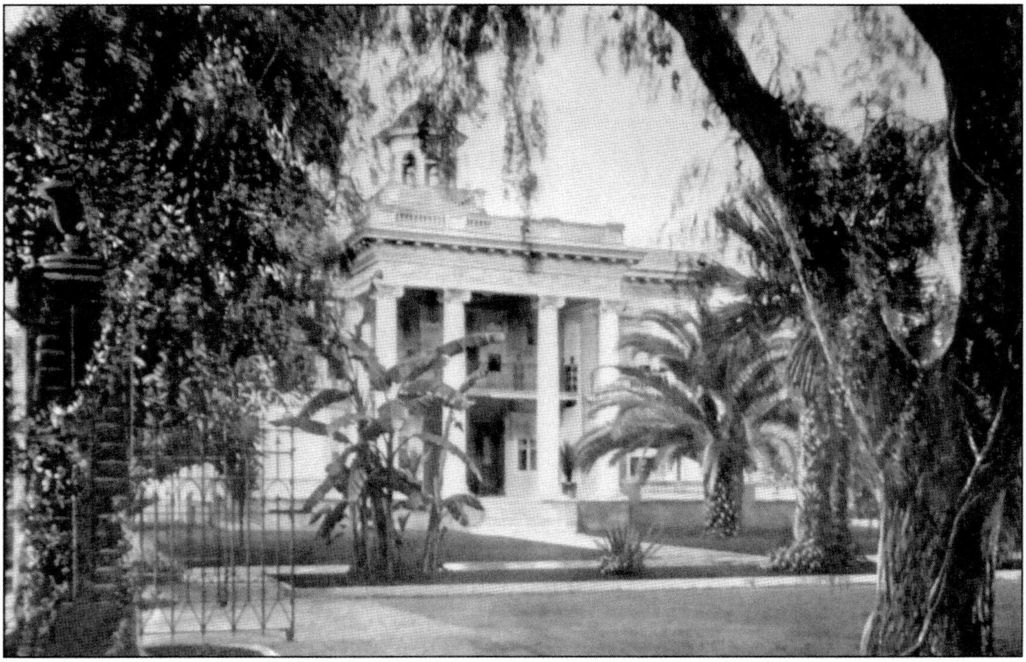

Gray Residence. When it was completed in 1902 for Mr. and Mrs. Harry Gray, this Colonial residence at 19 Chester Place was a showplace in yellow with white trim. In September 1903, Mrs. Gray discovered her bedroom had been ransacked by a burglar while the Grays were dining downstairs. Less than six months later, they sold the house for $40,000 and moved to Pasadena.

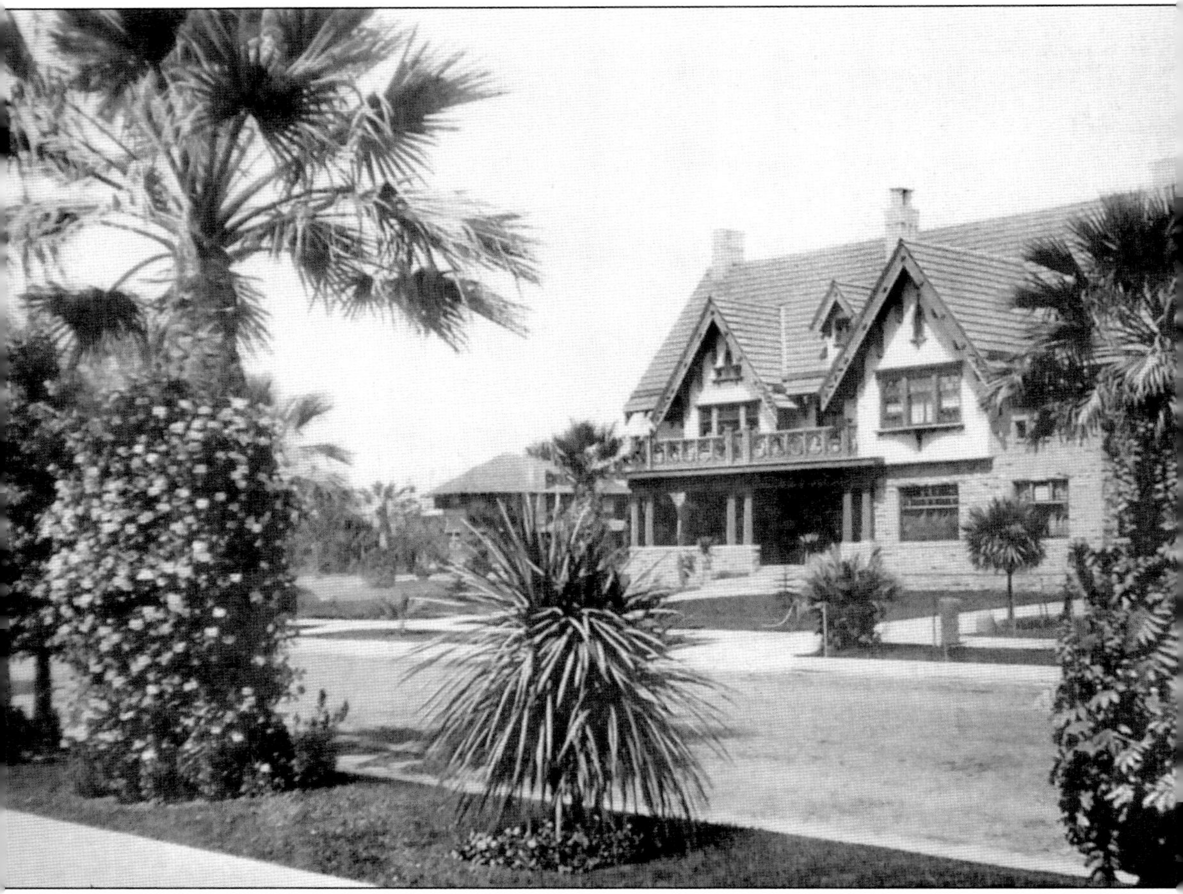

Vermilion Residence. A. S. Vermilion's name was rarely spelled the same way twice, but whether they identified her as Artemisia Vermilion or Artimisia Vermillion, the press was always in agreement on the beauty of her home. The *Los Angeles Times* described a gathering in "one of the handsomest interiors in the city, adapted admirably to the needs of large social functions" where "handsomely-gowned women gathered in ever-changing groups found fitting background in rich draperies and artistic furnishings." The house at 11 Chester Place was designed by Hunt and Eager in 1902. Upstairs were six bedrooms, each with its own bathroom. A reception room downstairs was decorated in white and gold, painted with exquisite designs in oil. Rugs could be removed from the polished floors downstairs, where large doorways connecting dining room to hall to living room allowed space "where maidens and escorts flitted to and fro, keeping time with the latest waltz or two-step."

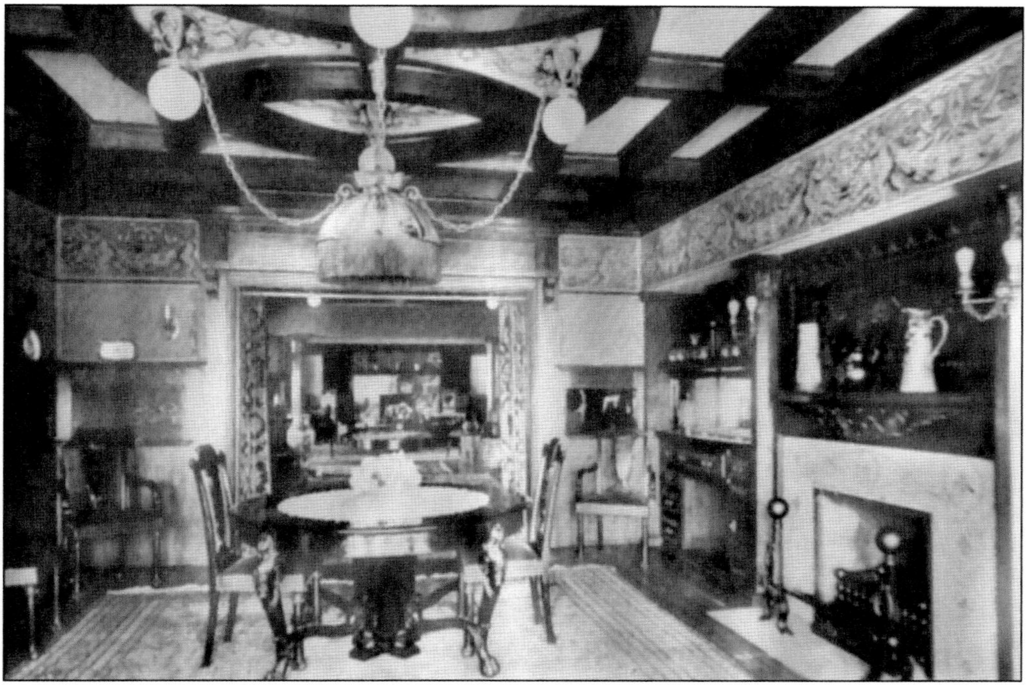

VERMILION INTERIOR. For at least one party, Mrs. Vermilion placed a centerpiece of white sweet peas on her dining room table, which was covered with a Battenberg table cover she bought in Germany. The adjoining breakfast room was perfumed with pink sweet peas.

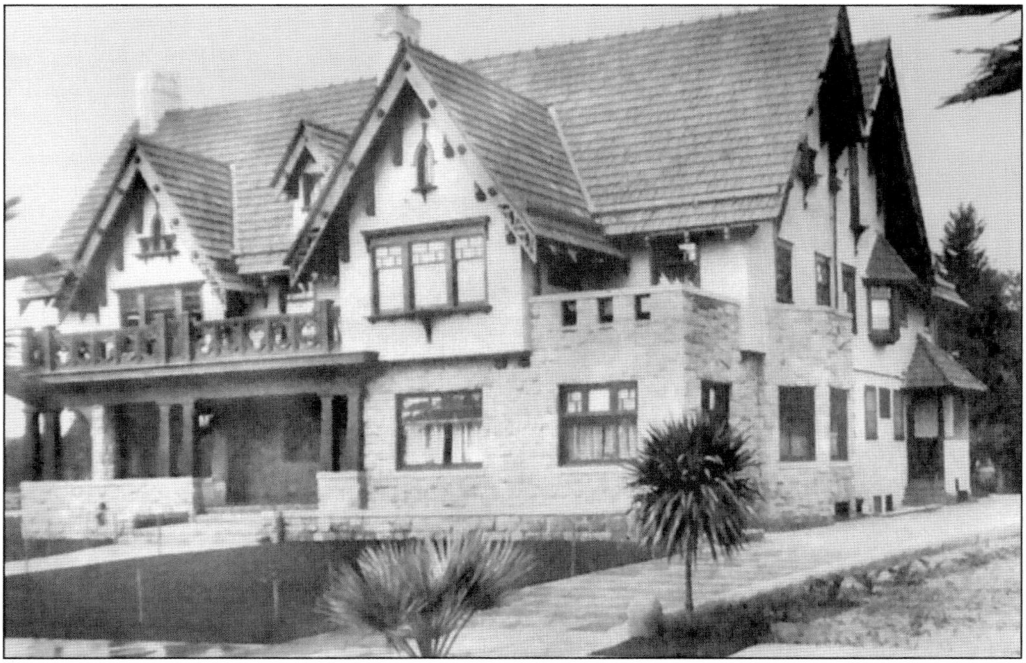

VERMILION HOME. Mrs. Vermilion, sadly, outlived her husband and all of her children. In 1896, she petitioned for guardianship of her grandson, six-year-old David S. Gottschalk. Her son, Harry, who had retired from railroad work to attend to her properties more than 10 years before, died at her home in 1915.

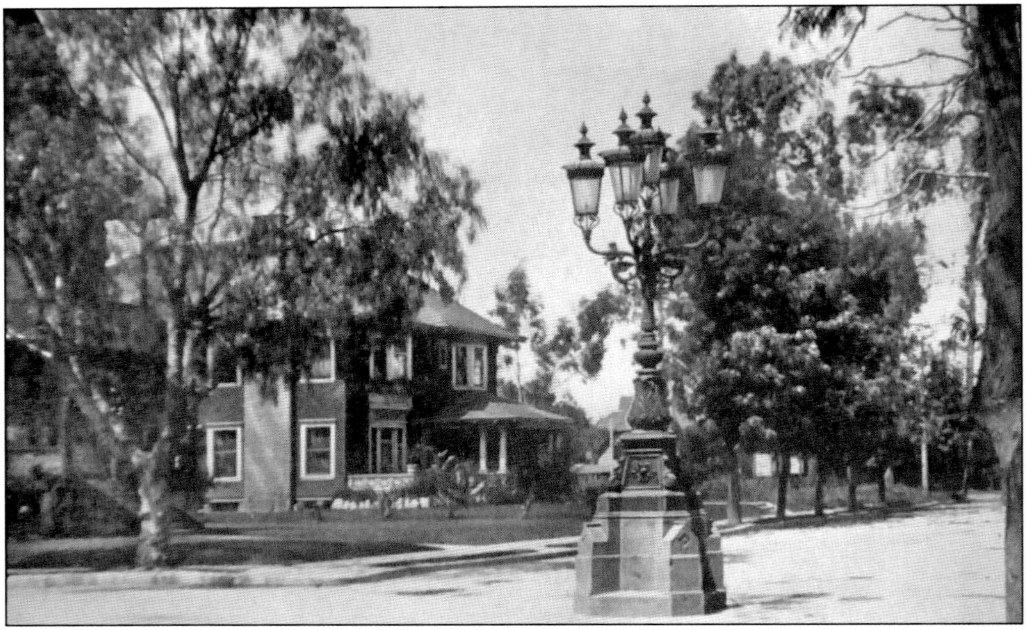

ST. JAMES PARK. "St. James Park is away out on Figueroa-street," wrote the *Los Angeles Times* in 1888. "It's not so public. . . . the grounds are pretty and well kept, and have more flowers about them. . . . if only it were nearer town and easier of access it would be the most beautiful and popular place of the town." Occupants of the surrounding mansions probably did not consider its relative inaccessibility a drawback.

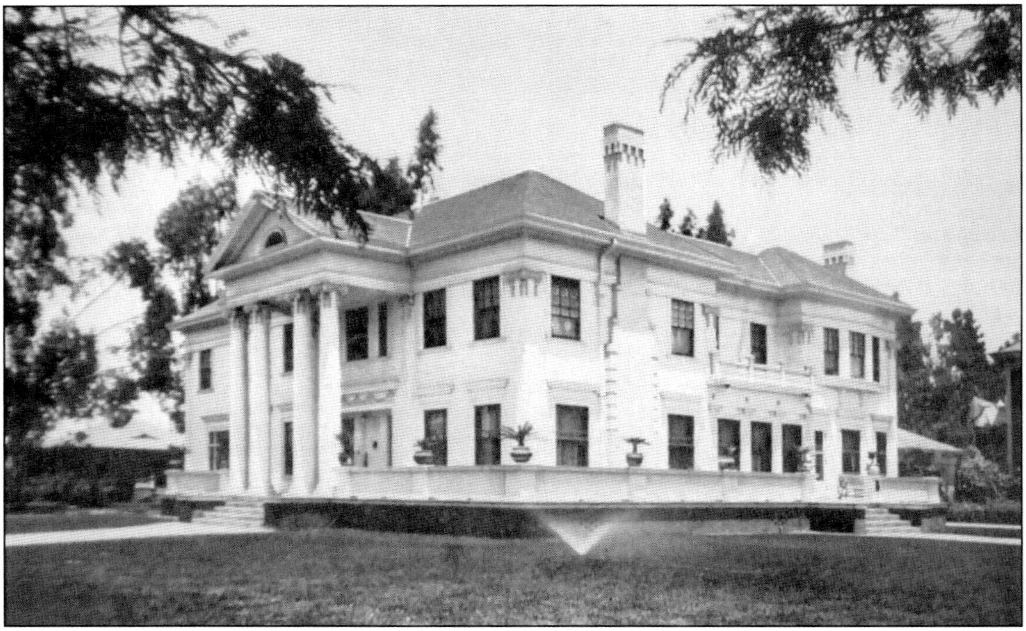

STEARNS-DOCKWEILER RESIDENCE. A 1917 wedding united the children of two prominent early California families when Katherine Stearns, resplendent in white satin and lace, married her neighbor, Lt. Thomas Dockweiler. He joined his father's law firm; she was active in social and charitable circles. After the deaths of her parents, the couple moved to 27 St. James Park, the house John Parkinson had designed for the Stearns family in 1900.

Four

Hoover Street to Western Avenue

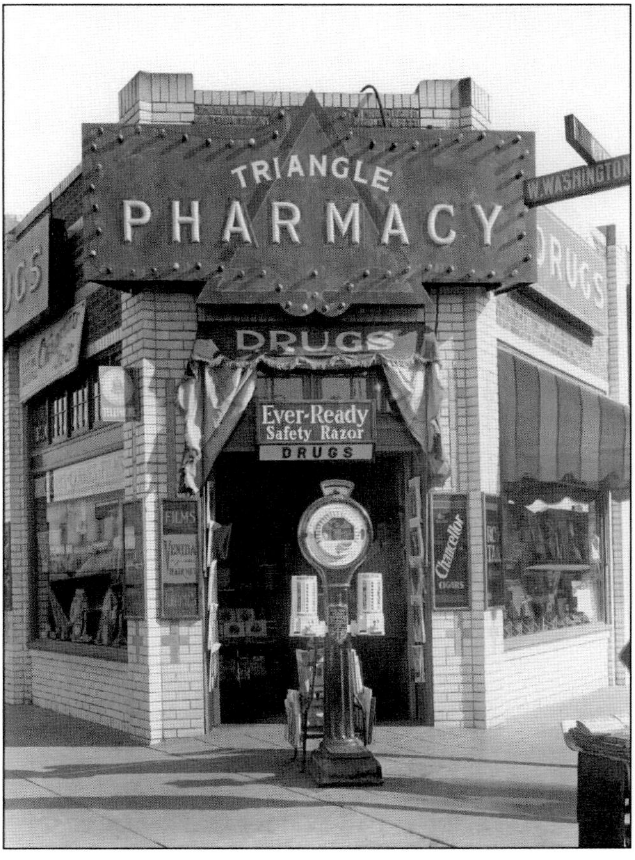

Triangle Pharmacy. Before the rise of chain pharmacies, every neighborhood had a corner drugstore. The Triangle Pharmacy at the corner of Washington and Hoover Streets carried a variety of items: film, hairnets, and cigars. Ever-Ready Safety Razors provoked a small flurry of patriotism in 1927, when one of their largest single orders was sent to England, because it was assumed that the traditional home of fine cutlery would not order blades from the United States unless they were extraordinarily well made. The Pacific Peerless Weighing Machine outside helped flappers maintain their slender, boyish figures. When the company's downtown office was robbed in 1925, the police recovered 60,444 pennies—600 pounds worth. (Courtesy of the University of Southern California, on behalf of the USC Specialized Libraries and Archival Collections.)

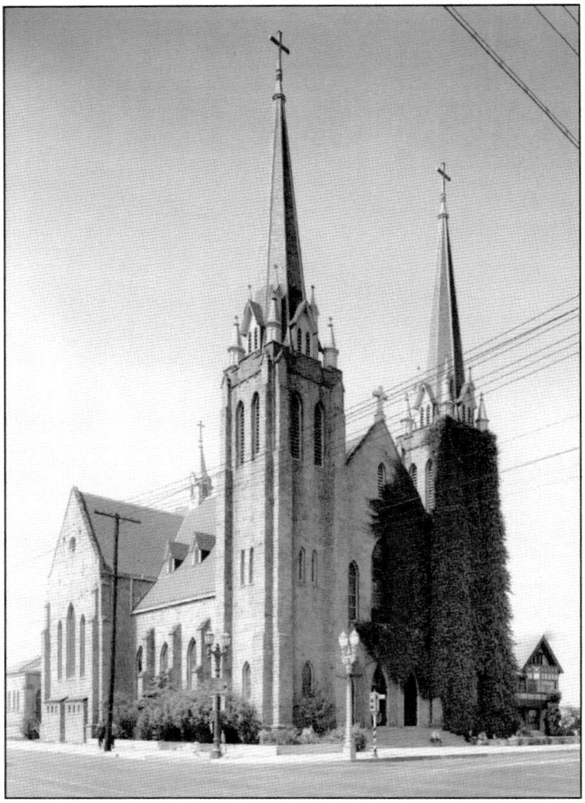

ST. AGNES CATHOLIC CHURCH (1941). A 1903 plan to build on Adams Boulevard at Budlong Avenue was derailed by neighbors, who objected to a church in their very exclusive neighborhood. They were, however, willing to offer $2,000 and an alternate site just blocks away at Vermont Avenue. The church was dedicated Thanksgiving 1907. Due to earthquake damage, the Gothic structure has been replaced with a modern building. (Courtesy of Bison Archives.)

FIRE STATION 8. In 1900, a firehouse was planned for Engine Company 8 on Hoover Street just north of Washington Street. Forty-five years later, assistant fire chief Wesley E. Augustine recalled that when he joined the department in 1909, he was one of only 175 men, and the most frequent request from passersby was, "May I come in and pet your horses?" (Courtesy of Los Angeles Fire Department Historic Archive.)

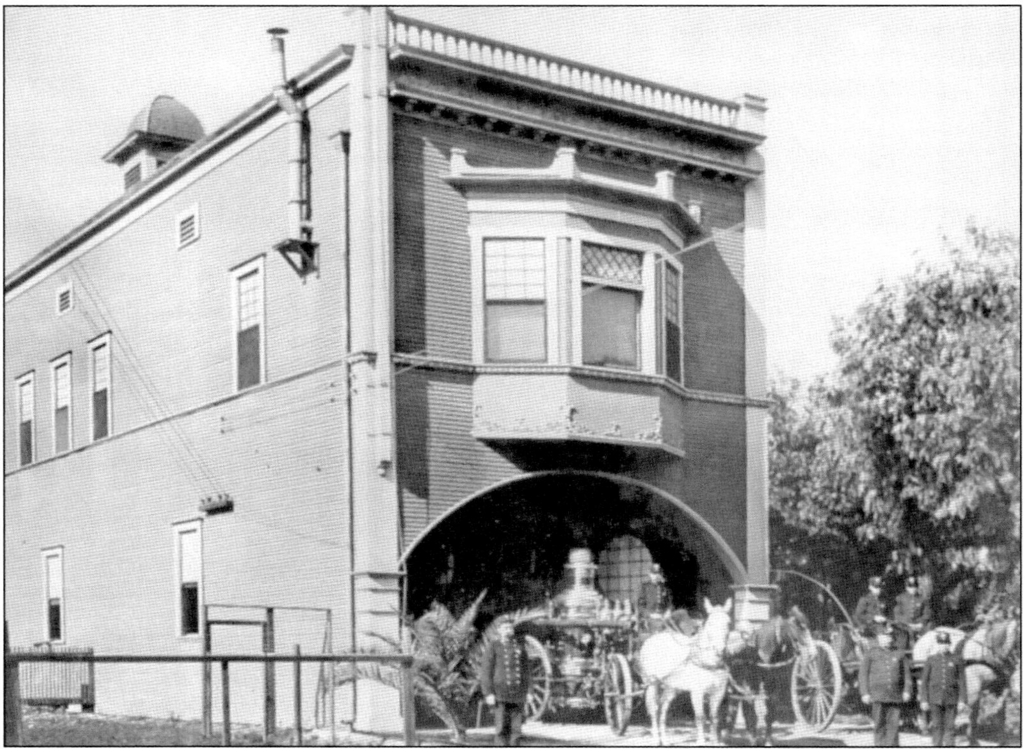

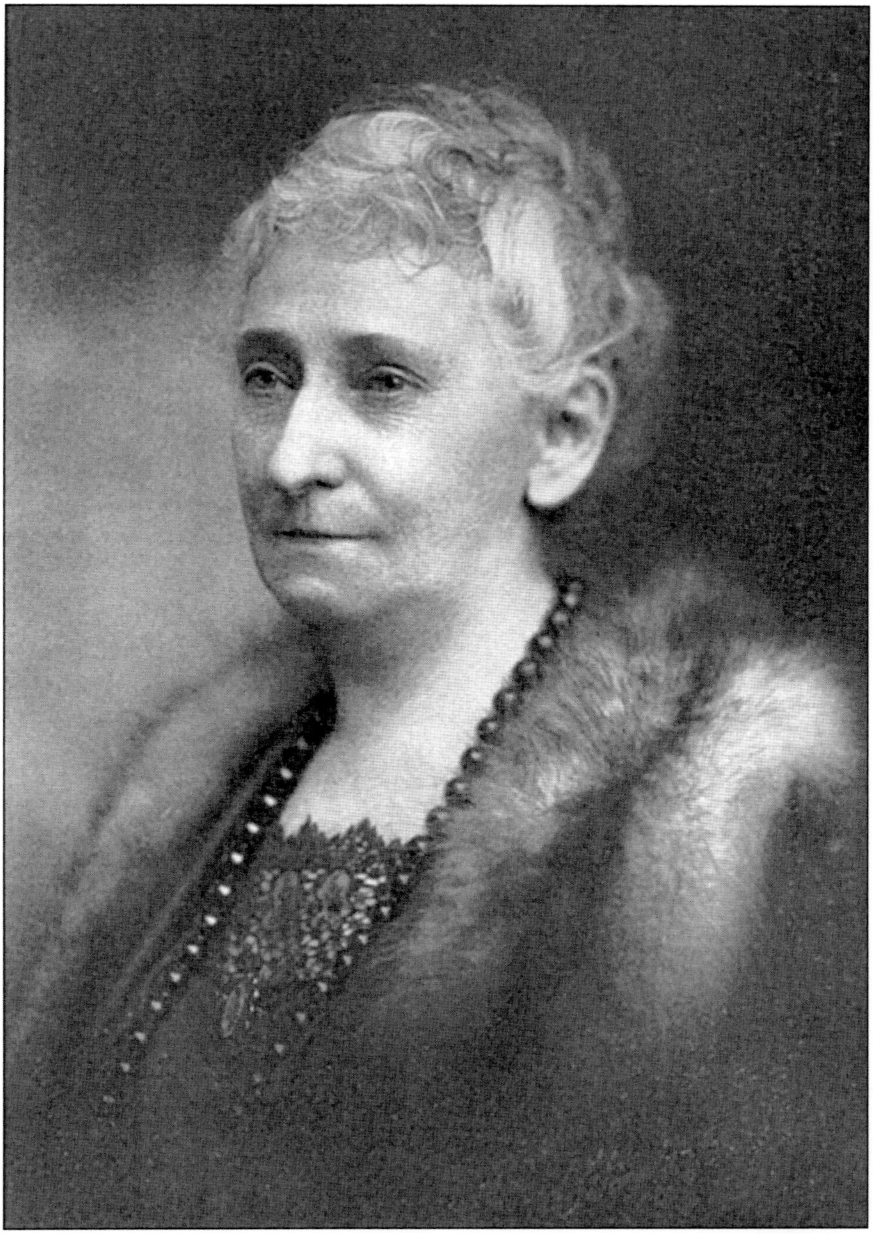

ADELIA EDWARDS HICKMAN. One of Adelia Hickman's poems, "In California," ended with "The investments are securest, the real estate the surest, the best thing for the tourist, in California." This was possibly a bit self-serving, since in 1907 she became the first woman to open her own real estate office in Los Angeles, called Union "Square" Realty. Her office was on a city square, but the name also had metaphorical significance: as a woman in a man's world, she had to give her customers a square deal or better. She believed strongly in both the city and the women who lived here and once said, "My message to every woman everywhere is to think success, then come to Los Angeles and realize it." Her home in 1915 was at 1125 West Twenty-fifth Street. Perhaps it inspired the lines: "The bungalows are the coziest, in California, the maidens are the rosiest, in California, the lovers are the thickest, the lovesick are the sickest, the autos go the quickest, in California."

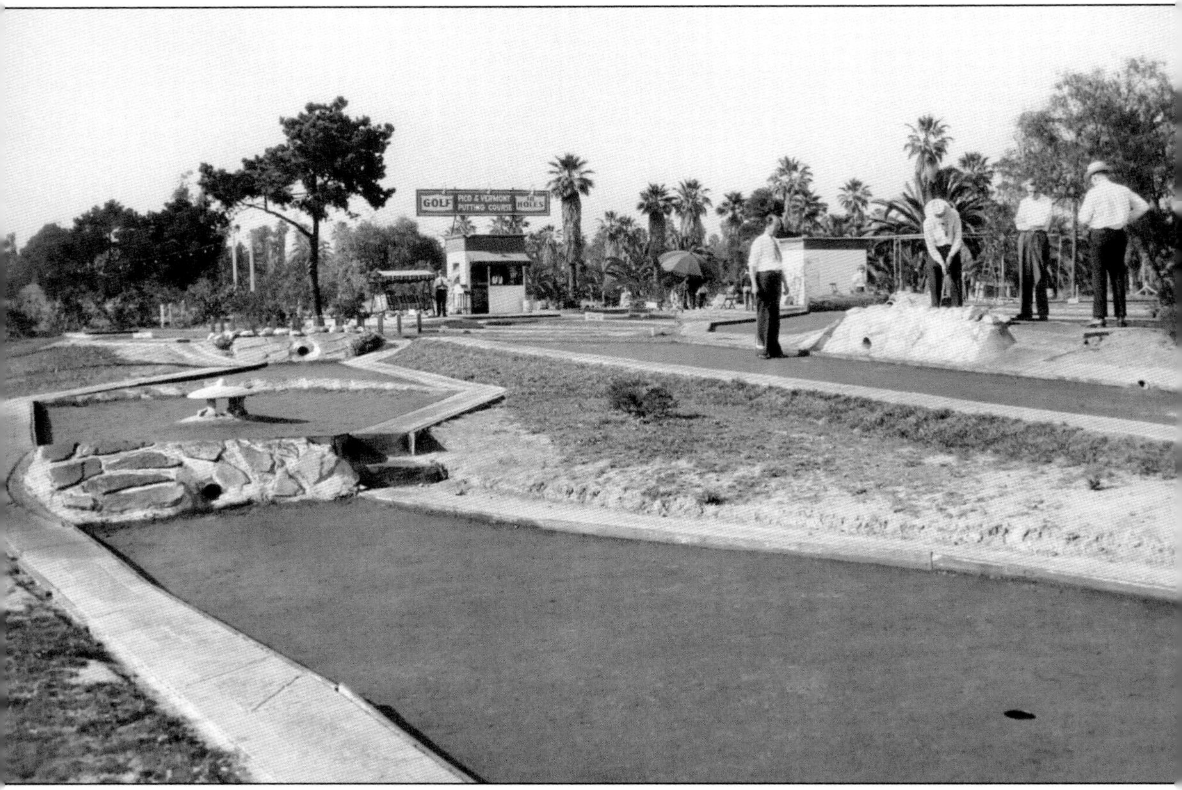

MINIATURE GOLF COURSE (1930). Miniature golf was immensely popular around 1930, and golf courses sprouted all over the city, sometimes within blocks of each other. In 1929, there were 10 or 12 golf courses in the entire city. By 1930, there were a dozen in West Adams alone, including this one at Vermont Avenue and Pico Boulevard. The manager of one course believed the phenomenal growth was because the whole family could have fun together with "no chance for anything smutty or suggestive, as there is at a good many picture shows." Maybe this was so, but economics took its toll. The next year, miniature golf courses were back to a handful of listings. (Courtesy of the University of Southern California, on behalf of the USC Specialized Libraries and Archival Collections.)

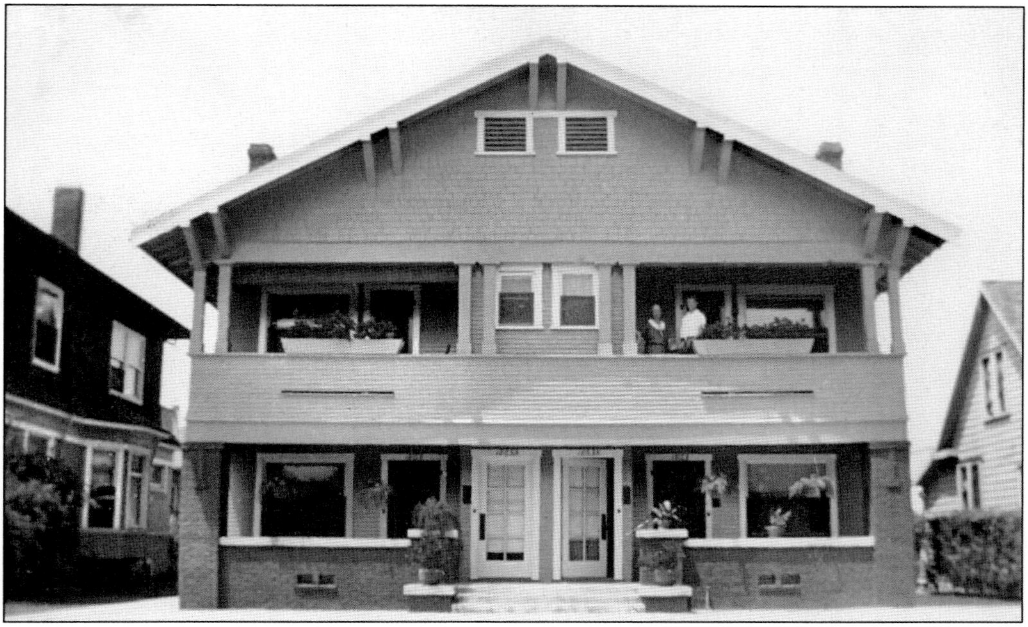

APARTMENT, 1863–1865 WEST TWENTY-FIFTH STREET. Apartment houses were not unusual in West Adams, some being built as far back as the 1890s. This craftsman-style building in the 1800 block of West Twenty-fifth Street has much of the same detail as the houses around it, with bracketed eaves, brick porch railings and columns, and a combination of clapboard and shingle siding.

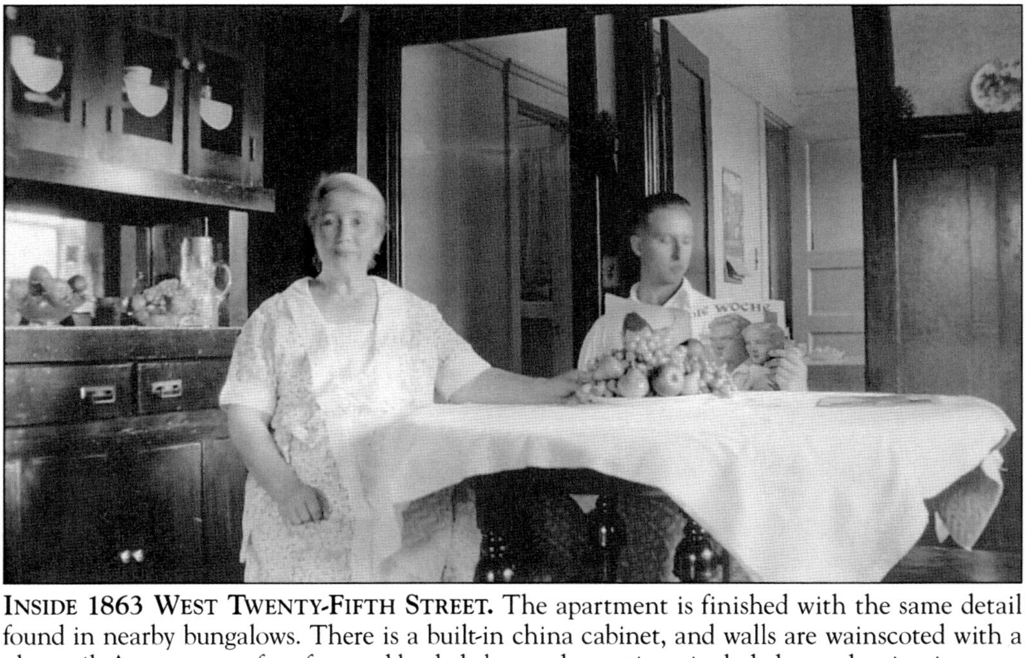

INSIDE 1863 WEST TWENTY-FIFTH STREET. The apartment is finished with the same detail found in nearby bungalows. There is a built-in china cabinet, and walls are wainscoted with a plate rail. Apartments often featured leaded glass and sometimes included a mechanism in upper units to open the door at the bottom of the stairs by pulling a lever. The young man is reading the German magazine *Die Woche*.

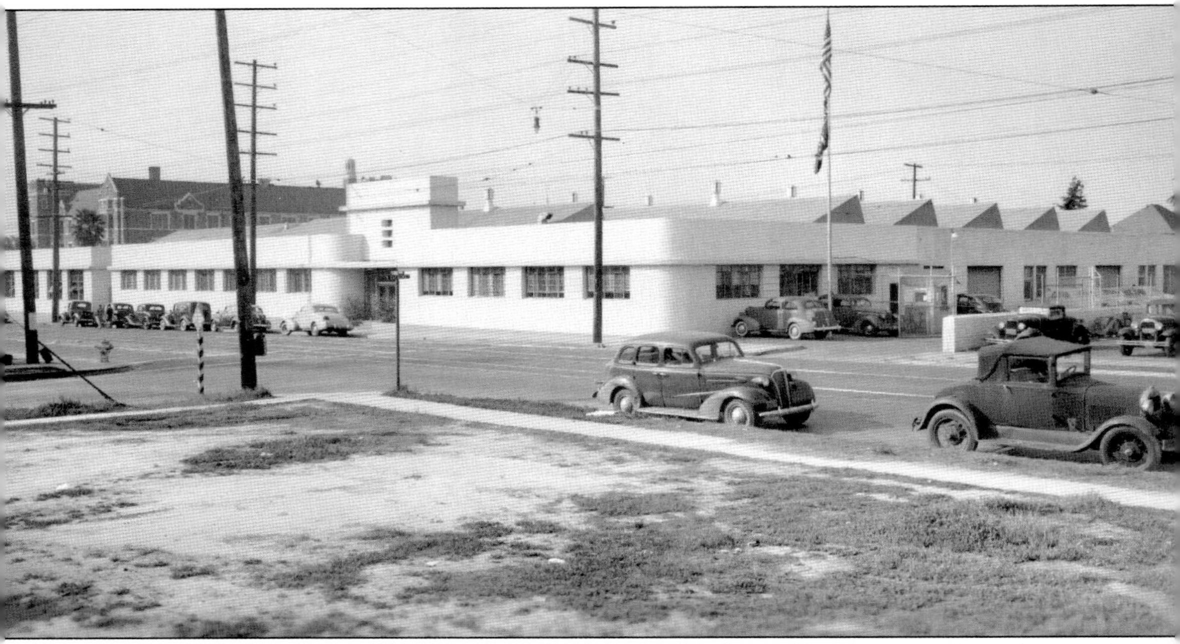

GILFILLAN. In 1912, Gilfillan Brothers Smelting and Refining Company was formed to supply precious metals to jewelers, dentists, and other businesses. By the 1940s, they were manufacturing radios and ultimately televisions from this very modern building on Venice Boulevard. During World War II, the company branched into military radar systems with such success that by 1950 they had ceased making televisions altogether. Eventually the business was moved to the San Fernando Valley to be near the Van Nuys Airport. Today it is a part of ITT Corporation, and its former location was razed to make room for the athletic field of Loyola High School next door. (Courtesy of ITT Corporation.)

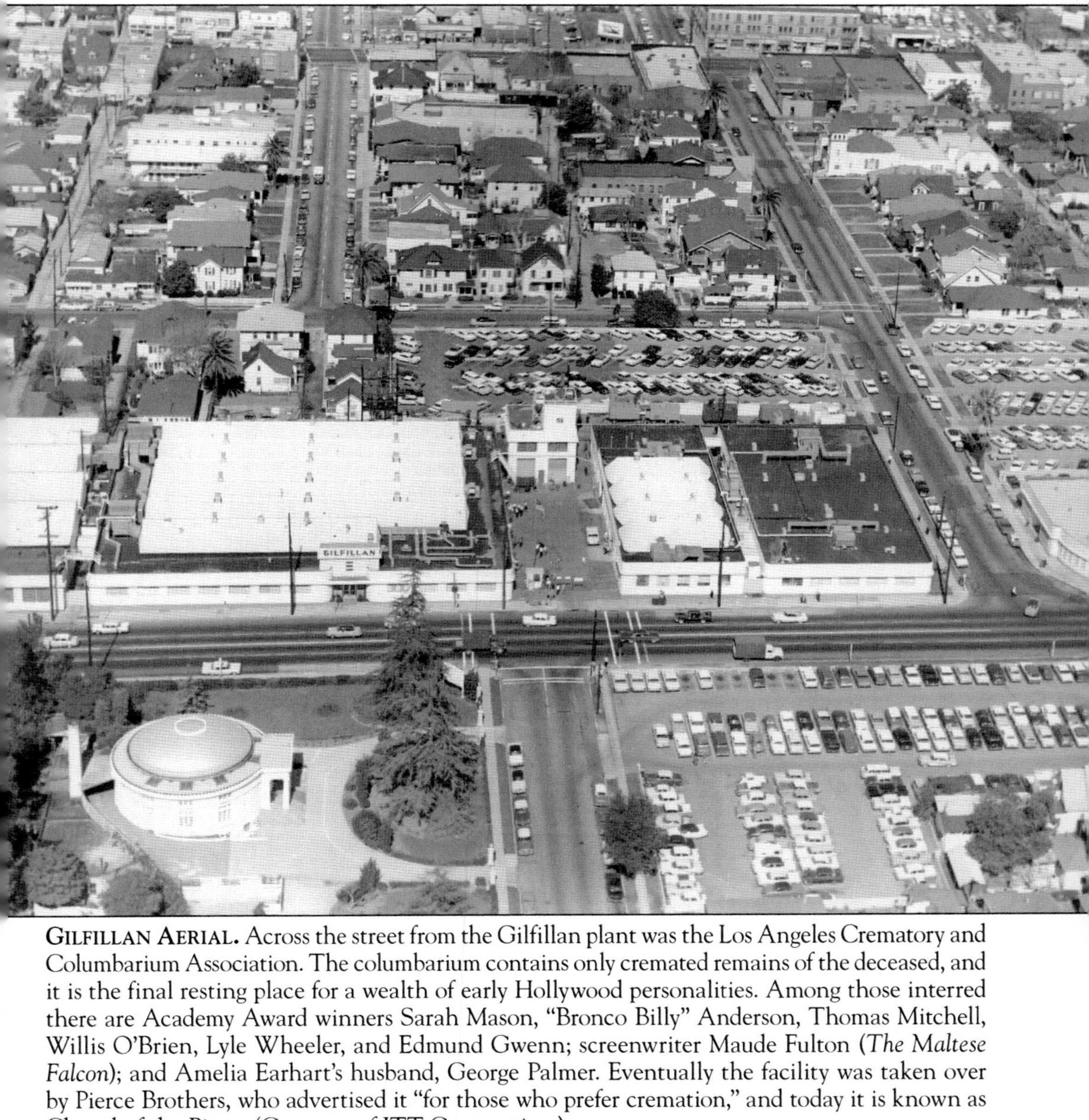

GILFILLAN AERIAL. Across the street from the Gilfillan plant was the Los Angeles Crematory and Columbarium Association. The columbarium contains only cremated remains of the deceased, and it is the final resting place for a wealth of early Hollywood personalities. Among those interred there are Academy Award winners Sarah Mason, "Bronco Billy" Anderson, Thomas Mitchell, Willis O'Brien, Lyle Wheeler, and Edmund Gwenn; screenwriter Maude Fulton (*The Maltese Falcon*); and Amelia Earhart's husband, George Palmer. Eventually the facility was taken over by Pierce Brothers, who advertised it "for those who prefer cremation," and today it is known as Chapel of the Pines. (Courtesy of ITT Corporation.)

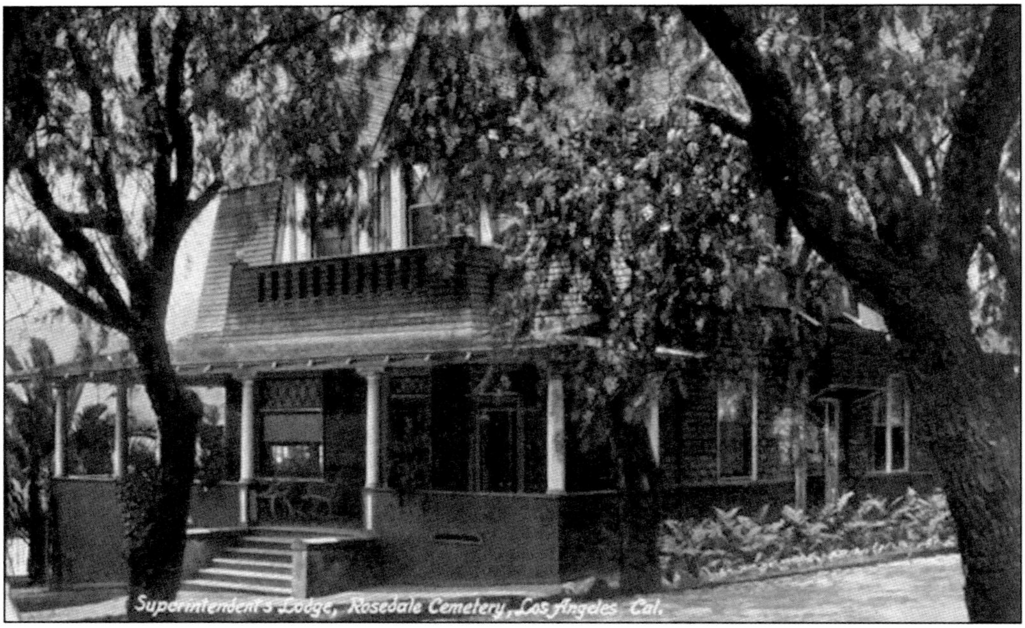

ROSEDALE CEMETERY SUPERINTENDENT'S LODGE. A reporter for the *Los Angeles Times* visited the new Rosedale Cemetery in November 1884. He pronounced the 65 acres between Washington Boulevard and Pico Street beautiful, with a view "that embraces the whole of the valley, and on clear days, the ocean." There had, at that time, been 12 interments. This bungalow housed an on-site caretaker.

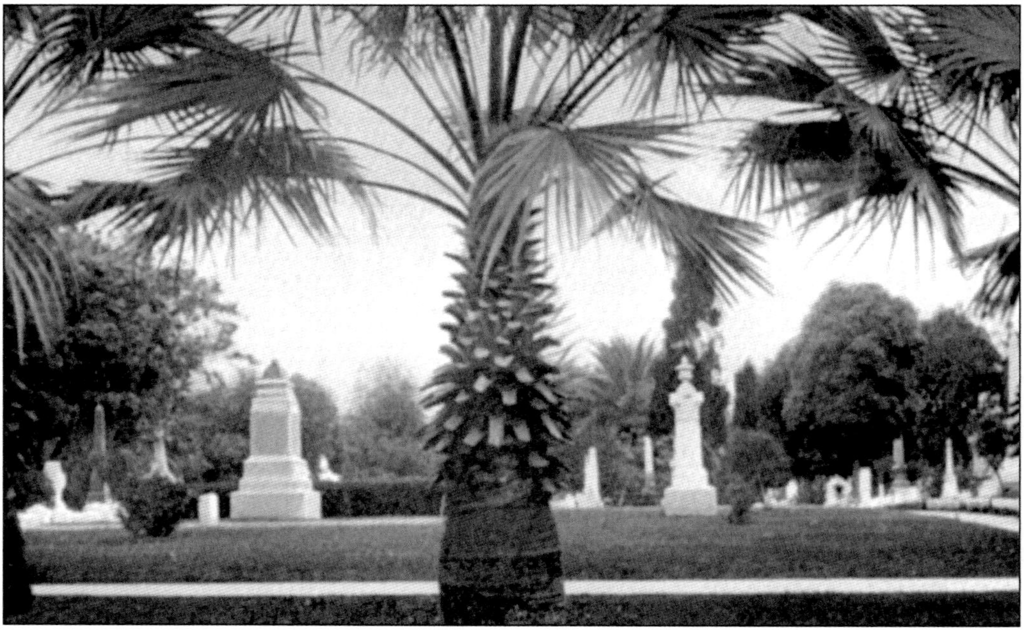

ROSEDALE CEMETERY. Rosedale Cemetery was open to all races and creeds. When West Adams resident Hattie McDaniel, who won an Oscar as Mammy in *Gone With the Wind*, expressed a wish to be buried in Hollywood, the cemetery there refused because of her race. In recent years, Hollywood Forever Cemetery invited the family to move her, but remembering the past slight, they chose to leave her at Rosedale.

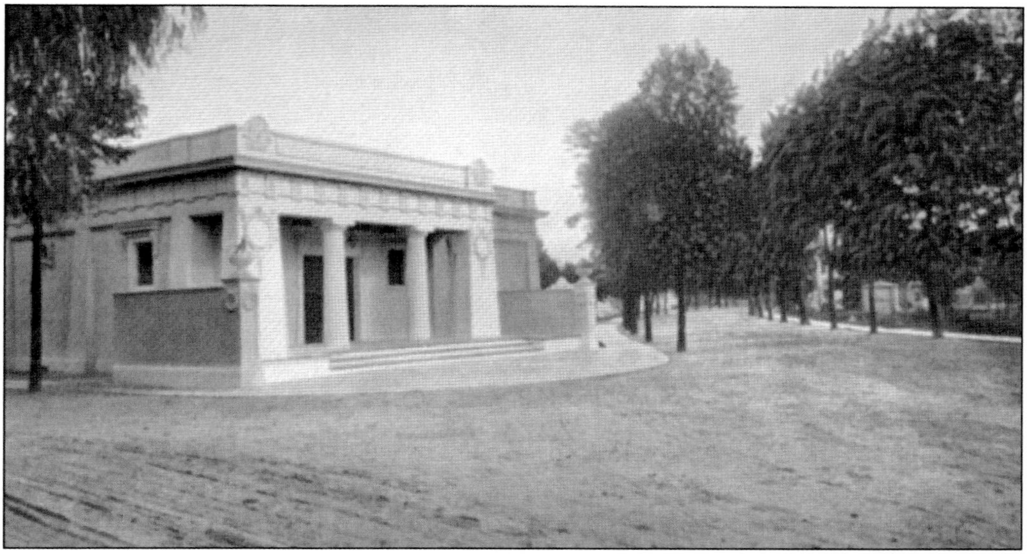

Rosedale Cemetery, Mausoleum. Property owners converged on the Health and Sanitation Committee of the city council in 1919 to protest Rosedale's plans to build a mausoleum. The committee agreed, but the decision was overruled by the Board of Public Works. Their visit was not a total loss, however. The committee also voted to label vehicles carrying dead bodies "Mortuary" and prohibit ambulances from being used for the purpose.

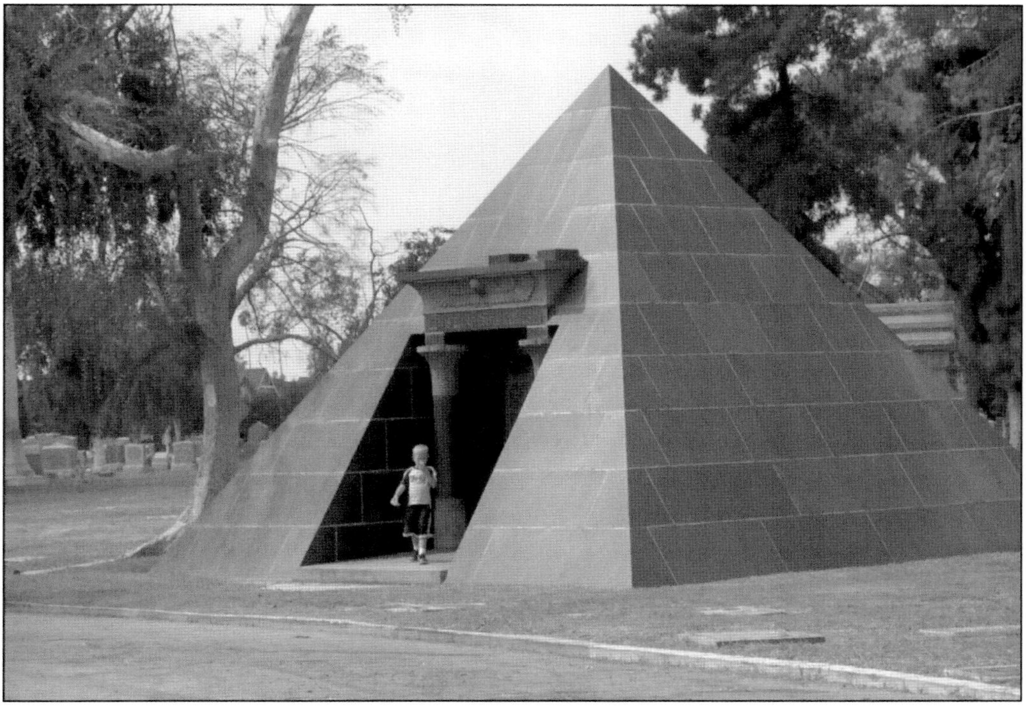

Lewis and Emma Grigsby Mausoleum. Angelus Rosedale Cemetery, as it is today known, features two pyramid-shaped mausoleums: this one, in polished black granite, and the Shatto monument in a rough red stone. When Emma Grigsby died in 1930, her husband donated chimes to a church in Washington, D.C., in her honor, echoing a gift of a 20-tone set of chimes the couple gave to Wilshire Boulevard Congregational Church in 1927.

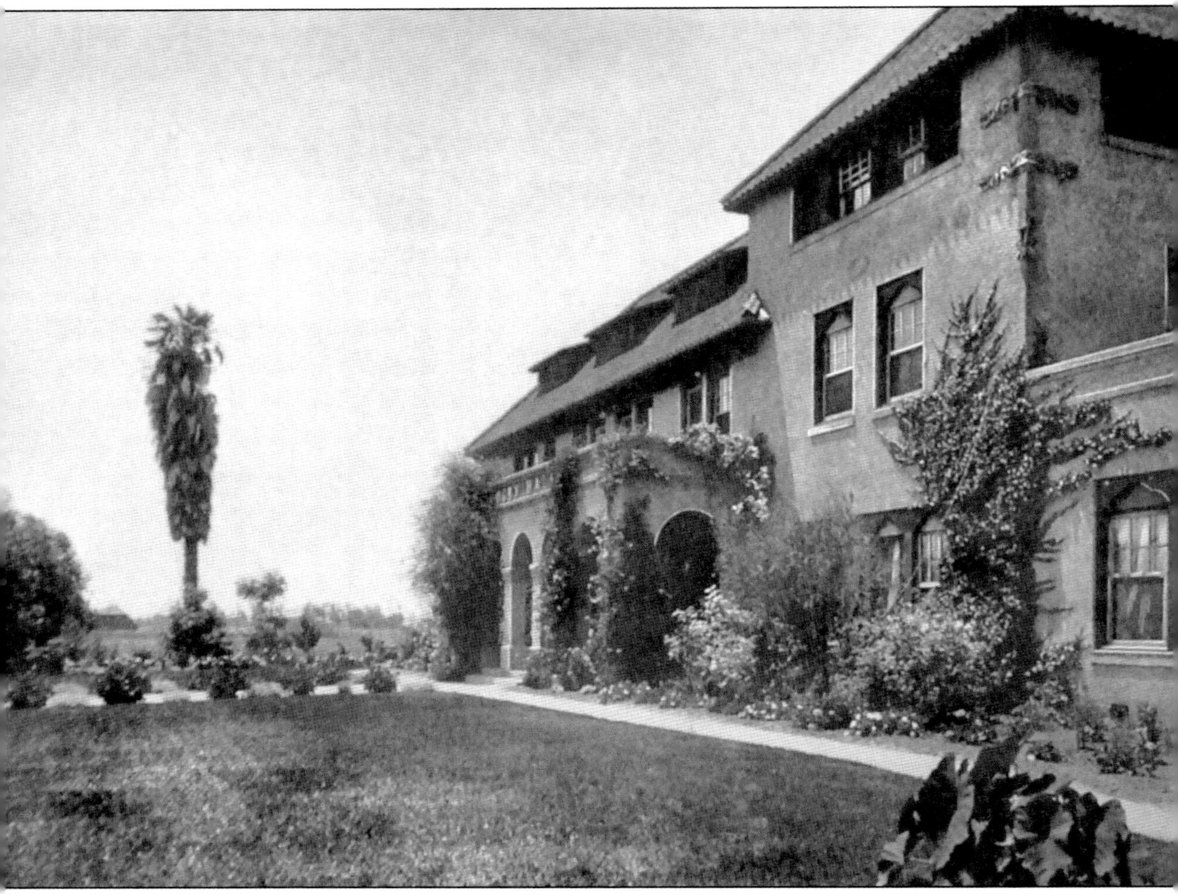

HARVARD MILITARY SCHOOL. Mayor Frederick Eaton's skillful trowel work elicited applause when the cornerstone was laid for Harvard Military School in 1900. "Character building will hold first place" at the boys' school, said Grenville C. Emery, headmaster and founder. Perhaps, but in 1907, the *Los Angeles Times* wrote, "An evil-smelling cigarette, several bottles of liquid joy that was not soda pop, and the peculiar desire of boys to cut one another's hair" led the school to cancel commencement ceremonies, much to the disappointment of the boys' girlfriends, who were forced to do without the graduation dance. Other classes managed to stay out of trouble, and the school grew. Over the years, various buildings were designed by Arthur B. Benton and John C. Austin in the mission style recommended by Charles Lummis.

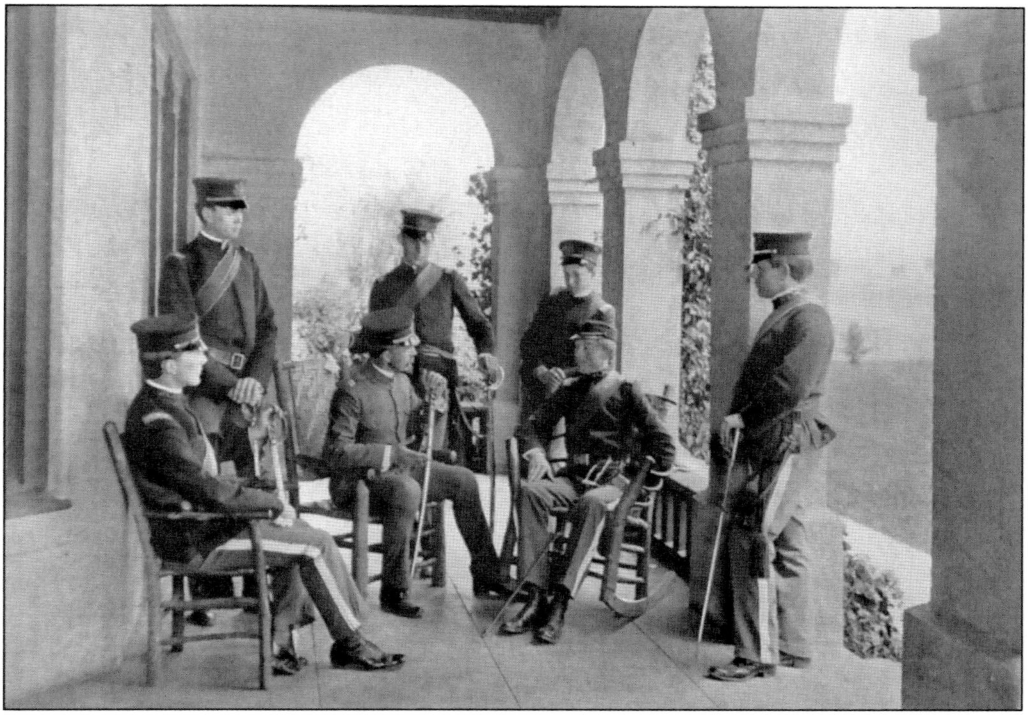

HARVARD MILITARY SCHOOL OFFICERS. Students were expected to learn to read intelligently, cipher accurately, and write a respectable letter to prepare them for college and a business or military career. Early morning reveille, uniforms, and daily drills were part of the school culture. Many wealthy and famous men, including J. Paul Getty, were once students.

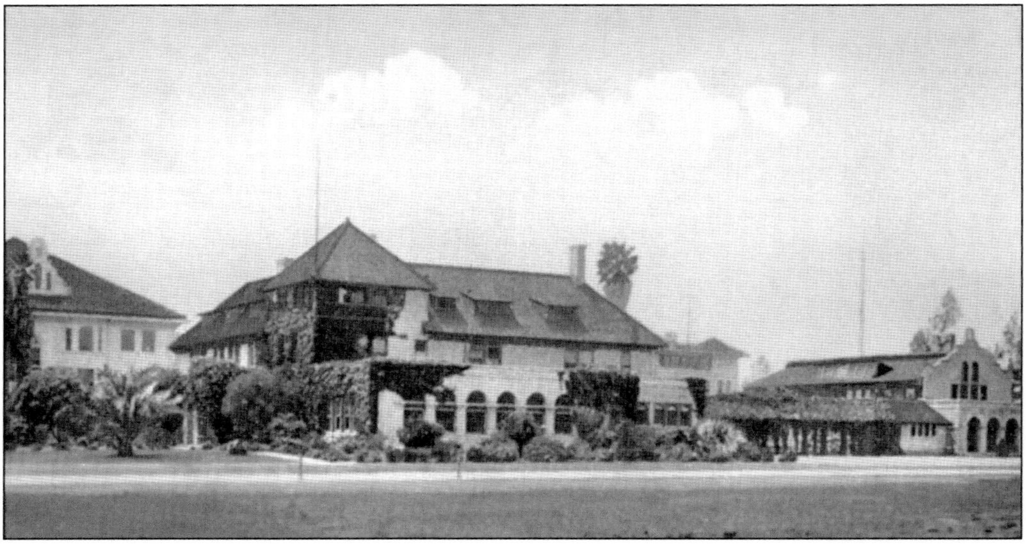

HARVARD MILITARY SCHOOL CAMPUS. Acres of land at Western Avenue and Sixteenth Street (now Venice Boulevard) gave ample space for playing fields, and the school's athletic teams excelled. In 1911, Emery offered the school to the Episcopal diocese, whose bishop felt "education . . . is more important than building cathedrals." In 1926, seeking more space, the school moved from West Adams and eventually became Harvard-Westlake. (Courtesy of Rory Cunningham.)

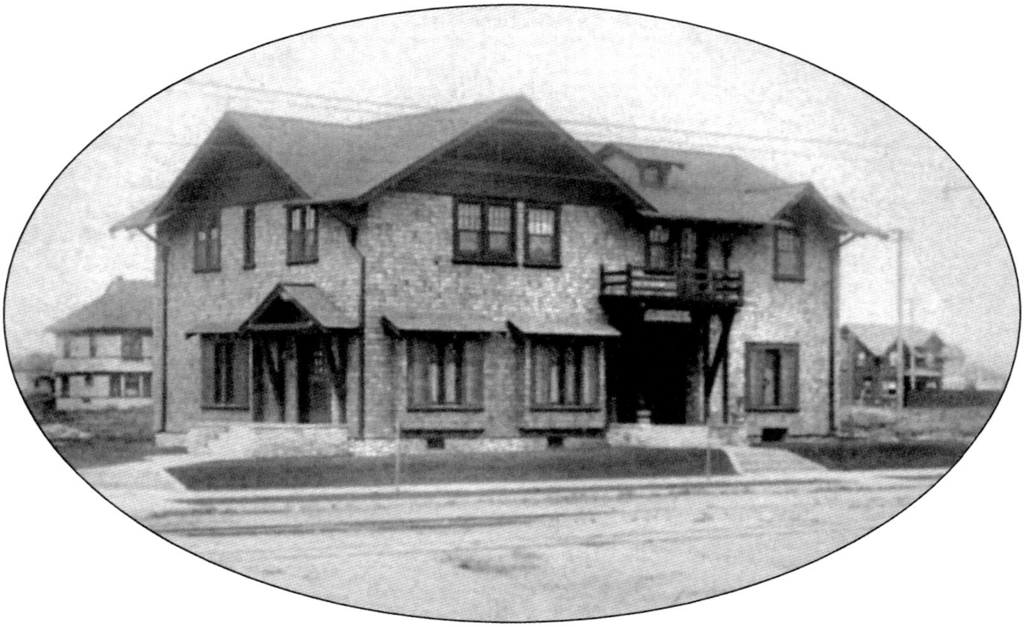

PIKE RESIDENCE. Eva Frances Pike was the head of the music department at Harvard Military School for 23 years—not too surprising, since the school was founded by her brother. Entertainment at her home at 2289 West Sixteenth Street usually featured musical performances. She was a proud member of the Daughters of the American Revolution, tracing her ancestry to Jonathan Parker, one of the Sons of Liberty who threw tea in Boston Harbor.

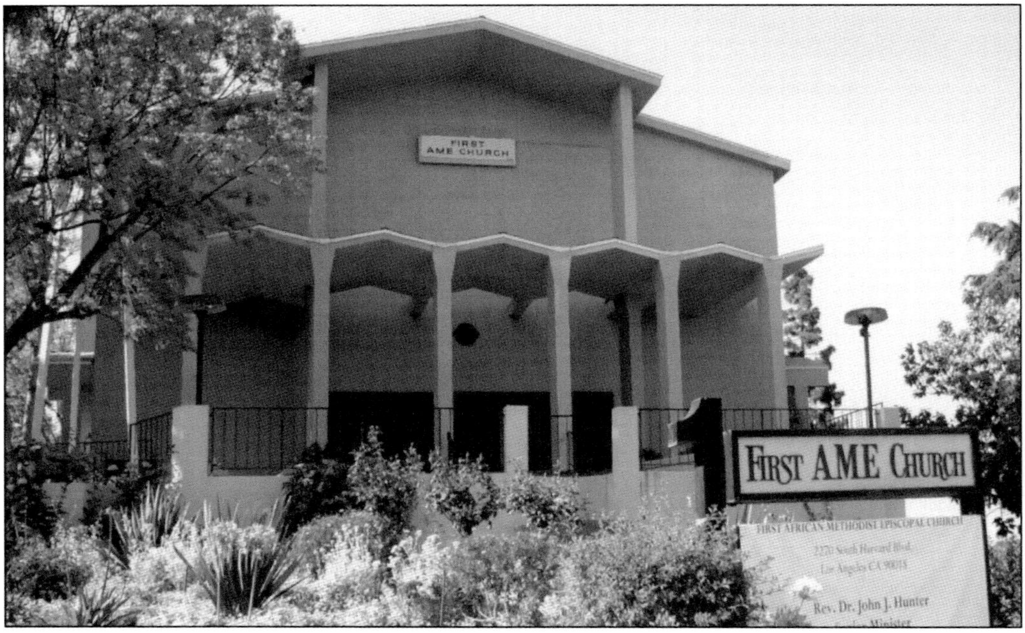

FAME. First African Methodist Episcopal Church is the oldest church in Los Angeles founded by African Americans. Begun by Biddy Mason in 1872, it has grown into one of the most important churches in the region. From an architectural good news standpoint, they have rescued and adapted several historic buildings, including a 1924 telephone company building on Adams Boulevard near Western Avenue.

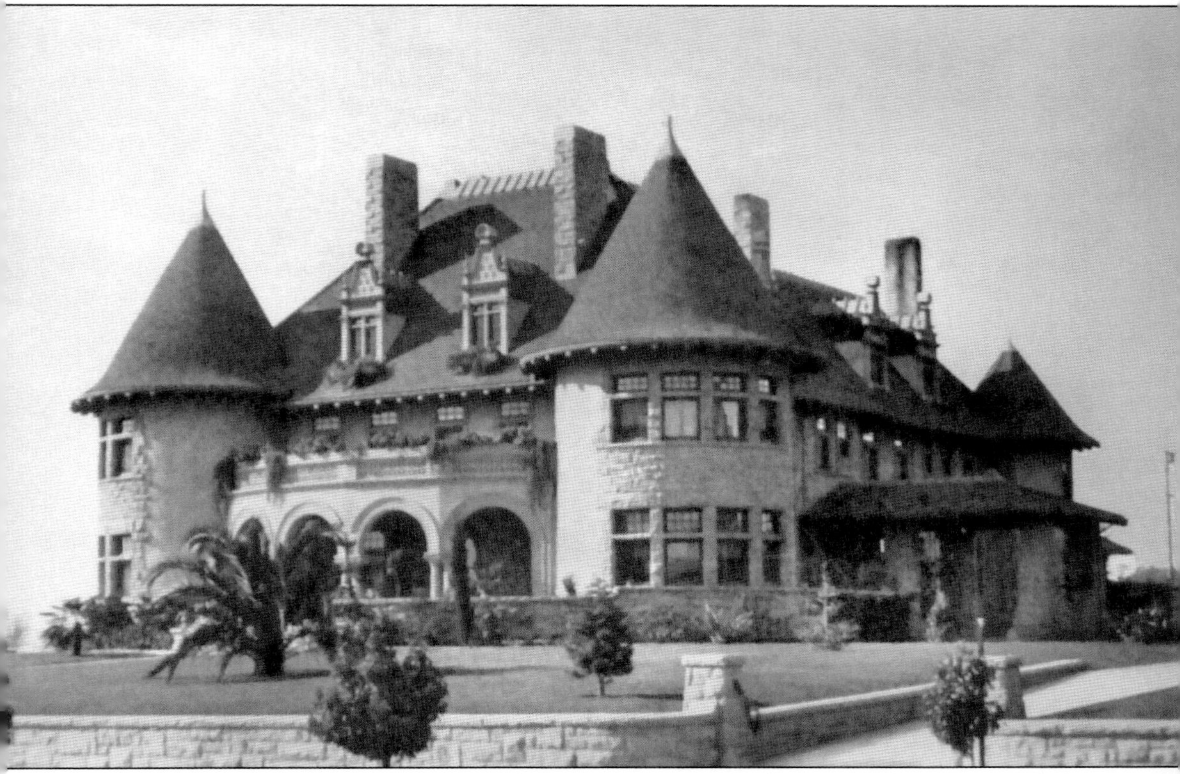

RINDGE RESIDENCE. Fredrick Hastings Rindge was born in Cambridge, Massachusetts, attended Harvard for a short time, and in 1883 inherited his father's substantial estate. Many buildings and streets in his hometown bear the Rindge name in acknowledgment of the family's philanthropy. Rindge married Rhoda May Knight, a teacher from Trenton, Michigan, just one week after they met in 1887. The couple moved to California, settling in West Adams. In 1892, Rindge purchased 13,000 acres of Rancho Malibu. He later expanded the ranch to 17,000 acres, encompassing much of present-day Malibu. Although a beach cottage was built on the ranch, this opulent mansion, designed by Frederick L. Roehrig and finished in 1906, was planned as their city home. Rindge never enjoyed the splendor of his house. His premature death in 1905, at age 48, left the 41-year-old Rhoda the manager of the family fortune. At a time when the idea of a woman in business was considered highly questionable, she built a railroad across Rancho Malibu, becoming the first female president of a U.S. railroad.

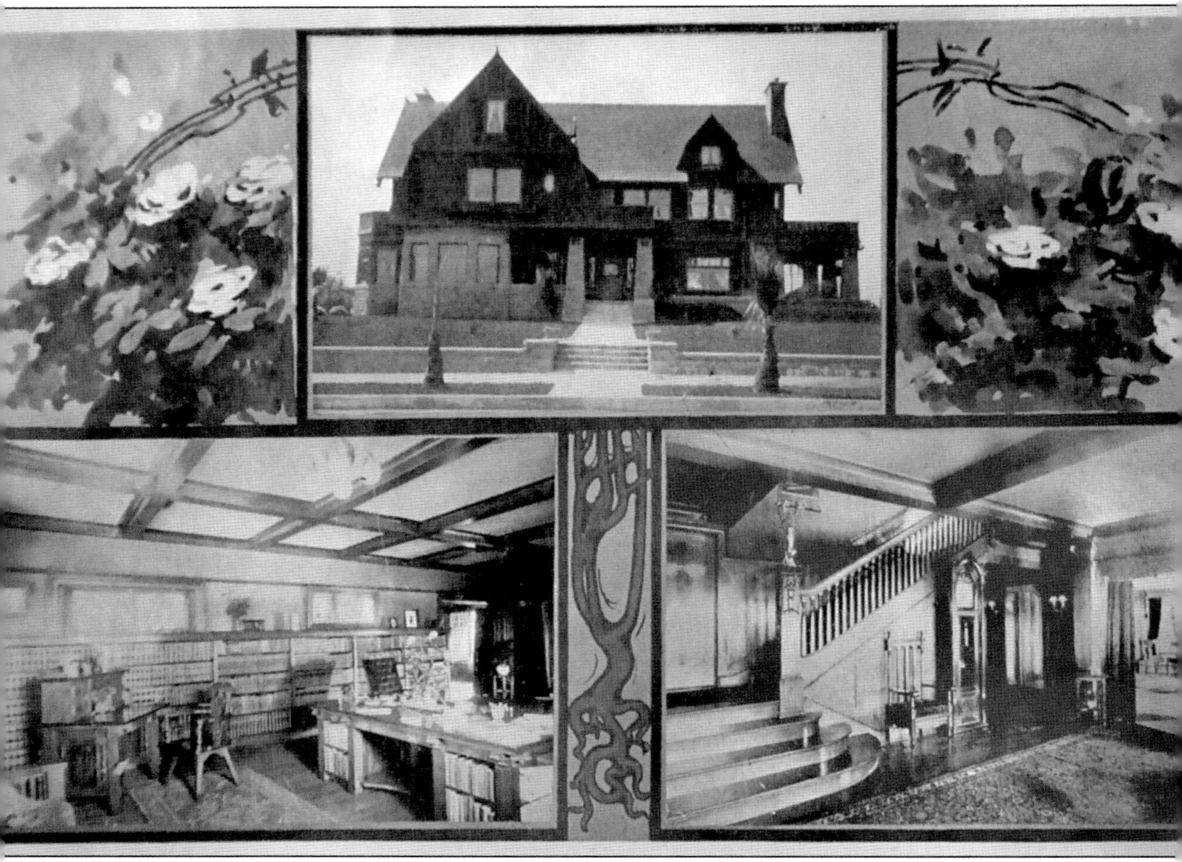

VARIOUS VIEWS OF THE COCHRAN RESIDENCE. George I. Cochran was a lawyer, born and educated in Canada, who moved to Los Angeles in 1888. His interests were extensive and included a multitude of clubs, schools, banks, water companies, and the West Adams Heights Association, but his primary title was president of Pacific Mutual Life Insurance, a position he held for 30 years. In 1905, Cochran's wife, Alice Maud, died. Two years later, he married her sister, Isabelle, who was described as tall and willowy, with soft brown eyes and hair. He brought her home to 2249 South Harvard Boulevard, a house designed by Train and Williams. The couple lived there until his death in 1949. In 1952, Isabelle presented a portrait of her husband to UCLA, where he was regent from 1919 to 1946.

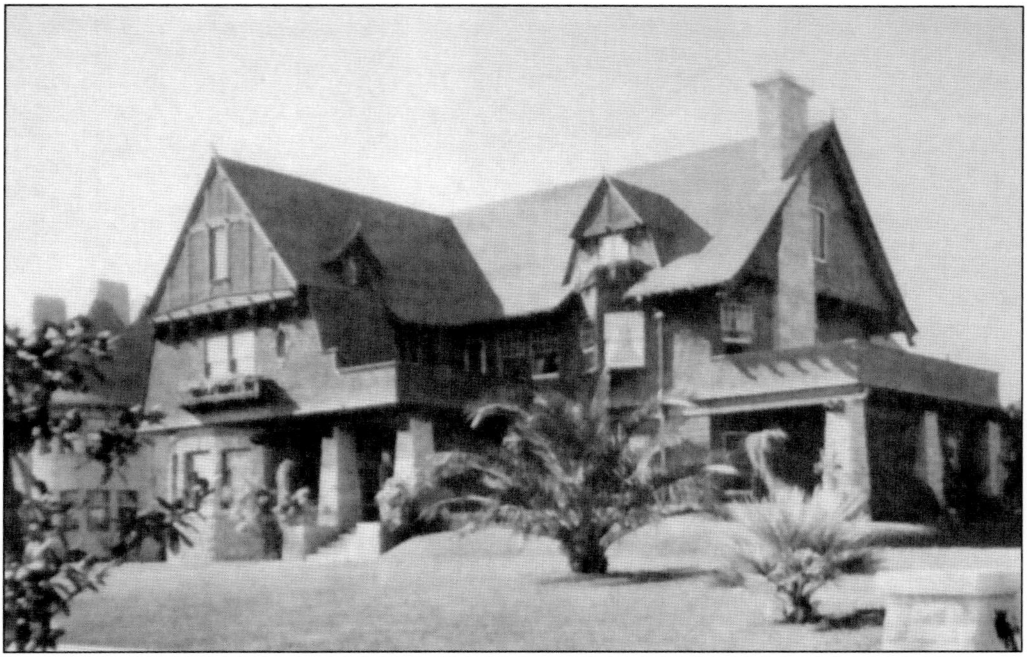

COCHRAN RESIDENCE. The Cochran family also had strong ties to USC. In 1928, he made a gift of $100,000 to the school, where his late father had been dean. His speech touched on his hope "that Los Angeles . . . will come to be one of the great educational and cultural centers of the world" and that "the University of Southern California will play a dominant part."

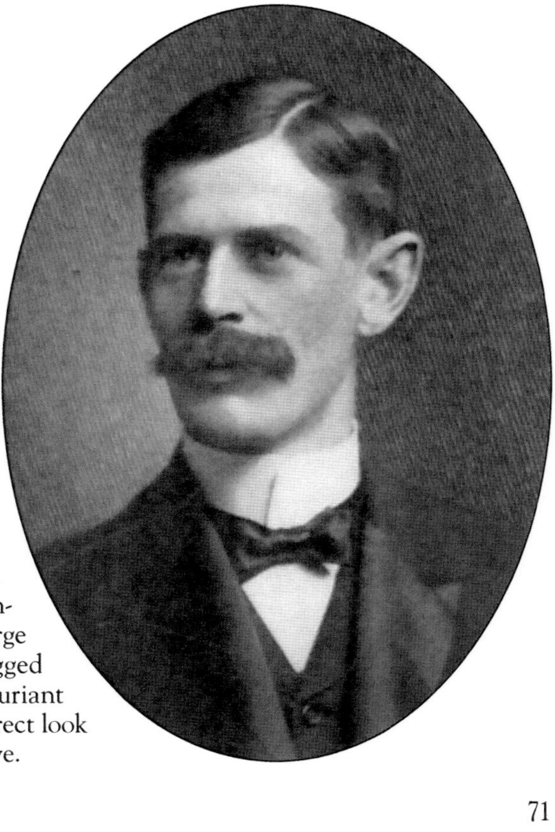

GEORGE IRA COCHRAN. Could a successful Los Angeles businessman have a chance as a movie star? The question was asked of Ben Piazza, casting director for Metro-Goldwyn-Mayer in 1934. One of his picks was George I. Cochran, whom he described as "a rugged type with rather regular features." The luxuriant mustache was gone by the 1930s, but his "direct look and carriage" were apparently still impressive.

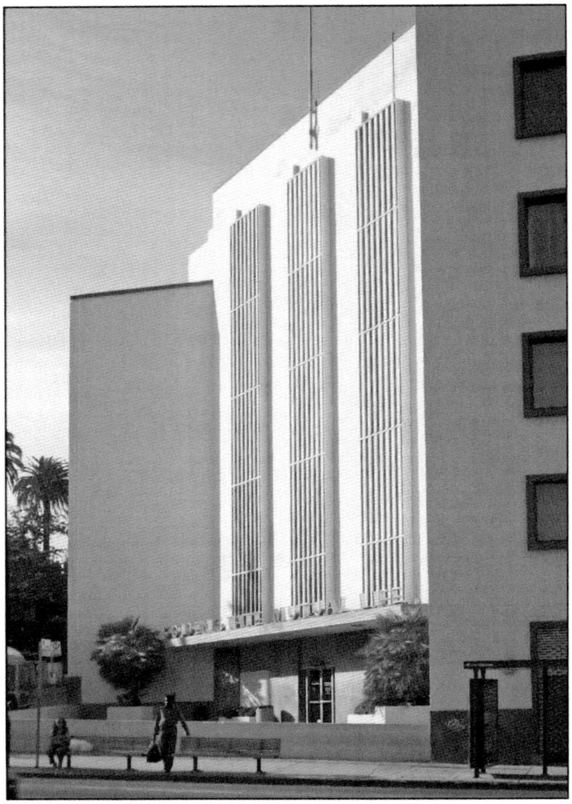

GOLDEN STATE MUTUAL LIFE INSURANCE. From its early days in a one-room office on Central Avenue, providing life insurance to the African American community, Golden State Mutual Insurance has grown into a multibillion-dollar business. Their office building at 1999 West Adams Boulevard, designed by Paul Williams, opened in 1949. Lobby murals by Hale Woodruff and Charles Alston depict the African American experience in California history.

HELLMAN RESIDENCE. Maurice S. Hellman had the rare distinction of being a native Angeleno. He began his career in the stationery business with his father, but by the age of 30, he had moved into the more lucrative arena of bond brokerage and ultimately banking. He built an impressive home in fashionable West Adams Heights at 2225 South Harvard Boulevard, securing the firm of Hunt and Eager as the architects.

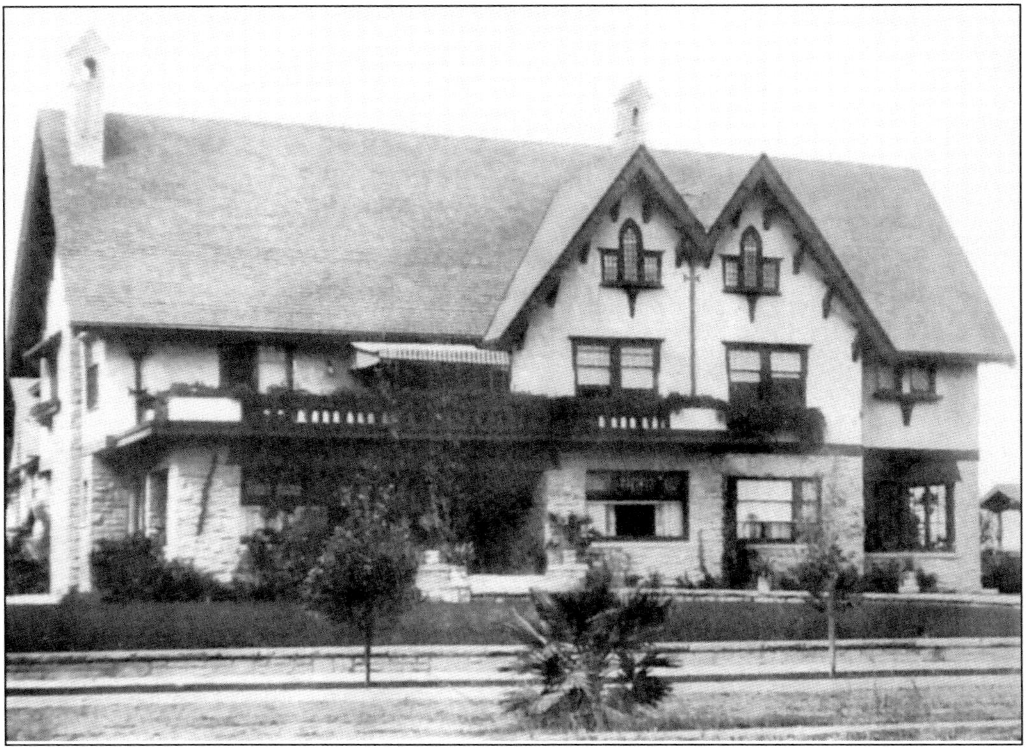

Five

THE BUNGALOWS

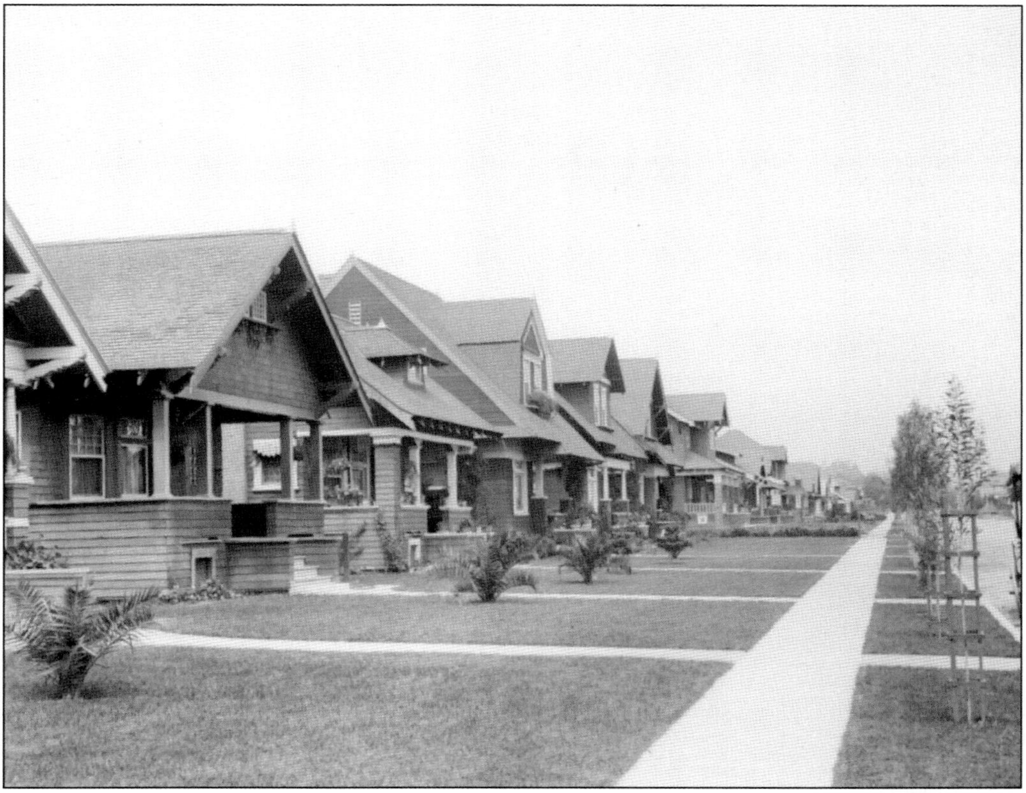

HOUSES ON HARVARD BOULEVARD (C. 1915). This row of houses on the 3000 block of Harvard Boulevard, looking north toward Adams Boulevard, are typical arts and crafts bungalows of Los Angeles. There are exposed rafter tails, bracketed eaves, wide porches, a combination of shingle and clapboard siding, and a palm tree in every yard. While the three houses closest to the camera still remain, the next three have been replaced by newer homes with less architectural detail. (Courtesy of University of Southern California, on behalf of the USC Specialized Libraries and Archival Collections.)

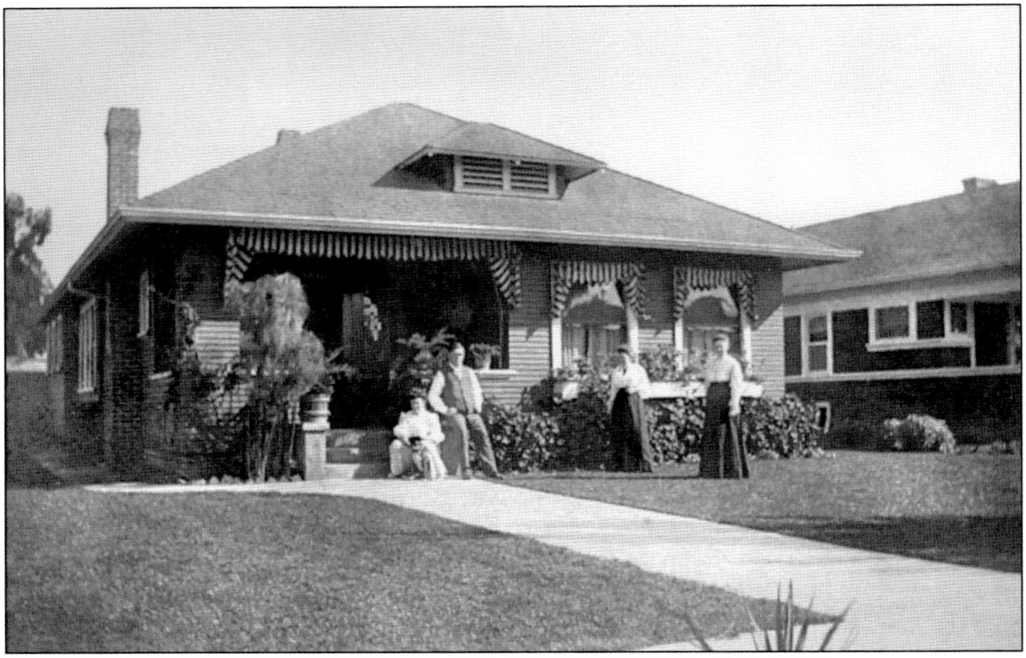

BUNGALOW, 2914 HARVARD BOULEVARD. "Feb 6–07. Thermometer 84°," this handsome family wrote on a postcard of their home on the 2900 block of Harvard Boulevard. Families flocked to Los Angeles, where many of middle-class means purchased bungalows. Facing west, this one captured the cooler breezes from the ocean only 10 miles away. Dormer vents ensured that fresh air flowed through the attic, cooling the home in the summer.

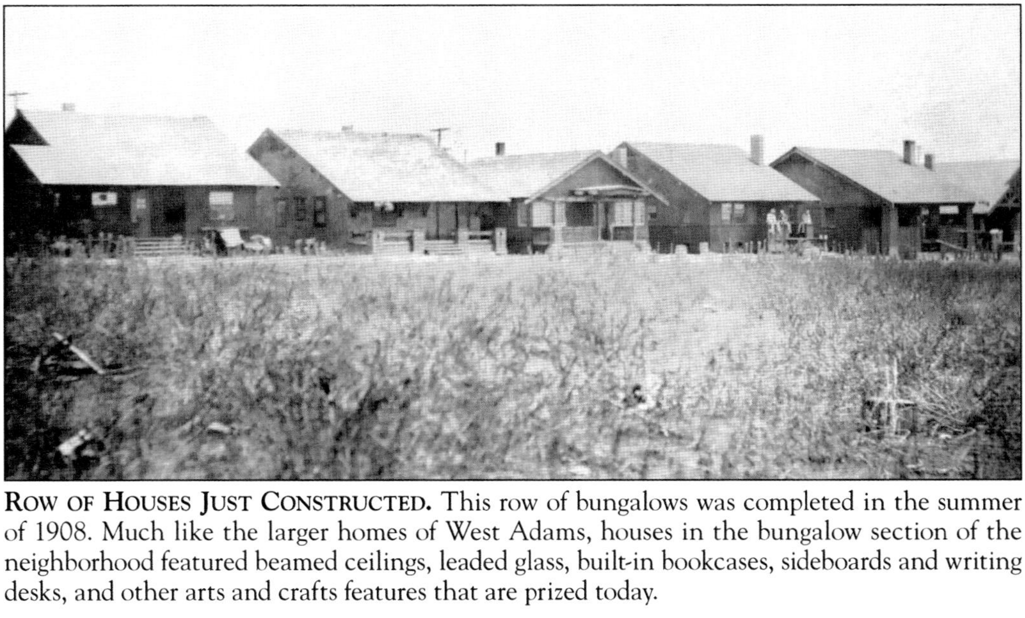

ROW OF HOUSES JUST CONSTRUCTED. This row of bungalows was completed in the summer of 1908. Much like the larger homes of West Adams, houses in the bungalow section of the neighborhood featured beamed ceilings, leaded glass, built-in bookcases, sideboards and writing desks, and other arts and crafts features that are prized today.

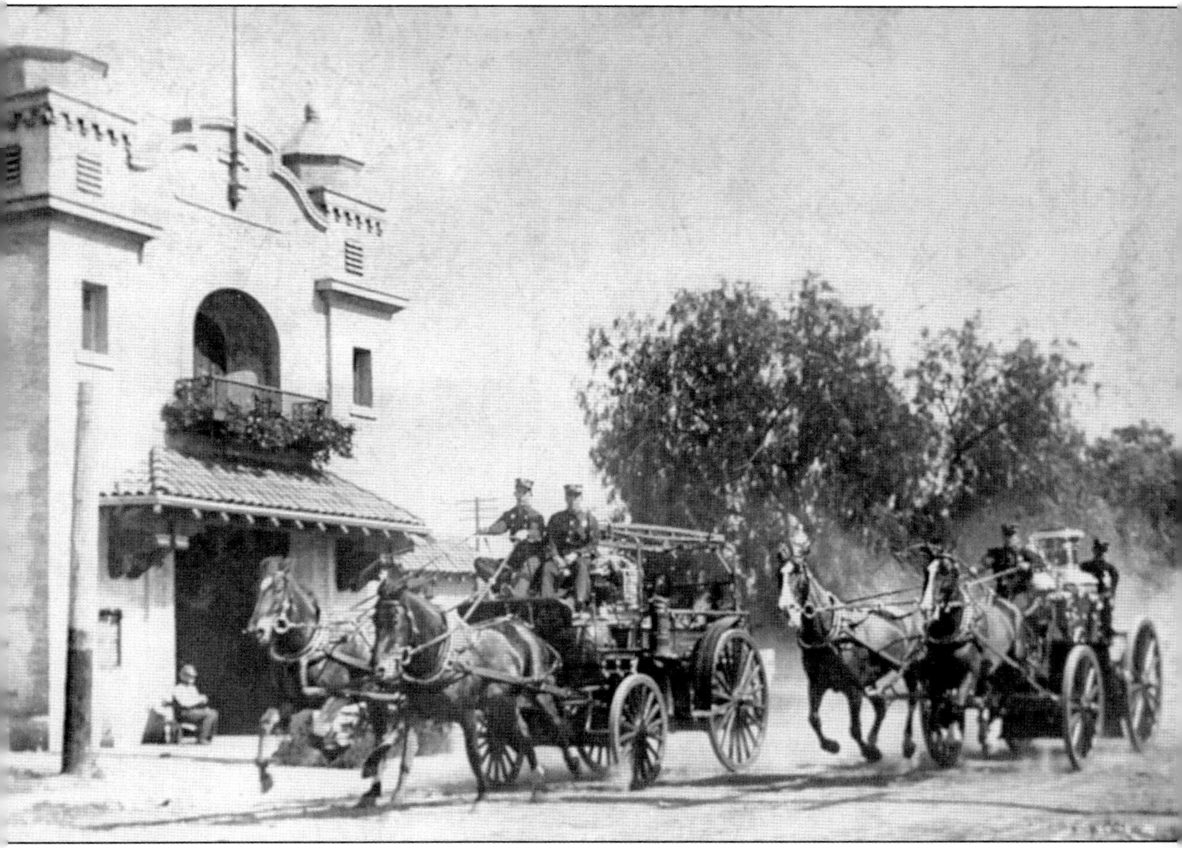

FIRE STATION 18. In 1904, fire chief Tom Strohm recommended building an engine house at Adams Street and Hobart Boulevard to house a combination chemical and hose wagon. The building was designed by John Parkinson but in early 1906 was still vacant. The hollow where it stood had an unfortunate tendency to become a lake during rains. Maple floors were warped and windows were broken in the empty building. Chief Strohm was out of office by then and said he did not want to criticize but felt there was a great need for fire protection in the West Adams area. Apparently the new fire chief listened because this picture is from around 1906. The problems were not over, however, and the station was closed in 1915 when money was tight, then reopened several years later. In 1984, the Community Redevelopment Agency planned a restoration, but the building is currently unoccupied and deteriorating. (Courtesy of Los Angeles Fire Department Historic Archive.)

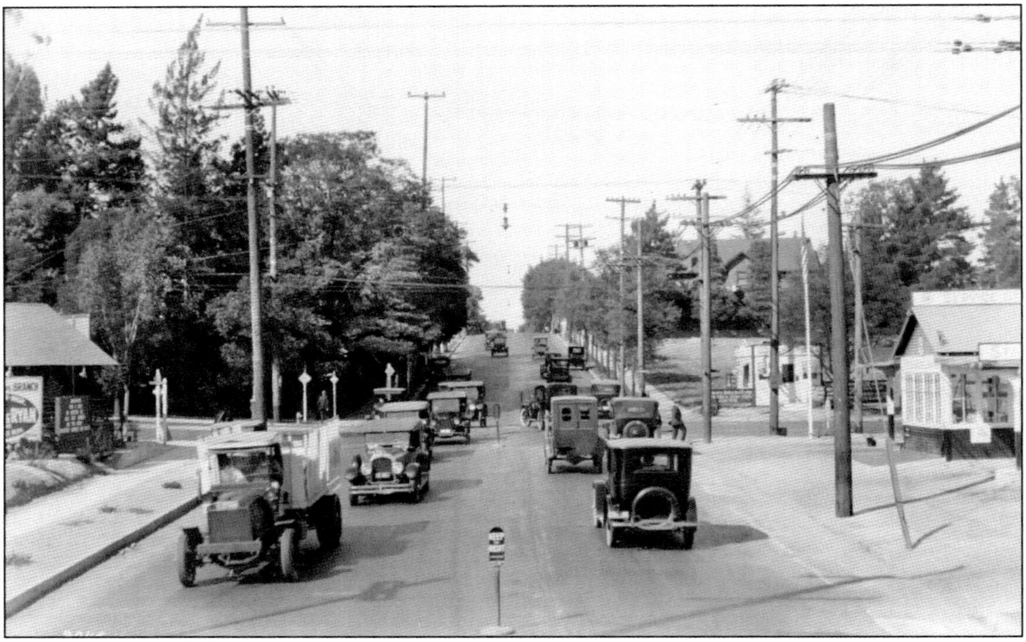

INTERSECTION OF WESTERN AVENUE AND ADAMS BOULEVARD (1924). This photograph, looking north on Western Avenue toward Adams Boulevard, shows a mixture of expensive cars and delivery vehicles. The trees on the left hide several luxurious homes, while the northeast corner became the site of the Golden State Life Mutual Insurance headquarters. (Courtesy of University of Southern California, on behalf of the USC Specialized Libraries and Archival Collections.)

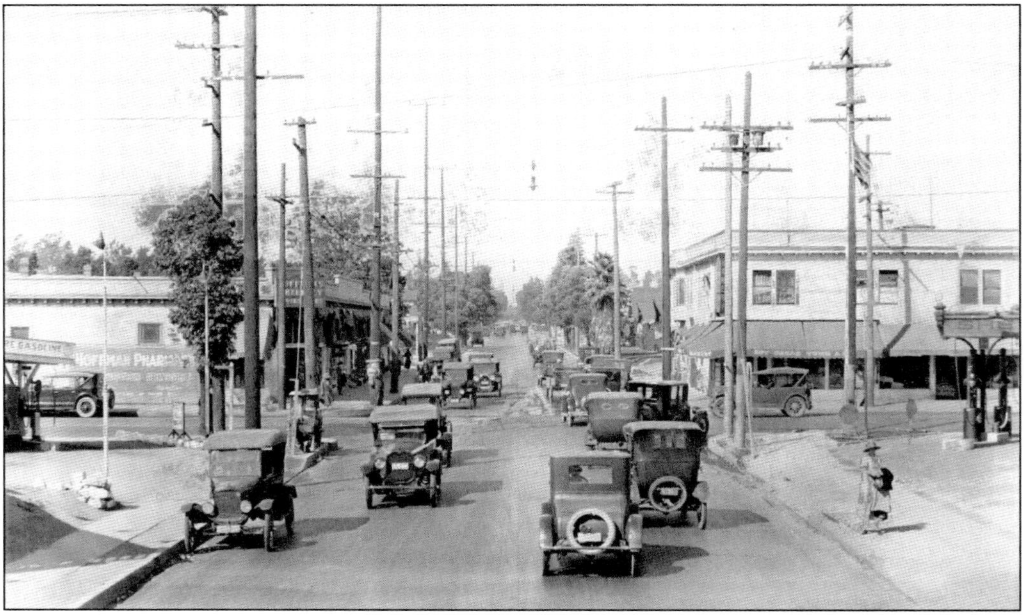

INTERSECTION OF WESTERN ADAMS AND JEFFERSON BOULEVARDS (1924). Taken the same year, this photograph, only a few blocks south of the one above, is in the middle-class area called "The Bungalows." The automobiles are a little more ordinary, and there are commercial buildings on two of the corners. The other two corners house filling stations. (Courtesy of University of Southern California, on behalf of the USC Specialized Libraries and Archival Collections.)

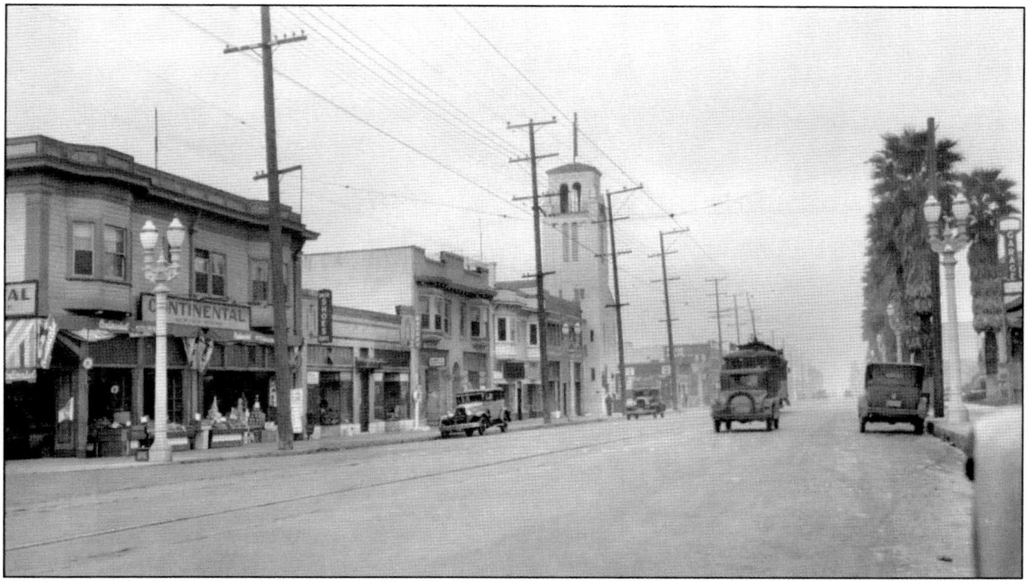

JEFFERSON BOULEVARD LOOKING WEST FROM SECOND AVENUE. St. Paul's Presbyterian Church, designed by Quentin Scott with a revolving cross, was made a reality when politician and former saloon owner Charles Crawford put a $3,554 diamond ring into the collection plate, followed with a donation of $25,000. Crawford's funeral was one of the first to be held there: 6,000 people showed up after he was murdered in 1931.

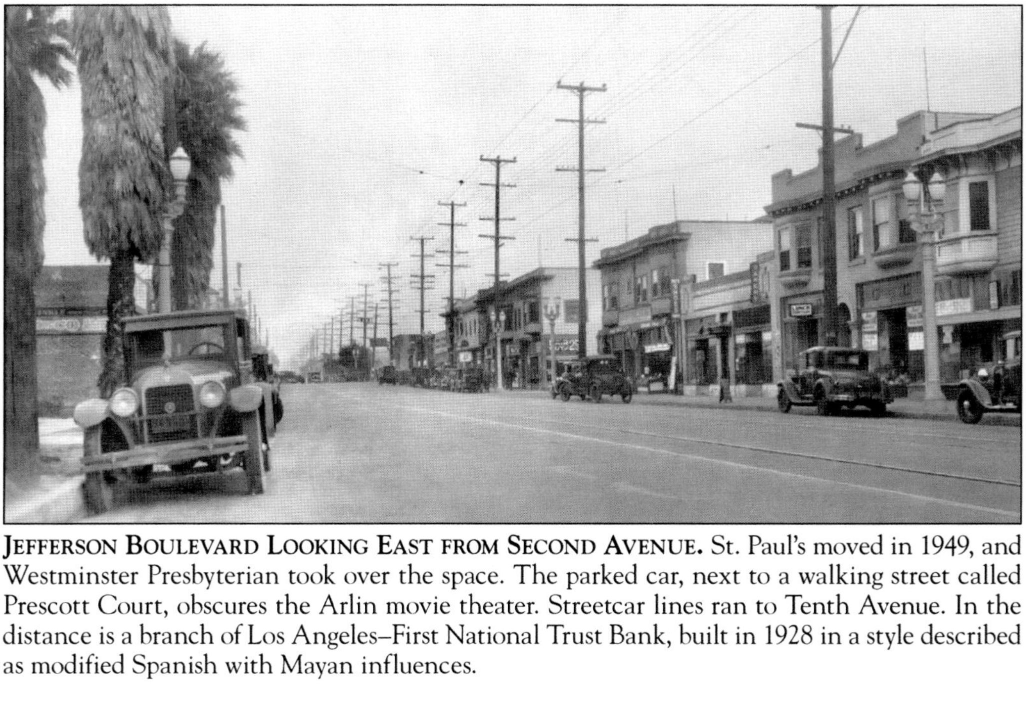

JEFFERSON BOULEVARD LOOKING EAST FROM SECOND AVENUE. St. Paul's moved in 1949, and Westminster Presbyterian took over the space. The parked car, next to a walking street called Prescott Court, obscures the Arlin movie theater. Streetcar lines ran to Tenth Avenue. In the distance is a branch of Los Angeles–First National Trust Bank, built in 1928 in a style described as modified Spanish with Mayan influences.

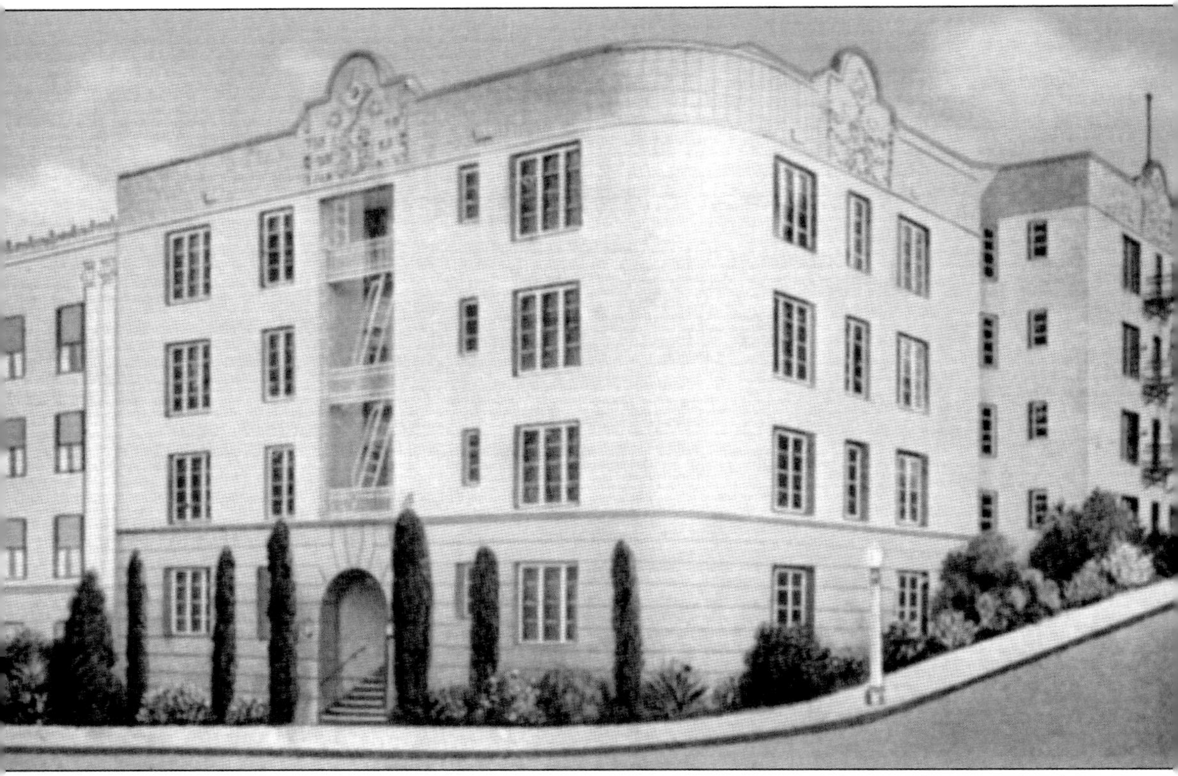

SHERLANDY APARTMENTS. "Unusual Rates to First Renters" were advertised in 1928 by the just opened Sherlandy apartment building at 2022 West Adams Street. Brides were at home with their many friends in the building designed by Lautzner and Anderson, but it also attracted some more unsavory characters. One resident was arrested when vice-squad officers grew curious about the rush of business at a gas station, only to find the lady in question in possession of a gallon of Prohibition-era liquor. Even the brides sometimes had problems. In 1949, a resident teamed up with another wife to demand divorces as well as bring criminal charges against the bigamist married to both of them. (Courtesy of Rory Cunningham.)

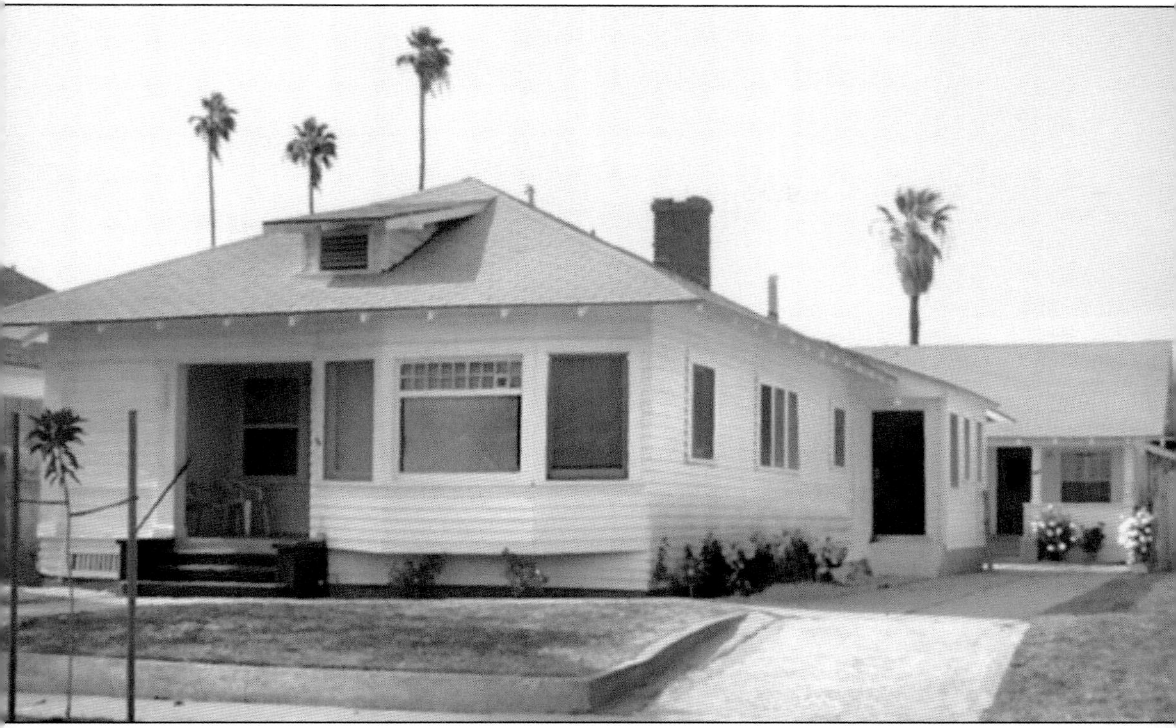

BUNGALOW, 2171 WEST TWENTY-NINTH STREET. When police were called to this modest bungalow in July 1915, they were in such a hurry they ran over a mail carrier, breaking his leg. The reason for the call was that neighbors had not seen the occupant, Frances Harrison, for some days, and her bedroom window was covered with flies. Once inside, officers found the woman's chloroformed, decomposing body. The "Diamond Widow," as the divorcée was known for the number of diamonds she possessed, was missing her valuable jewelry, all her money, and her live-in boyfriend, Calvin Whittington. In 1917, Whittington was arrested in Texas and returned to Los Angeles, but he was eventually released for lack of evidence.

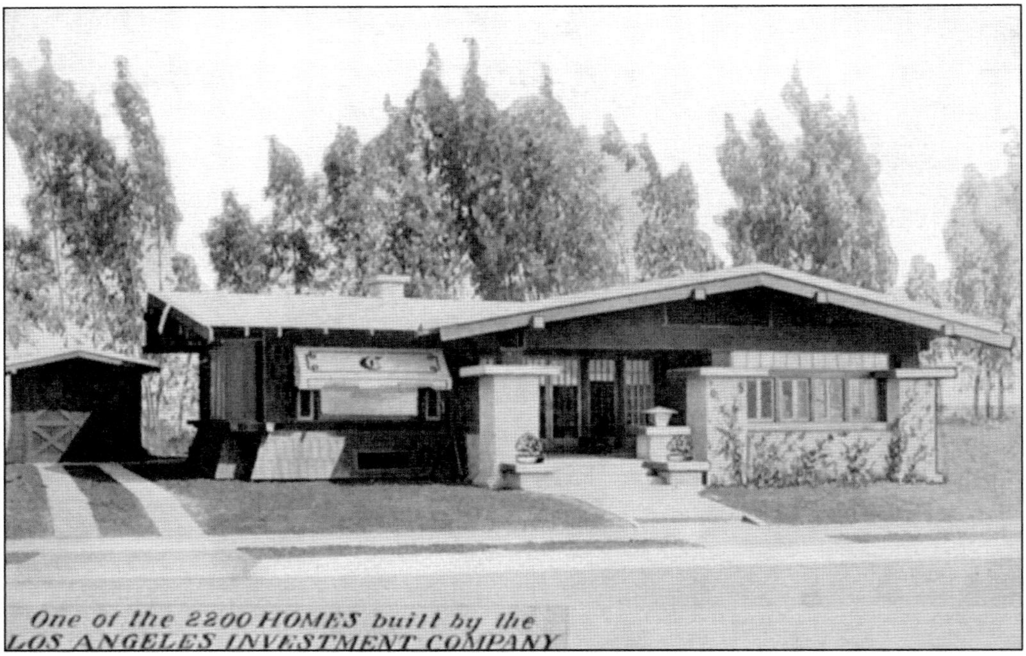

BUNGALOW. A note on this card announces that I. J. Hirsch was "removing from apartments" to "a nice bungalow" at 2135 West Twenty-ninth Street. The picture on the front, however, was a general advertisement for the Los Angeles Investment Company, the largest cooperative building company in the world in 1907. By 1915, when Hirsch bought his bungalow, the company was embroiled in lawsuits alleging fraud and embezzlement. (Courtesy of Rory Cunningham.)

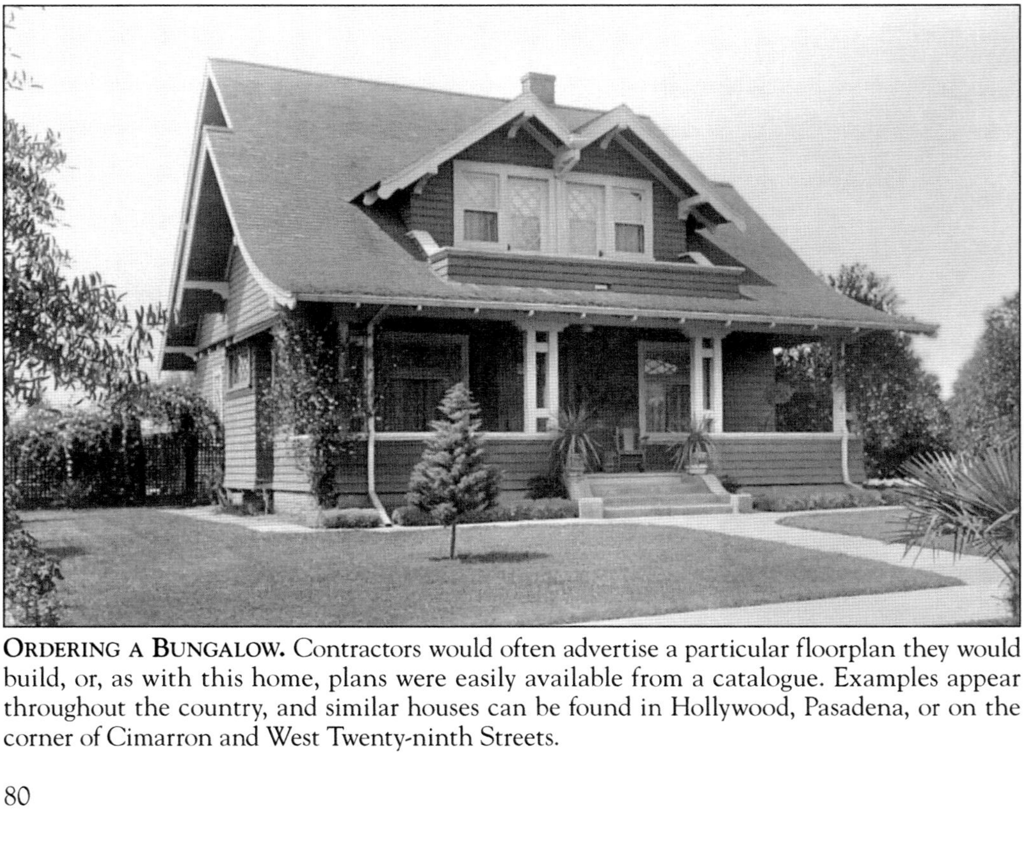

ORDERING A BUNGALOW. Contractors would often advertise a particular floorplan they would build, or, as with this home, plans were easily available from a catalogue. Examples appear throughout the country, and similar houses can be found in Hollywood, Pasadena, or on the corner of Cimarron and West Twenty-ninth Streets.

Six

Western Avenue to Arlington Avenue

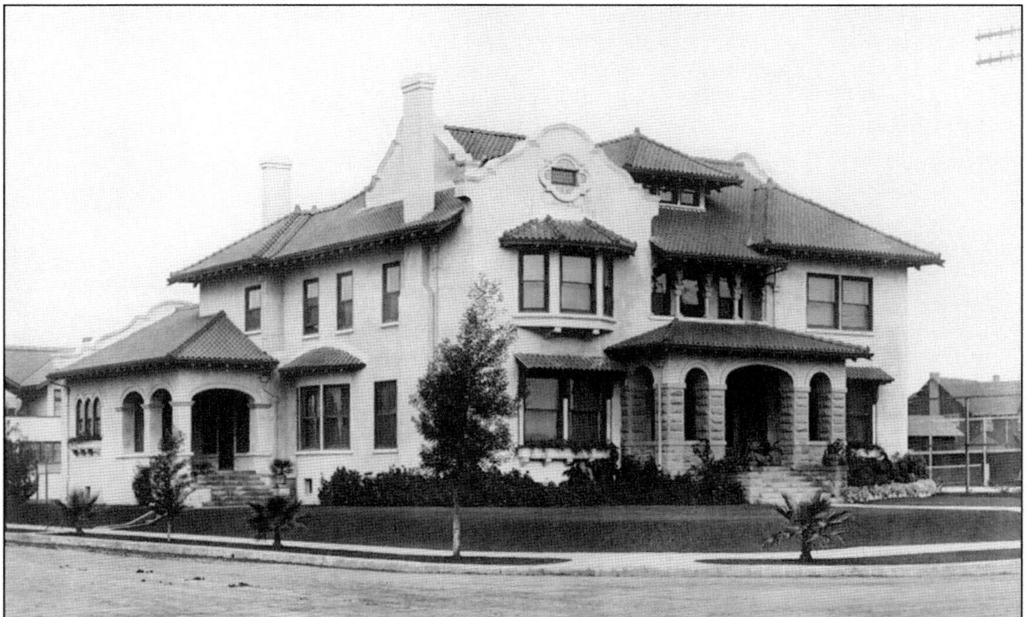

Cuzner Residence (around 1905–1910). Guy Cuzner was general manager of the Kerckhoff-Cuzner Mill and Lumber Company, of which his father was president. William Kerckhoff had his own mansion on Adams Boulevard several miles away. Cuzner built his mission-style home at 2091 South Harvard Boulevard in 1905. The porch columns are not cast concrete but solid pieces of stone carved for the purpose. In more recent years, the entire home was gutted by an arsonist's fire, but a subsequent owner has completely rebuilt the interior. (Courtesy of the University of Southern California, on behalf of the USC Specialized Libraries and Archival Collections.)

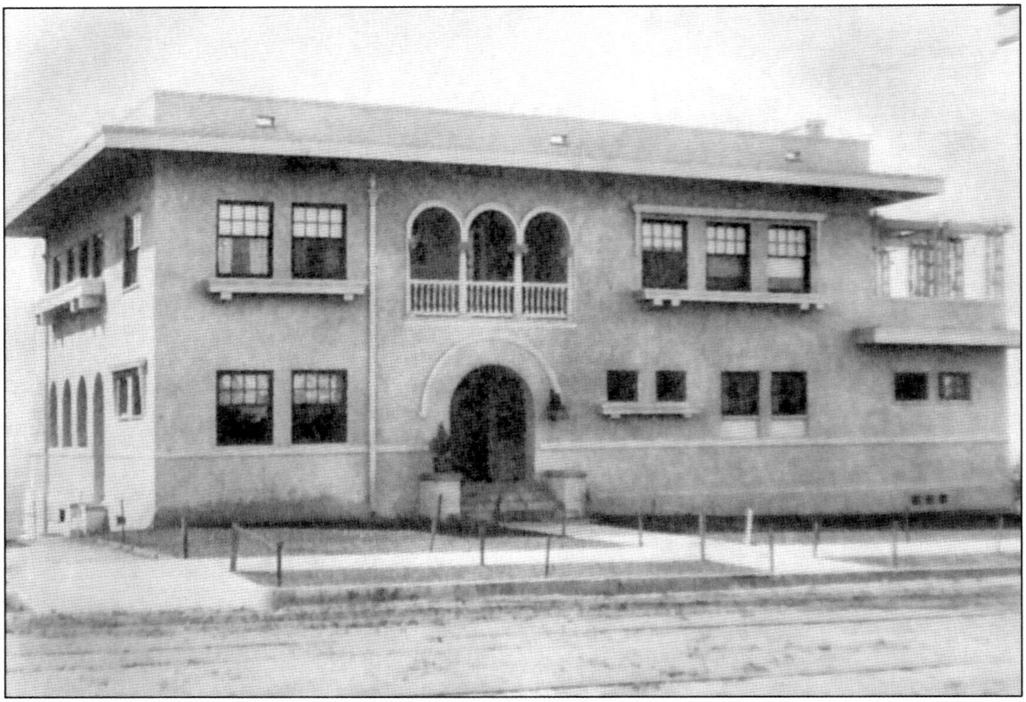

Wing Residence. In 1903, two years after he and his wife, Charlotte, relocated from Chicago, Dr. Elbert Wing bought several lots at Adams and Hermosa Streets with the intent of demolishing the existing houses for a larger home. The next year, he hired Hunt and Eager to design a Spanish-style house with roof garden. Dr. Wing was president of the Municipal League with a particular interest in hygiene.

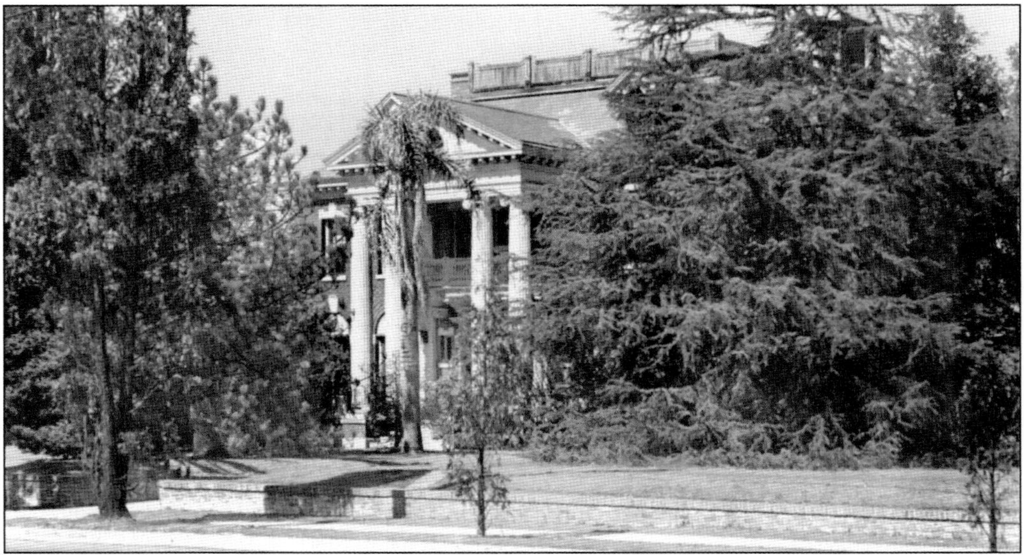

Britt Residence (1939). A. F. Rosenheim designed a home for Eugene W. Britt, a prominent attorney, at 2141 West Adams Boulevard. The classic Georgian Colonial building with matching garage cost $50,000 in 1910. The building was restored and used as a headquarters for the 1984 Olympics in Los Angeles. It is currently the offices of the LA 84 Foundation, formally called Amateur Athletic Foundation. (Courtesy of Bison Archives.)

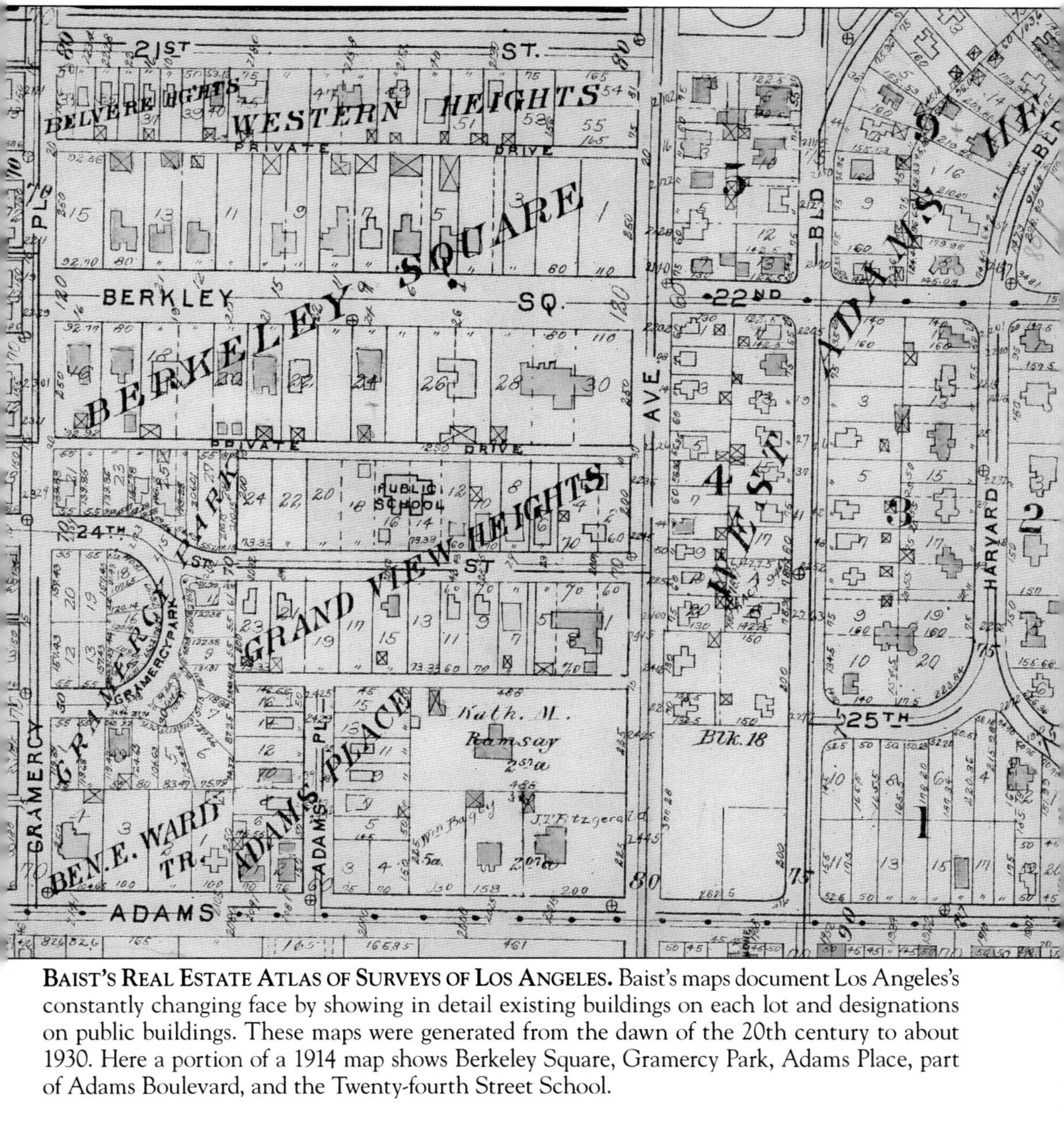

BAIST'S REAL ESTATE ATLAS OF SURVEYS OF LOS ANGELES. Baist's maps document Los Angeles's constantly changing face by showing in detail existing buildings on each lot and designations on public buildings. These maps were generated from the dawn of the 20th century to about 1930. Here a portion of a 1914 map shows Berkeley Square, Gramercy Park, Adams Place, part of Adams Boulevard, and the Twenty-fourth Street School.

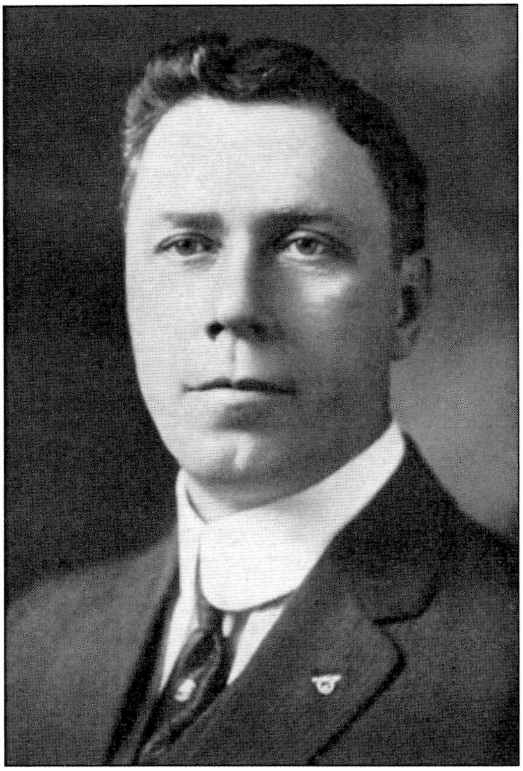

George Edmund Van Guysling. In 1889, George Van Guysling constructed the first practical motion picture camera, using glass plates and pneumatic stops, and used it to document an eclipse in West Africa for the U.S. Scientific Corps. He assisted in production of an early motion picture produced in California, *A Daring Hold-Up in South California*, released in September 1906. He was vice president and general manager of Biograph Films Company.

Van Guysling Residence. George E. Van Guysling is shown here with his sister, Bertha, in front of their residence, believed to be on Adams Place, which later became St. Andrews when it was extended to Twenty-fourth Street around 1920. As a private developer in 1908, he purchased undeveloped land, which became the Gramercy Park tract, bordering the gated enclave of Berkeley Square and the elegant mansions of West Adams Boulevard.

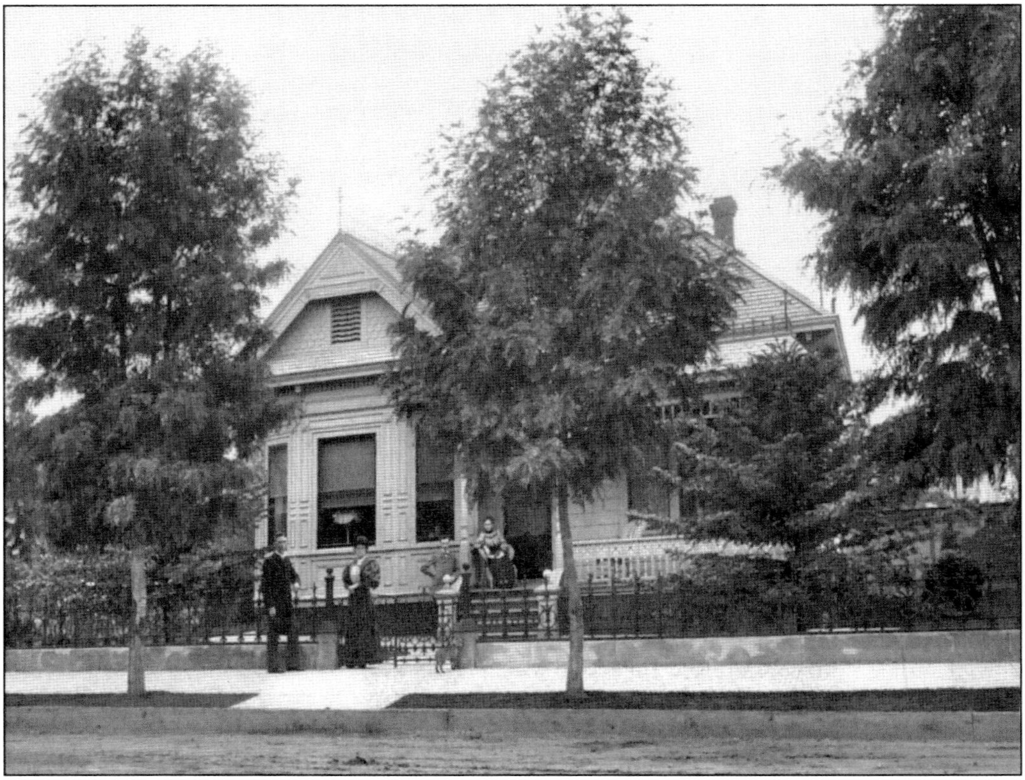

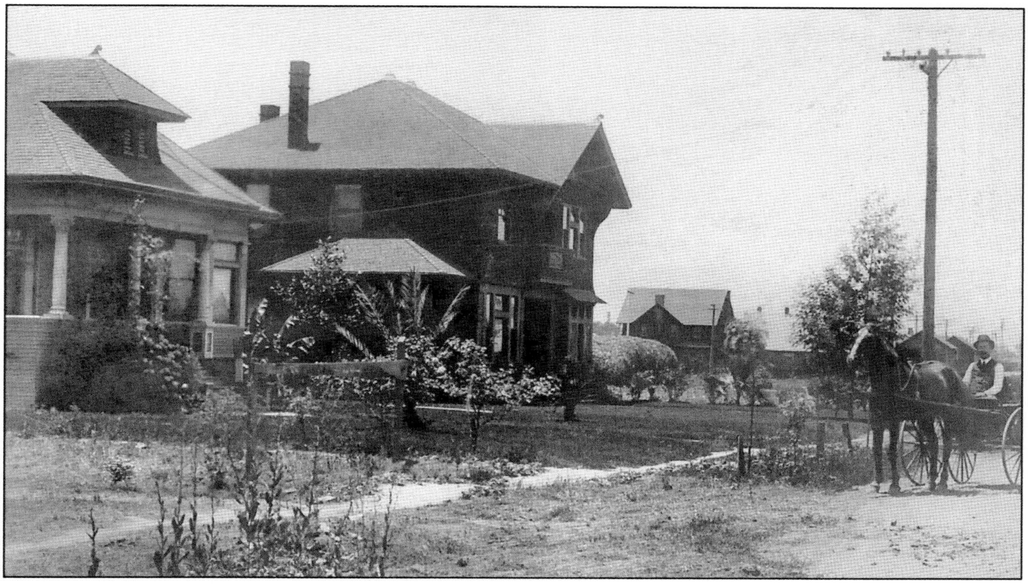

MILLS RESIDENCE. Twenty-fourth Street was still being developed when this photograph was taken. The two-story home shown here was purchased after World War II by Don Mills, of the famous Mills Brothers singing group, who remodeled it in a more contemporary style. Mills lived in the house for over 50 years before passing away in 1999.

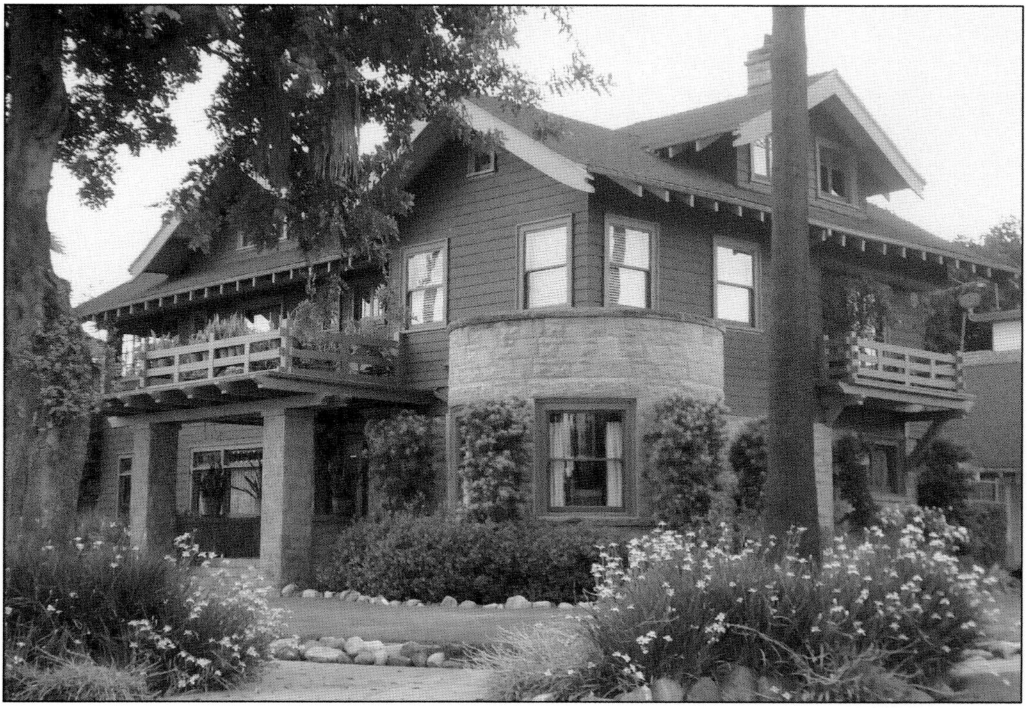

TWENTY-FOURTH STREET RESIDENCE. This transitional 1910 home bears Victorian design elements, such as the rotunda, leaded glass, and window surround moldings, and also elements of the more modern arts and crafts style, such as the stained redwood clapboard siding, the second-floor sleeping porches, and the curved dragon uplifts on the gabled roof and dormers. The building permit estimated the total cost of the house at $6,000.

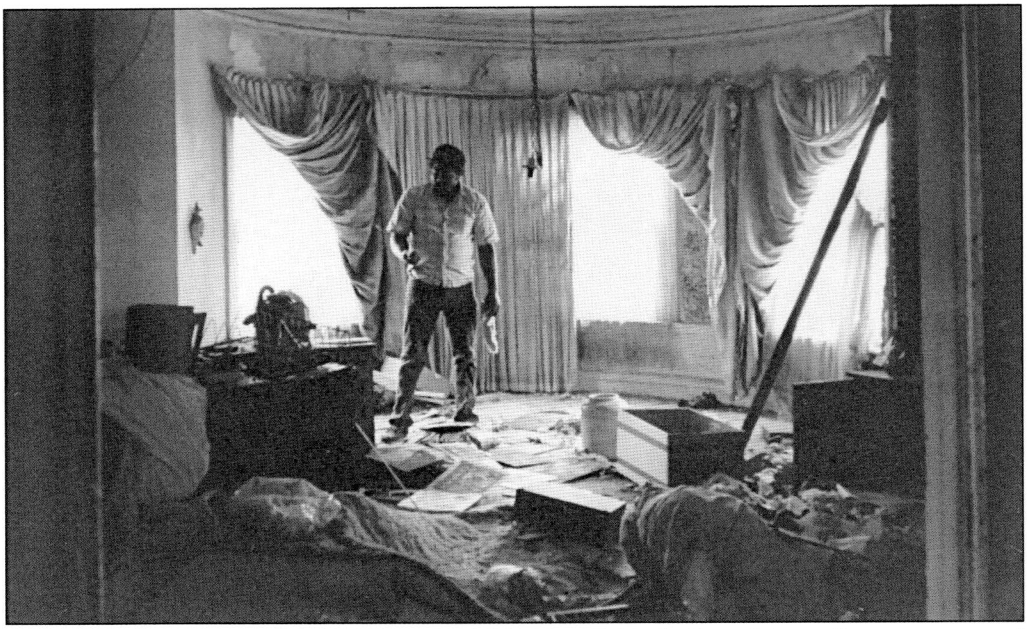

TWENTY-FOURTH STREET INTERIOR, PRE-RESTORATION. After the Santa Monica Freeway was routed through the heart of West Adams, taking many houses in the process, the neighborhood changed dramatically. Large homes were turned into rooming houses, and many were subdivided into multiple-family dwellings. Absentee landlords, constantly changing tenants, and too much deferred maintenance took its toll on many of the grand houses in the area, leaving them in poor condition.

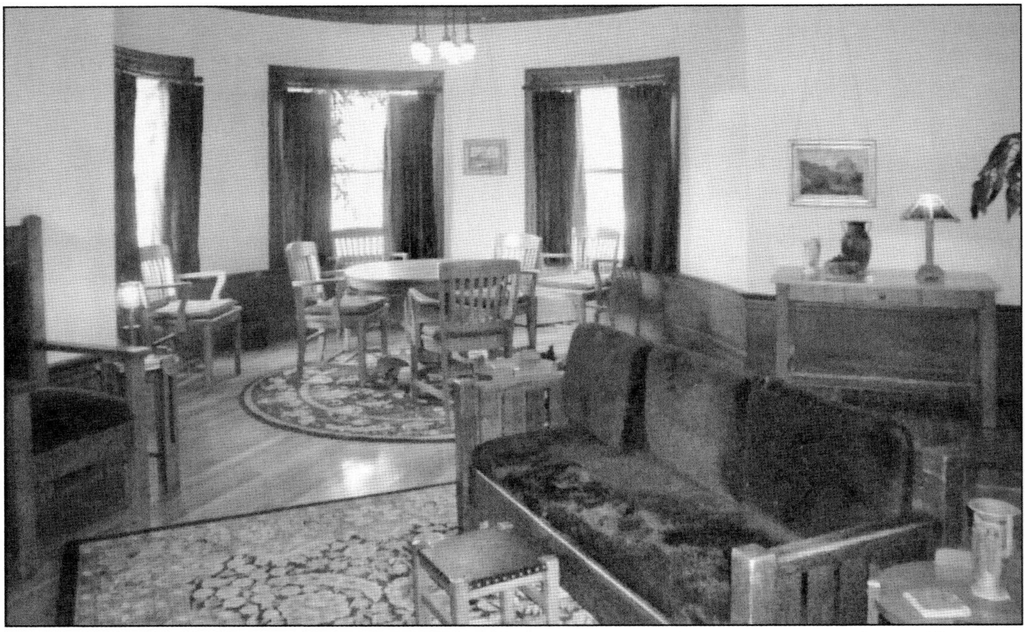

TWENTY-FOURTH STREET INTERIOR, POST-RESTORATION. In recent years, fans of historic architecture have restored many West Adams homes. Longtime residents have joined with newcomers, forming neighborhood organizations aimed at improving life in the community. Many houses have been painstakingly restored, and this is a prime example of a homeowner who has brought his residence back to its original glory with a massive investment of time, taste, and love.

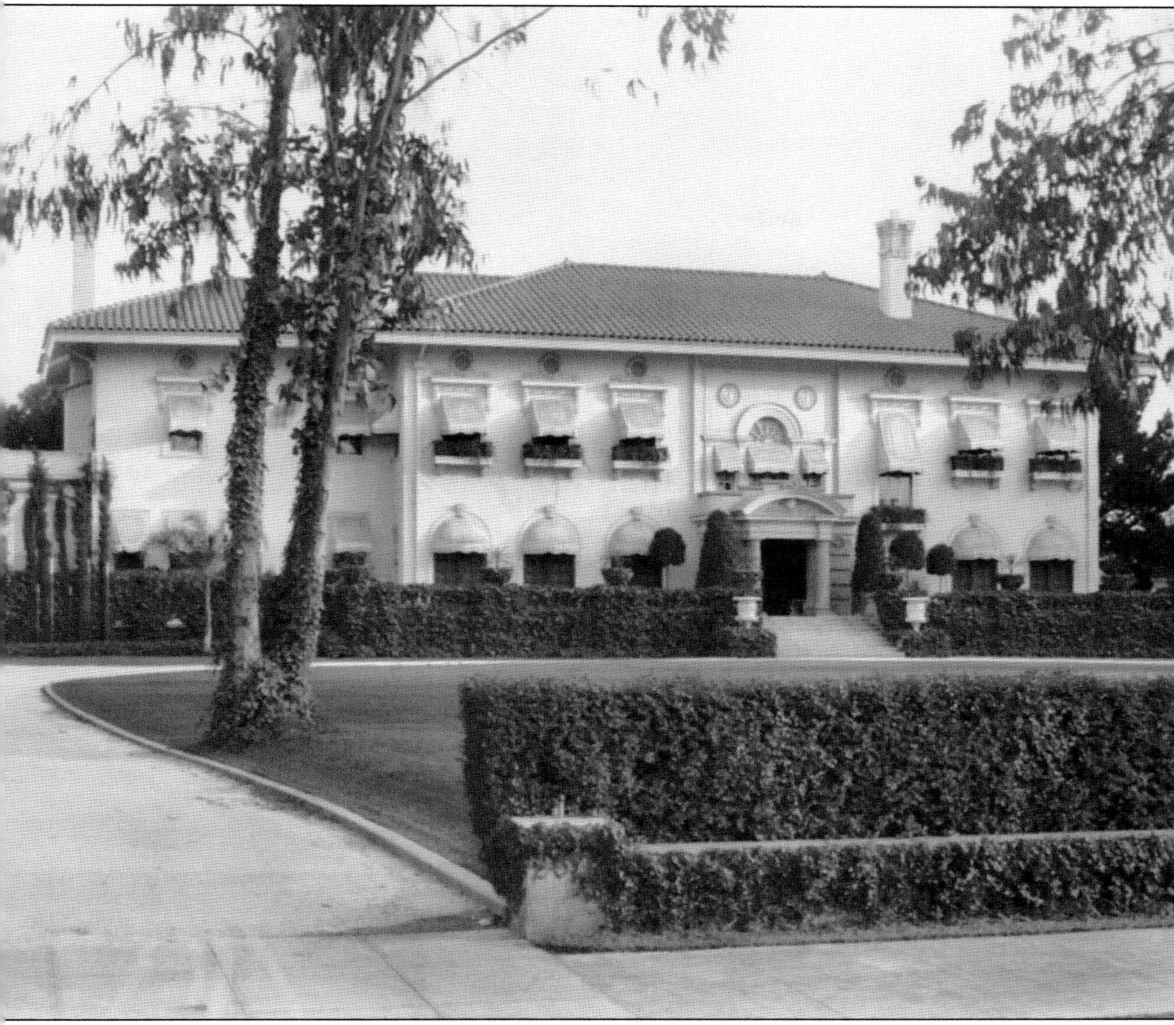

MURPHY RESIDENCE (C. 1910). Today Daniel Murphy's legacy is seen mostly in the private Catholic school that bears his name, but in his lifetime, he was an oil executive and owner of a cement company. Murphy and his wife, Antoinette, were devout Catholics. While they were in Italy, intending to adopt a son, a little girl reached out and tugged on Antoinette's dress. Accepting the gesture as a sign from God, the Murphys adopted the child and named her Bernadine. The family was noted for their generosity, and Murphy was granted the title of Commander of the Equestrian Order of the Holy Sepulcher by Pope Pius XI. Bernadine was, in her own right, later made a papal countess. Their Italian Renaissance–style home at 2076 West Adams Boulevard was a showplace. The garden, copied after one in Venice, was mentioned as a popular film location as early as 1936. (Courtesy of University of Southern California, on behalf of the USC Specialized Libraries and Archival Collections.)

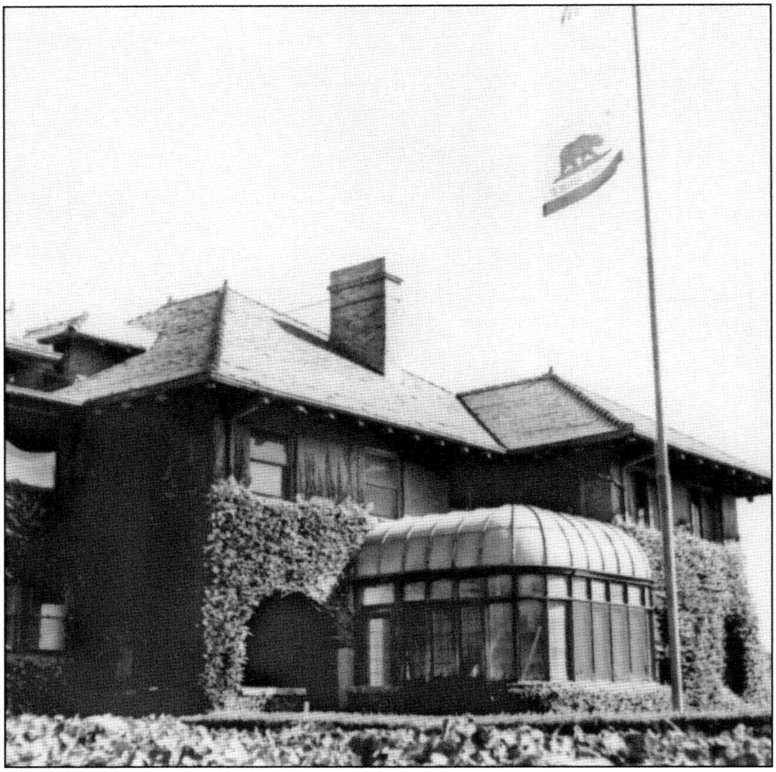

McCan-Clark Residence. New Orleans native David McCan built this 15-room home in 1906. He was the founder of the McCan Mechanical Works, which included parts for the Mount Wilson Observatory among its products. His wife, Martha, was one of the most socially prominent women in the city. Eventually McCan abandoned her and fled to Buenos Aires, where he died in 1919 at the age of 35. (Courtesy of Clark Library.)

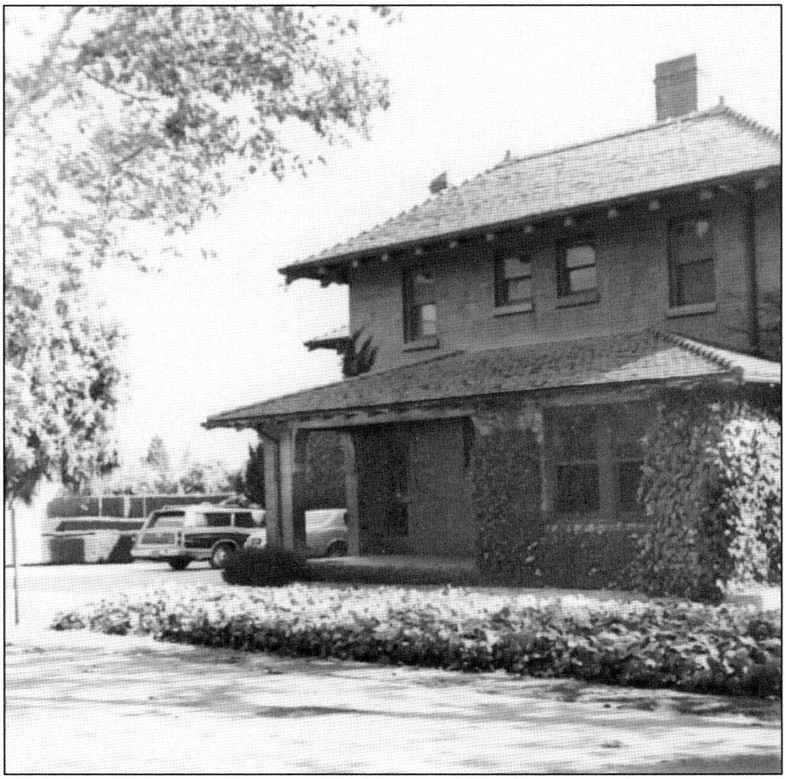

William A. Clark Residence. In 1910, William A. Clark Jr., heir to one of the nation's largest mining fortunes, bought the McCan residence and its contents for $90,000. Over the next several decades, he purchased all the other properties on the entire city block, removed the houses, and created a compound containing gardens, an observatory, and a private library. (Courtesy of Clark Library.)

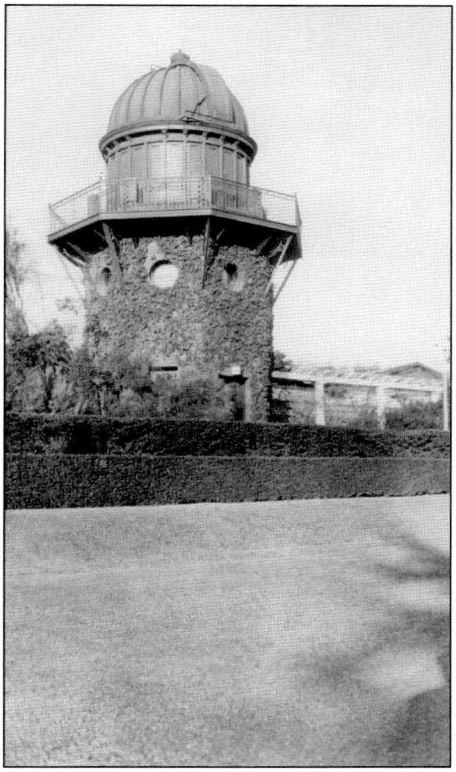

Clark Observatory. This observatory was built in 1917 on the grounds of William A. Clark's estate. The dedication ceremony included 100 members of the Astronomical Society of Los Angeles, all seated on the tennis court. Clark apparently did not foresee the growth of both light and air pollution, which ultimately rendered the telescope of little use. In the early 1950s, it was torn down. (Courtesy of Clark Library.)

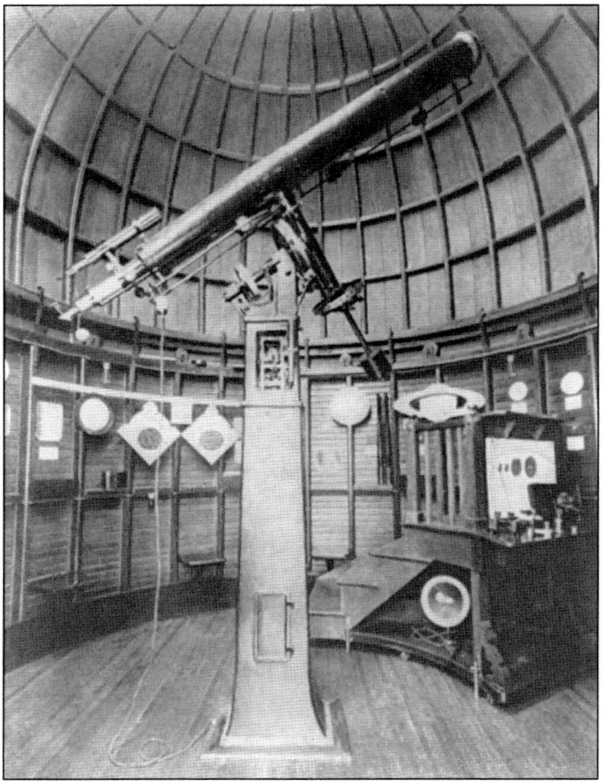

Clark Observatory Interior. The observatory on William A. Clark's property was not only for his enjoyment but for that of the public as well. A curator, Mars Baumgardt, was employed, and by applying to his office for a visit, anyone could receive the services of an instructor in its operation. On view were a number of photographs, models, and even a collection of meteors. (Courtesy of Clark Library.)

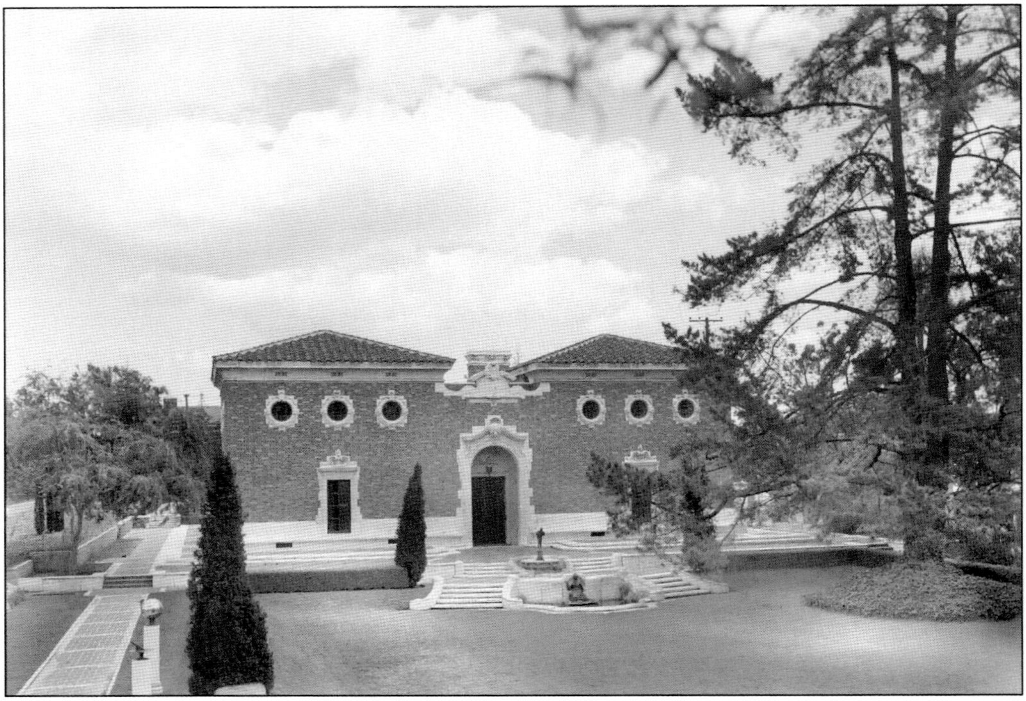

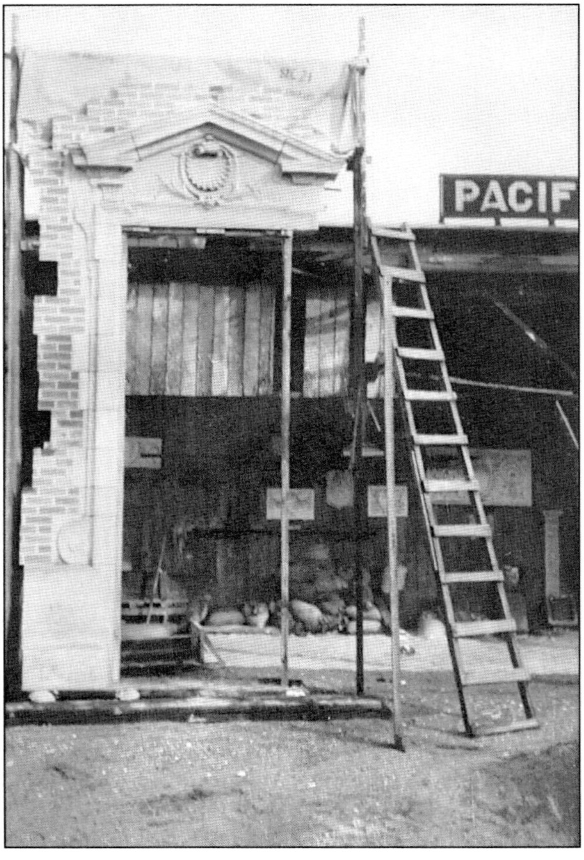

CLARK LIBRARY. In 1925, William A. Clark Jr. began construction of this private library for his collection of rare books and papers. Designed by Robert Farquhar in an Italian Renaissance Revival style, it required 60,000 rose-colored bricks. The interior features murals and paintings by Allyn Cox. It was ultimately donated to UCLA and today houses the largest collection of English literature outside of England. (Courtesy of Clark Library.)

CLARK LIBRARY DESIGNATED CULTURAL MONUMENT. William Andrews Clark Jr. traveled Europe extensively, studying libraries and museums to get ideas for what he wanted his library to look like. Here one of the doors is being manufactured locally. When the City of Los Angeles created the Historic Cultural Monument designation in the early 1960s, the library was the 28th to be dedicated. Today there are nearly 1,000 such monuments. (Courtesy of Clark Library.)

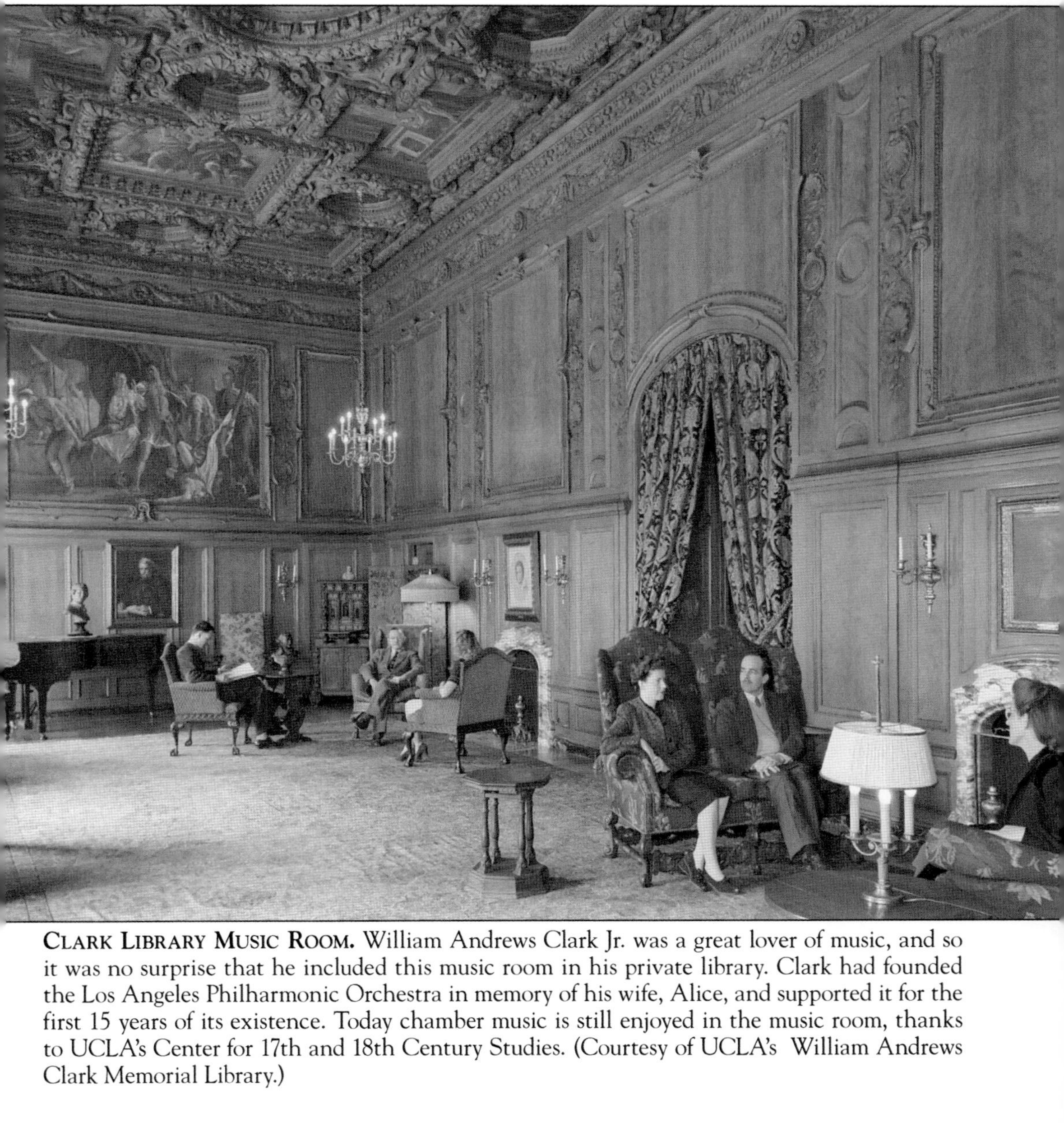

Clark Library Music Room. William Andrews Clark Jr. was a great lover of music, and so it was no surprise that he included this music room in his private library. Clark had founded the Los Angeles Philharmonic Orchestra in memory of his wife, Alice, and supported it for the first 15 years of its existence. Today chamber music is still enjoyed in the music room, thanks to UCLA's Center for 17th and 18th Century Studies. (Courtesy of UCLA's William Andrews Clark Memorial Library.)

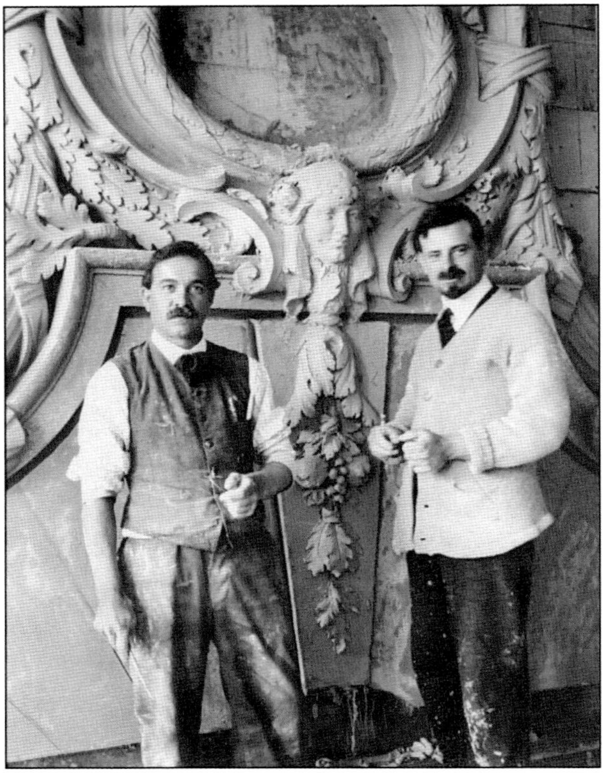

ARTISTS WORKING ON THE CLARK LIBRARY. These two artists stopped in their work on one of the bas-relief elements of the Clark Library to pose for a photographer. The interior of the library features numerous murals and paintings by Allyn Cox, including scenes of Apollo and the Nine Muses and a panel depicting Shakespeare's Antony and Cleopatra. (Courtesy of Clark Library.)

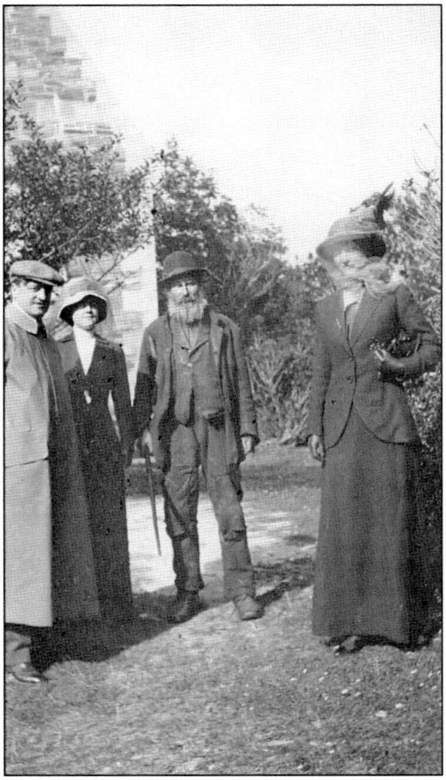

CLARK FAMILY IN IRELAND. William Andrews Clark Jr. and his wife, Alice McManus Clark, traveled frequently. They are shown here in Ireland in 1913 while visiting Blarney Castle, along with a local Irishman and Cora Saunders (far right). Alice Clark would not live to enjoy all of the improvements her husband was making to their property, dying of cancer in 1918 at the age of 34. (Courtesy of Clark Library.)

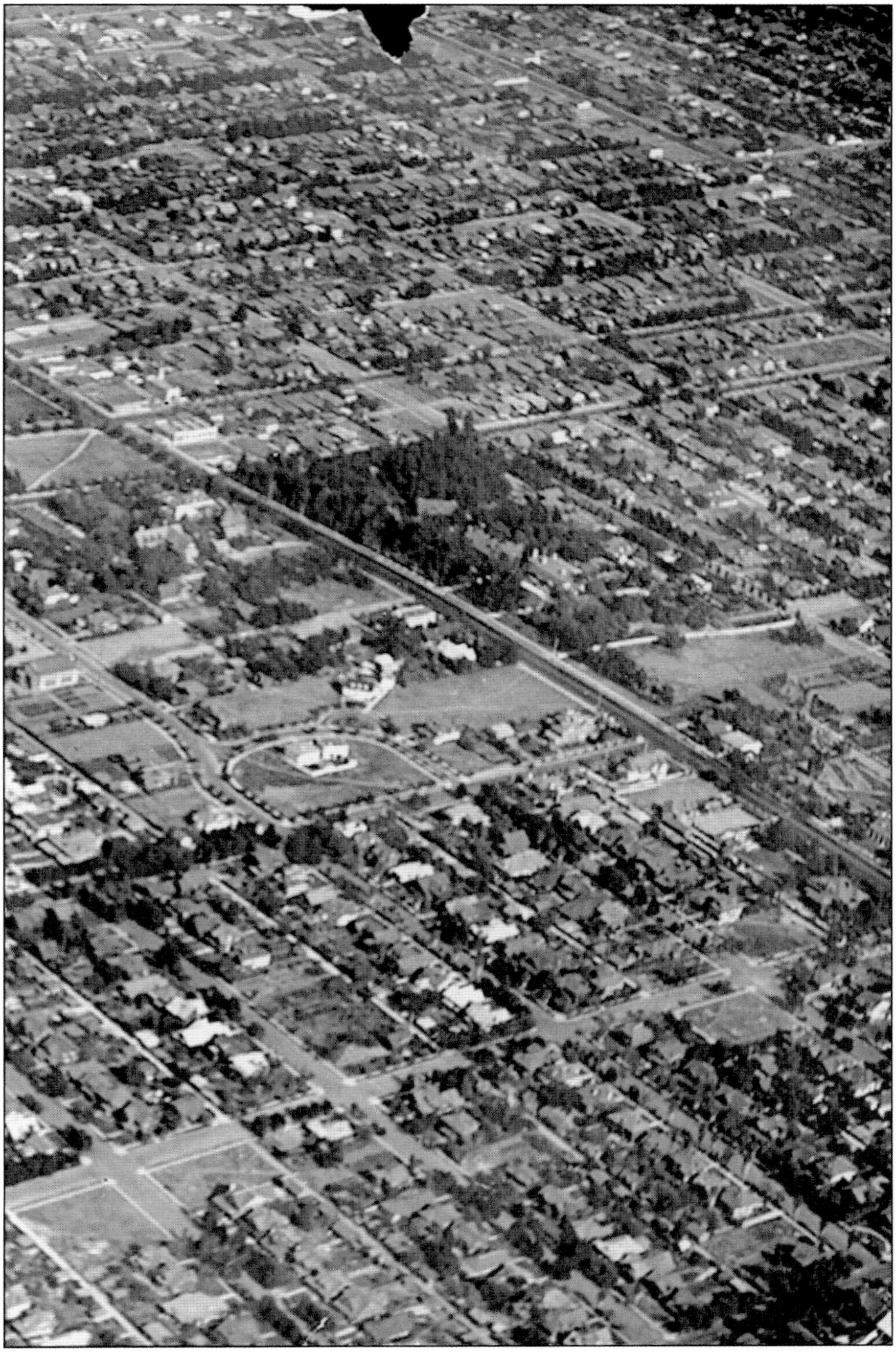

Aerial View of Kinney Heights (c. 1918). Adams Boulevard runs diagonally through the center of this photograph. Mansions and large homes can be seen built along it. Just as it runs off the right side of the photograph, the William Andrews Clark home is visible. The circular street in the center of the photograph is Gramercy Park, which was originally developed by George Van Guysling. The lower part of the photograph is Kinney Heights. (Courtesy of University of Southern California, on behalf of the USC Specialized Libraries and Archival Collections.)

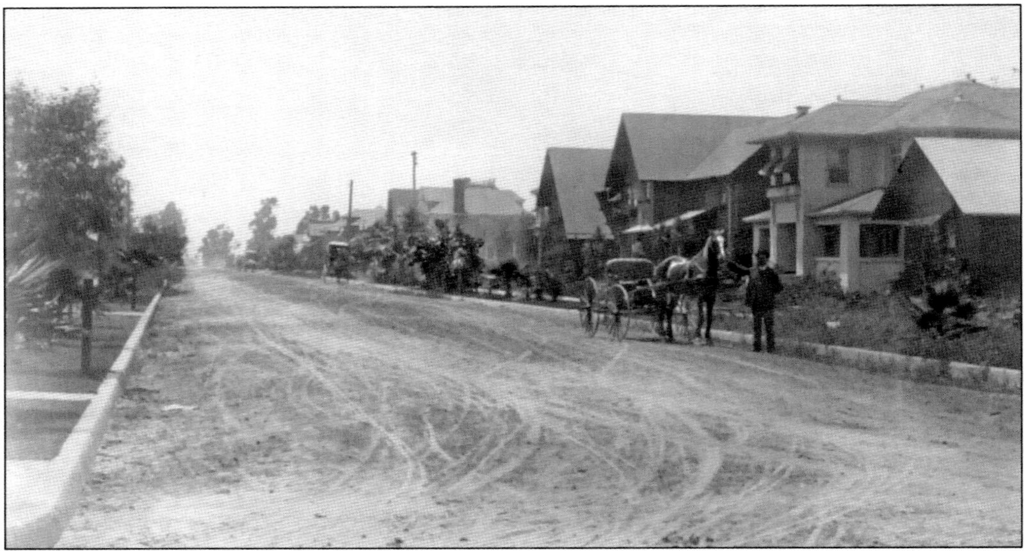

TWENTY-FOURTH STREET. From the time it was established in 1901, until her retirement 40 years later, Amelia Foshay was principal of Twenty-fourth Street School. A cousin of the superintendent of schools, James A. Foshay, she cared deeply enough about education to ride sidesaddle through this neighborhood to encourage families to enroll their children in the brand-new kindergarten.

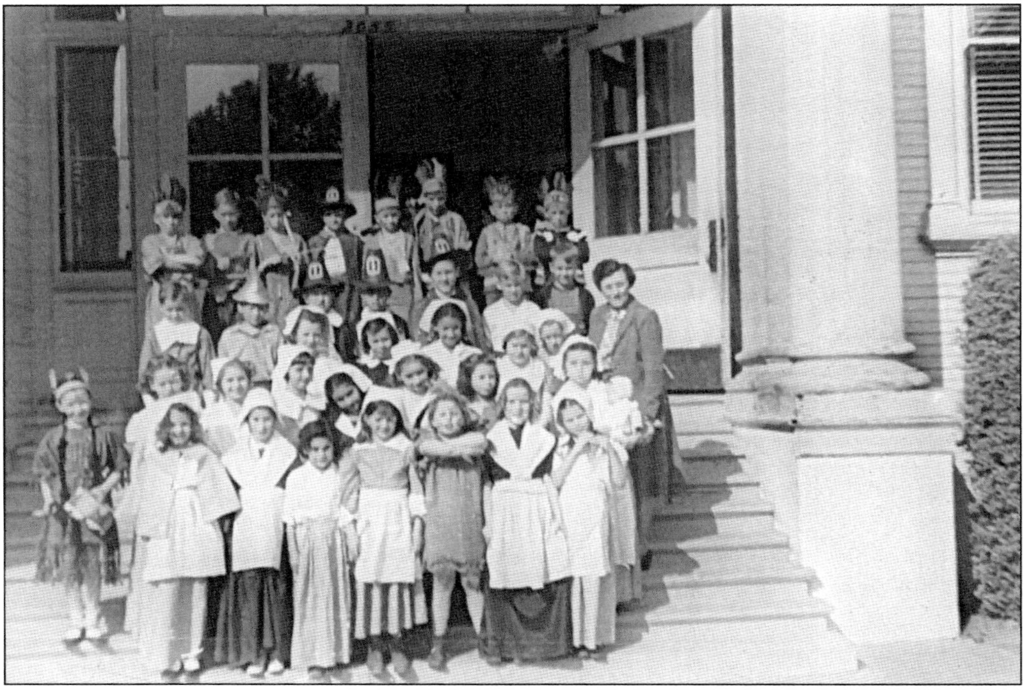

TWENTY-FOURTH STREET SCHOOL (1943). It was said Amelia Foshay was invited to every prominent wedding in the city. No doubt her former students pronounced "I do" loud and clear. To help children overcome stage fright, she had them mount a tree stump twice a week to recite their own poems and speeches. "It scared me to death," reminisced one erstwhile pupil, "but I've never been scared since." (Courtesy of Wally Matsuura and Elizabeth C. Sutherland.)

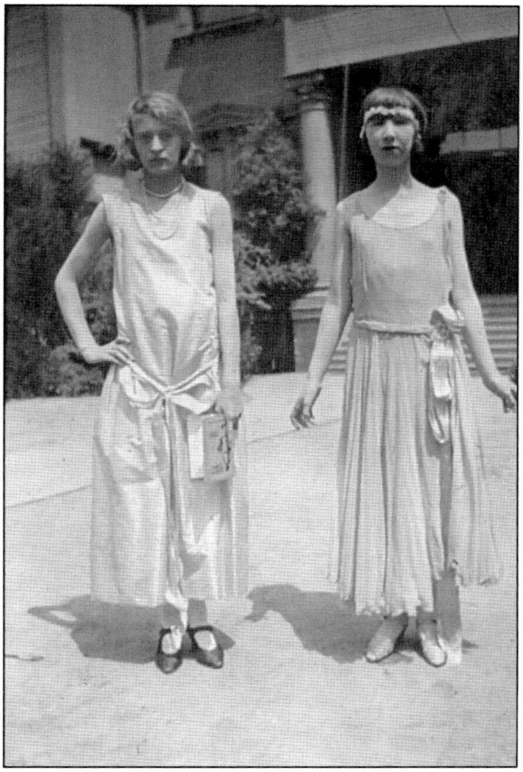

TWENTY-FOURTH STREET SCHOOL. Although fashionable hemlines hovered near the knee in 1925, the models in this fashion show wore them a bit longer, most likely because the dresses belonged to their mothers. (Courtesy of Wally Matsuura and Elizabeth C. Sutherland.)

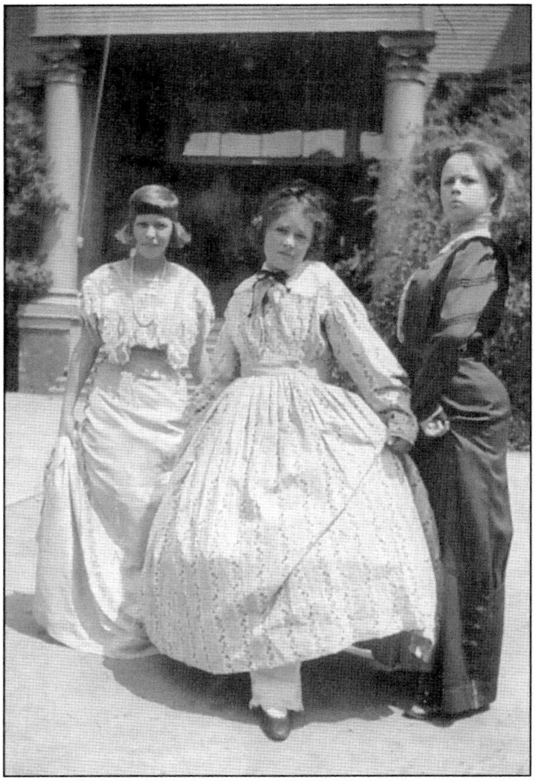

MORE TWENTY-FOURTH STREET SCHOOL. Or possibly their grandmothers, as these dresses would have been fashionable during the Revolutionary and Civil Wars, through Victorian times, and up to the dawn of the 20th century. (Courtesy of Wally Matsuura and Elizabeth C. Sutherland.)

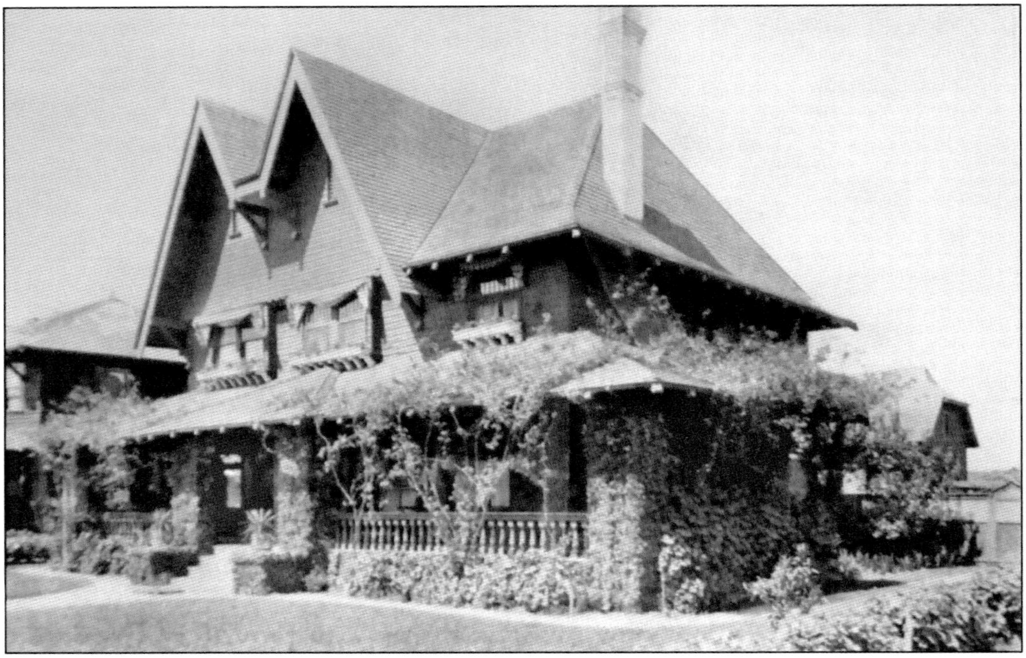

GARNSEY RESIDENCE. It was only natural that L. T. Garnsey would have a home at 2241 West Twenty-fourth Street in Kinney Heights. His Garnsey Investment Company had sold many of the lots for development. Before investing in real estate, Garnsey had a career in railroading. He was president of the Los Angeles and Redondo Railway, and his name was connected with some of the largest railroads of the Southwest.

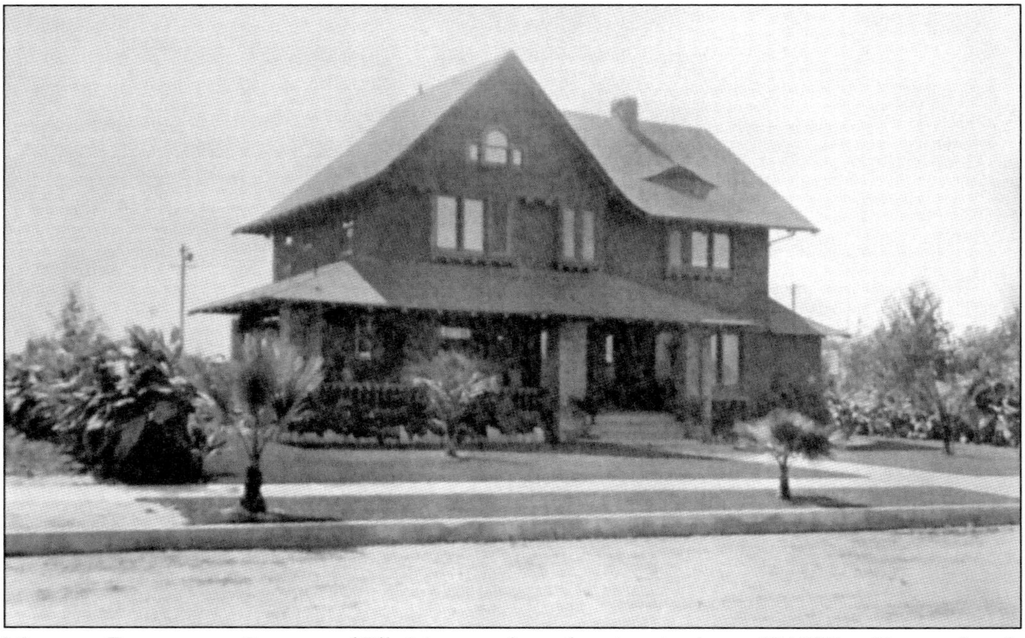

MORGAN RESIDENCE. Cosmo and Ella Morgan planted a wisteria vine at 2244 West Twenty-fourth Street that became the centerpiece of garden parties during their many decades in the house. A sugar broker in Los Angeles, as a young man, Cosmo was private secretary to Cecil Rhodes. One early job was grading diamonds, a skill that was probably handy when he proposed to his wife.

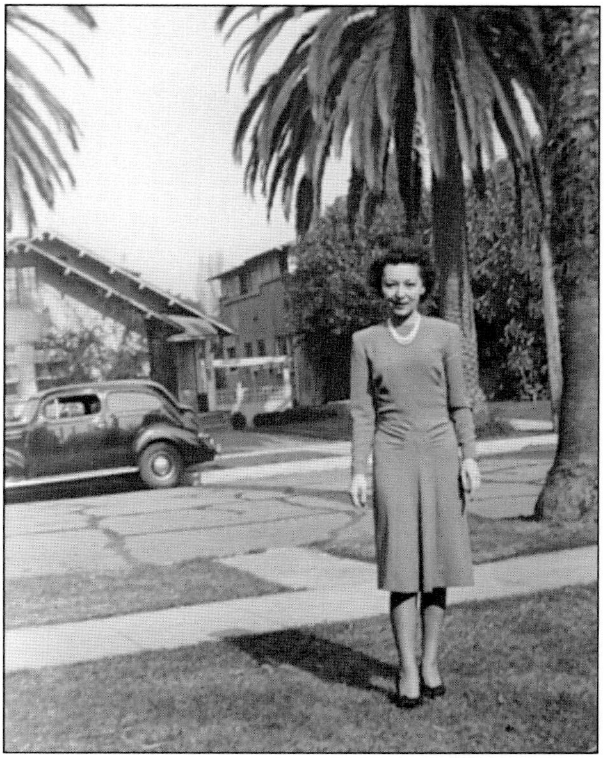

MELBA MATSUURA. Named for opera soprano Nellie Melba by her flamboyant actress mother, Melba Matsuura was exceptionally elegant. When she represented Japanese American women on a Rose Parade float, she outshone much younger women. The Twenty-fourth Street bungalow she and her husband owned is still occupied by their son, Wally. The house visible behind her was gutted, but a recent owner beautifully re-created the interior. (Courtesy of Wally Matsuura.)

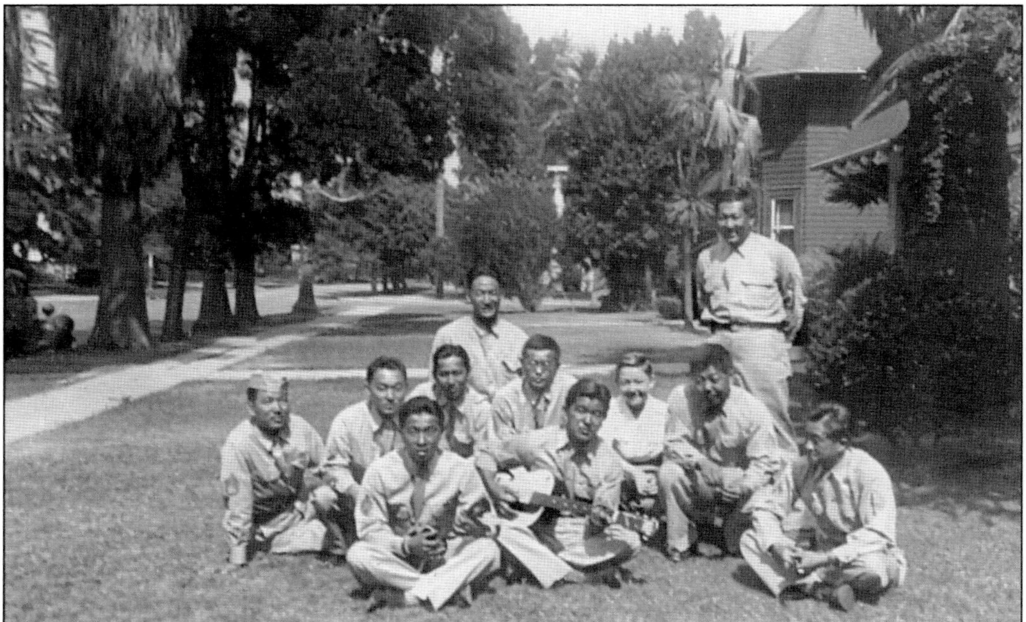

JAPANESE TRANSLATORS. During World War II, Japanese translators were vitally important but still unwelcome at the USO. The Matsuura family invited the men, who had mostly grown up in Hawaii, to enjoy the hospitality of their home on Twenty-fourth Street. Melba Matsuura saved her food stamps in order to be sure to have something especially delicious to feed them. (Courtesy of Wally Matsuura.)

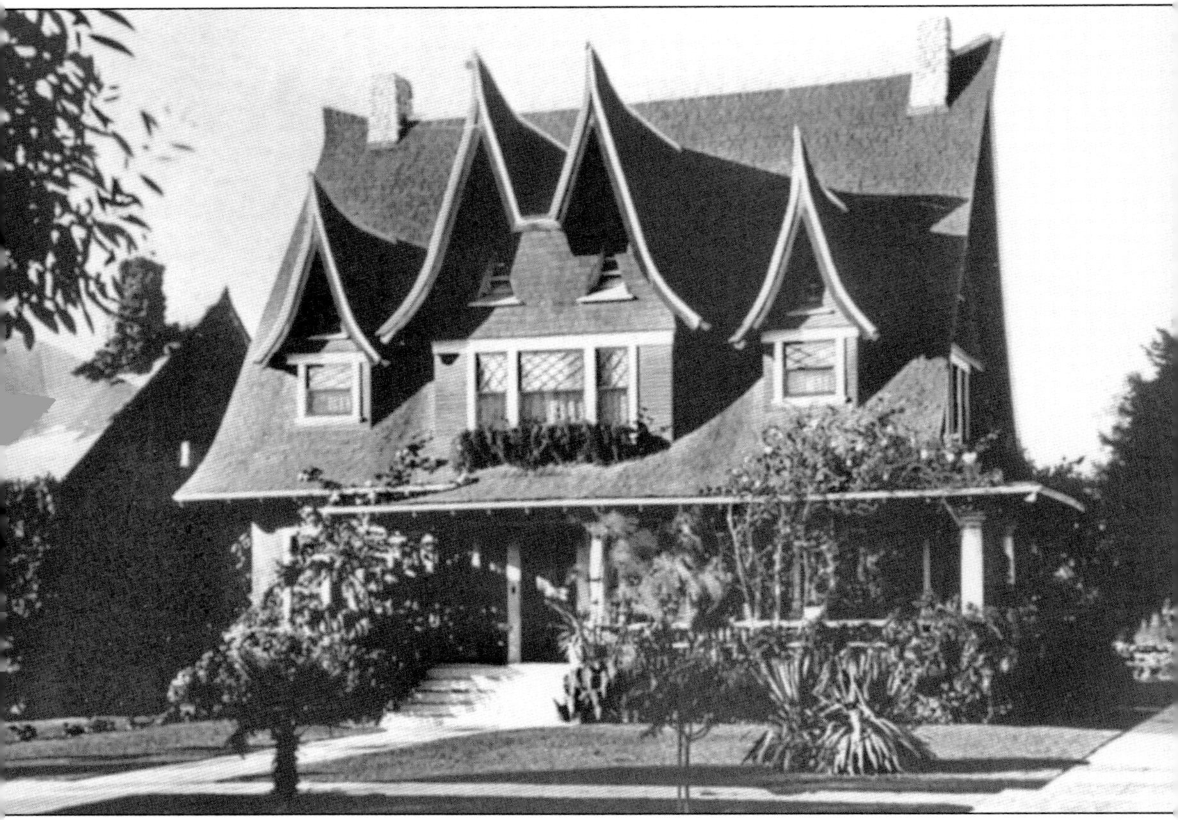

DUPUY RESIDENCE. Joseph Pierre Dupuy began his singing career as a boy soprano in a church choir a year after his family emigrated from Bordeaux. As an adult, his beautiful tenor voice gained acclaim. In 1913, impresario L. E. Behymer commemorated the three silver dollars Dupuy had earned at his first Los Angeles concert with a buckskin purse containing 25 coins—one for each year Dupuy sang in the city. Charles E. Shattuck designed an eight-room frame house at 2301 West Twenty-fourth Street for the singer in 1902. By the 1990s, the house was abandoned, badly deteriorated, and looked like a scary haunted house . . . inhabited by transients and drug dealers, rather than a witch in a pointy hat that matched the roofline. Architectural features, including the porch columns, were stolen, and several small fires had destroyed once lovely hardwood floors. The neighbors fought the owner—the City of Los Angeles—for many long, frustrating years, but the community center in the South Seas House is now an important success story of West Adams preservation. (Courtesy of Barbara Dupuy Hammer.)

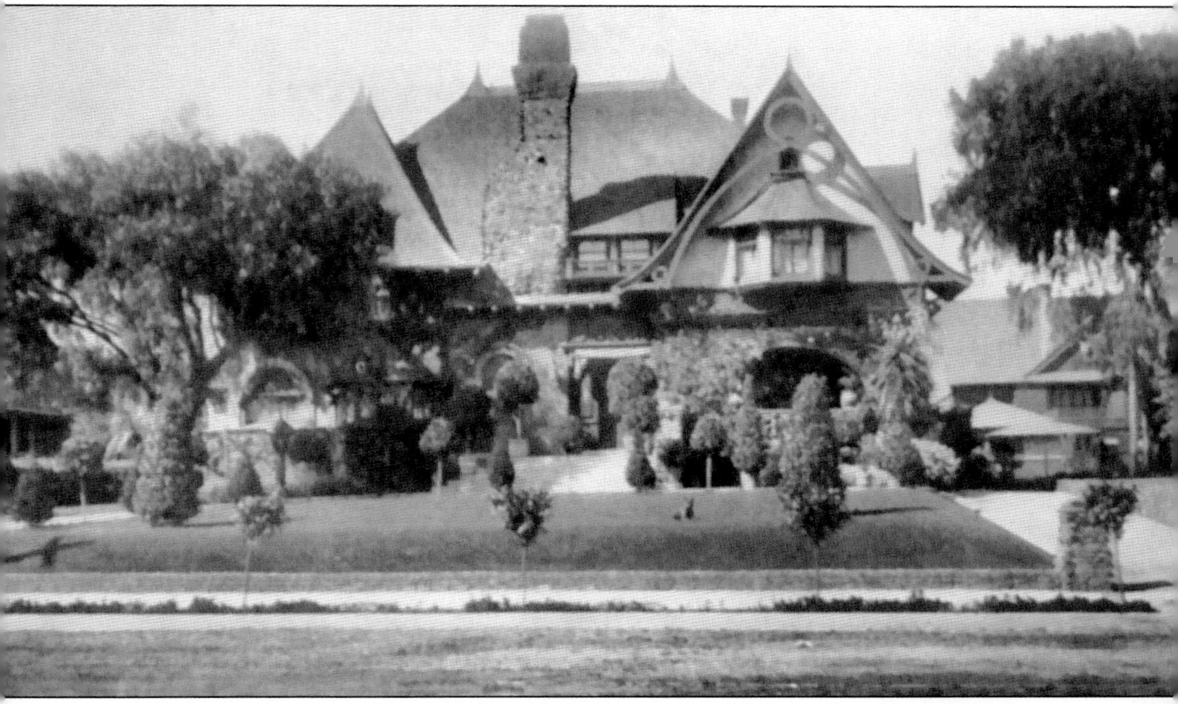

FITZGERALD RESIDENCE. In addition to his role as a partner in Blanchard and Fitzgerald Music Company, and later business director of the Los Angeles Symphony, James T. Fitzgerald was a very articulate and clever man. He once wrote, "Not to love the music of the Los Angeles Symphony Orchestra is not only a misfortune but a deformity," and complained in print about an accusation that he did not respond as a gentleman should to a request from La Loie Fuller for tickets to a concert. He stated, "I do not believe Miss Fuller would use such coarse language or make such statements. If she did, she is no gentleman either." In a long letter written after he and his wife were caught behind German lines in 1914, he included the poignant wish, "certainly there will come a time in the course of mankind's uplift . . . when differences between nations will be settled by a mental process. God speed the day!" His 12-room house at the corner of West Adams Boulevard and Arlington Avenue was designed by J. Cather Newsom in 1904.

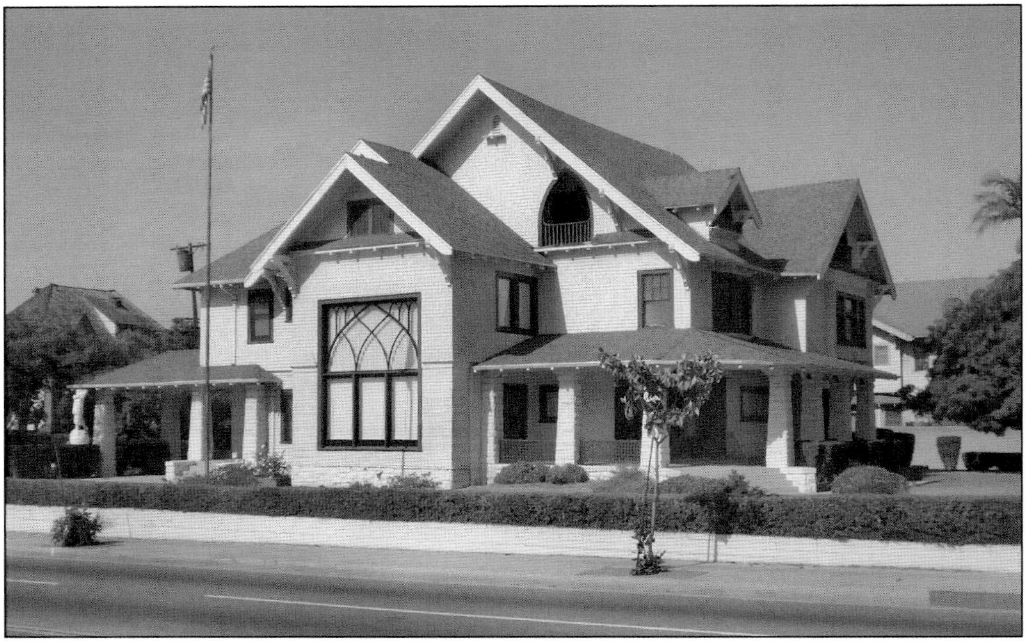

MARQUIS RESIDENCE. Neighbors questioned zoning ordinances when a "Fisher and Sons Funeral Home" sign first sprouted on the lawn of 2302 West Twenty-fifth Street, but it just heralded filming of HBO's *Six Feet Under.* With its beautiful old homes, West Adams is a popular location for movies and television. The 1904 house was originally owned by Auguste Marquis and is now the home of the Filipino Federation of America.

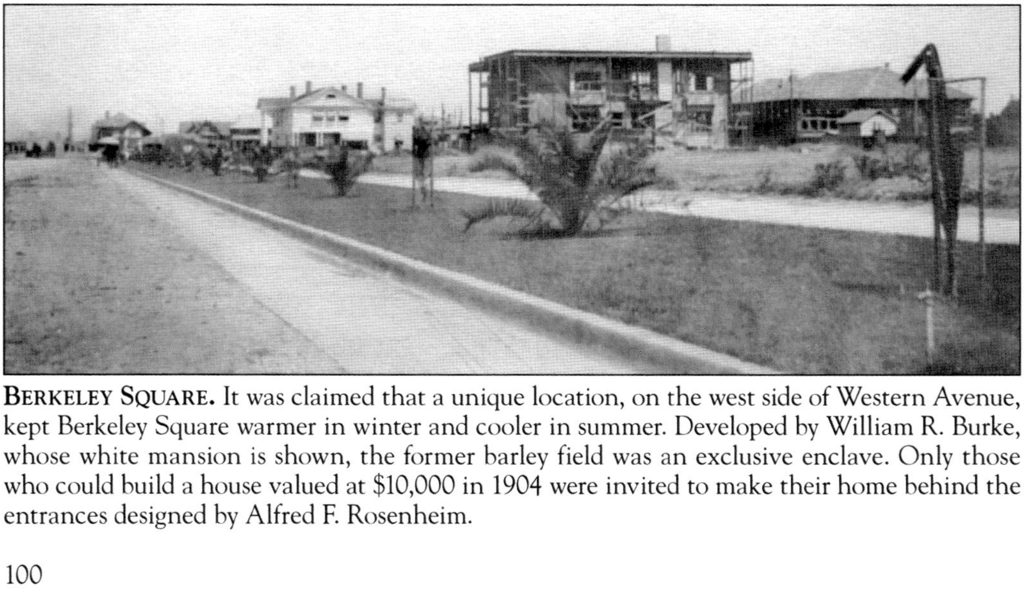

BERKELEY SQUARE. It was claimed that a unique location, on the west side of Western Avenue, kept Berkeley Square warmer in winter and cooler in summer. Developed by William R. Burke, whose white mansion is shown, the former barley field was an exclusive enclave. Only those who could build a house valued at $10,000 in 1904 were invited to make their home behind the entrances designed by Alfred F. Rosenheim.

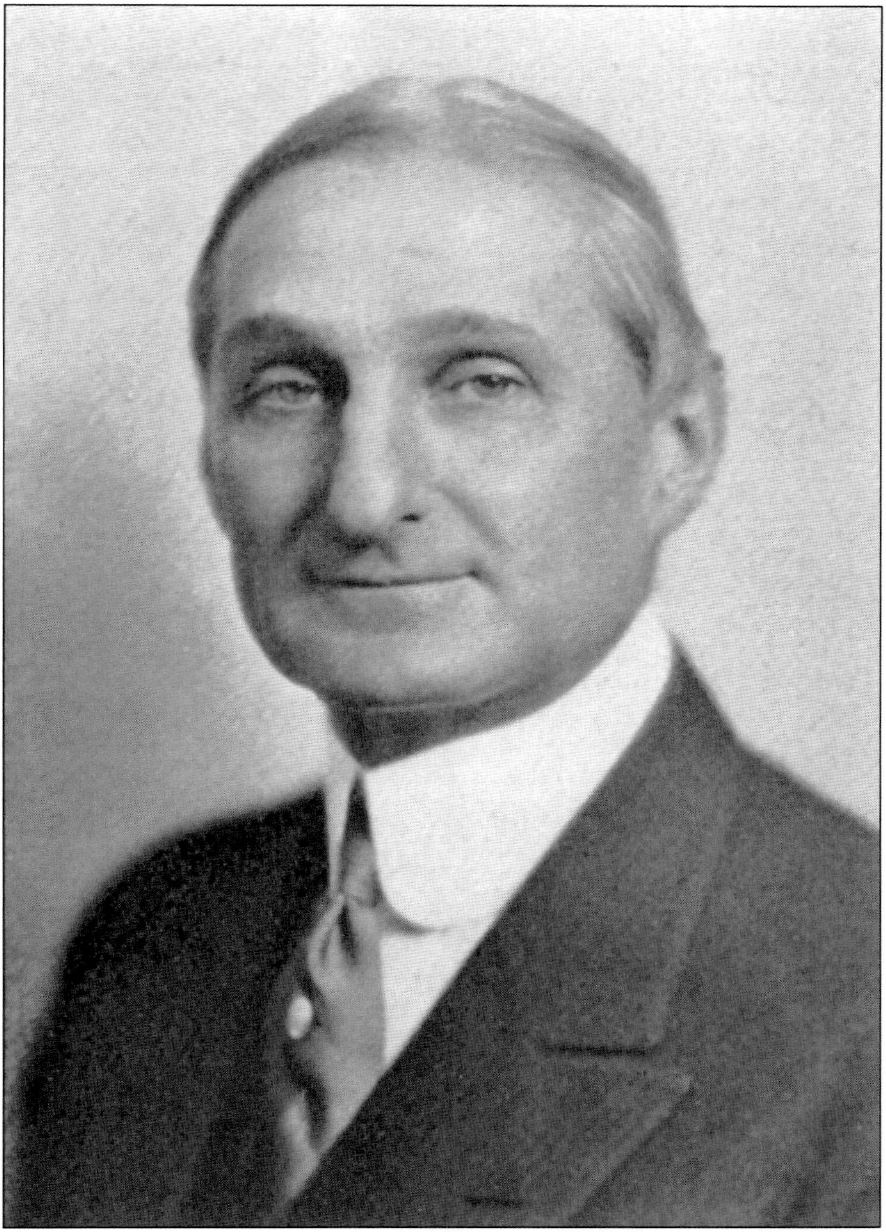

William Gibbs McAdoo. This secretary of the treasury defied superstition when his first gift to his fiancée was an opal, which, tradition says, is a stone that brings bad luck. Eleanor was the daughter of President Wilson, and the couple wed in the White House, but McAdoo never quite succeeded in his own presidential ambitions. He and Al Smith were so closely tied for the Democratic nomination in 1924 that they deadlocked, and the nomination went to a third candidate. In 1922, the McAdoos bought 5 Berkeley Square from Willis G. Hunt, who became their neighbor when he built a house next door. After 20 years of marriage, Eleanor divorced McAdoo because their interests no longer coincided. He said it was because her health did not permit her to join him in Washington, and, "After all, we have had 20 years of happiness." By the next year, the 71-year-old senator had consoled himself with a marriage to a public service nurse 45 years his junior.

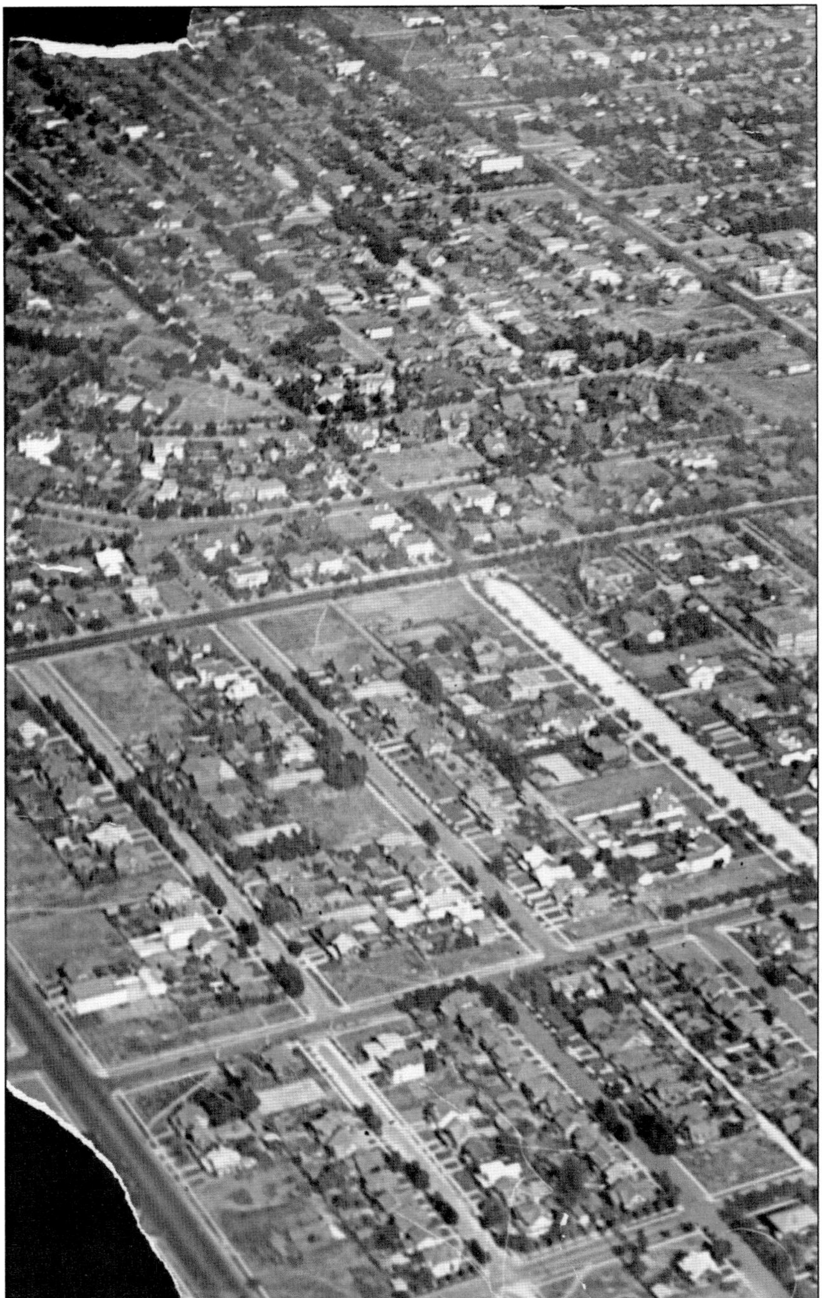

AERIAL VIEW OF WESTERN HEIGHTS (C. 1918). Berkeley Square is the wide street on the right in this photograph, where some of the largest homes in Los Angeles were located. At the bottom left is Washington Boulevard, and between the two is Western Heights, which was first laid out in 1904. This photograph, taken in 1918, shows that numerous lots are still undeveloped. Many would be filled with small apartment buildings. Across Western, which bisects the photograph, is West Adams Heights, also known as "Sugar Hill." Today the Santa Monica Freeway runs through the heart of this photograph. (Courtesy of University of Southern California, on behalf of the USC Specialized Libraries and Archival Collections.)

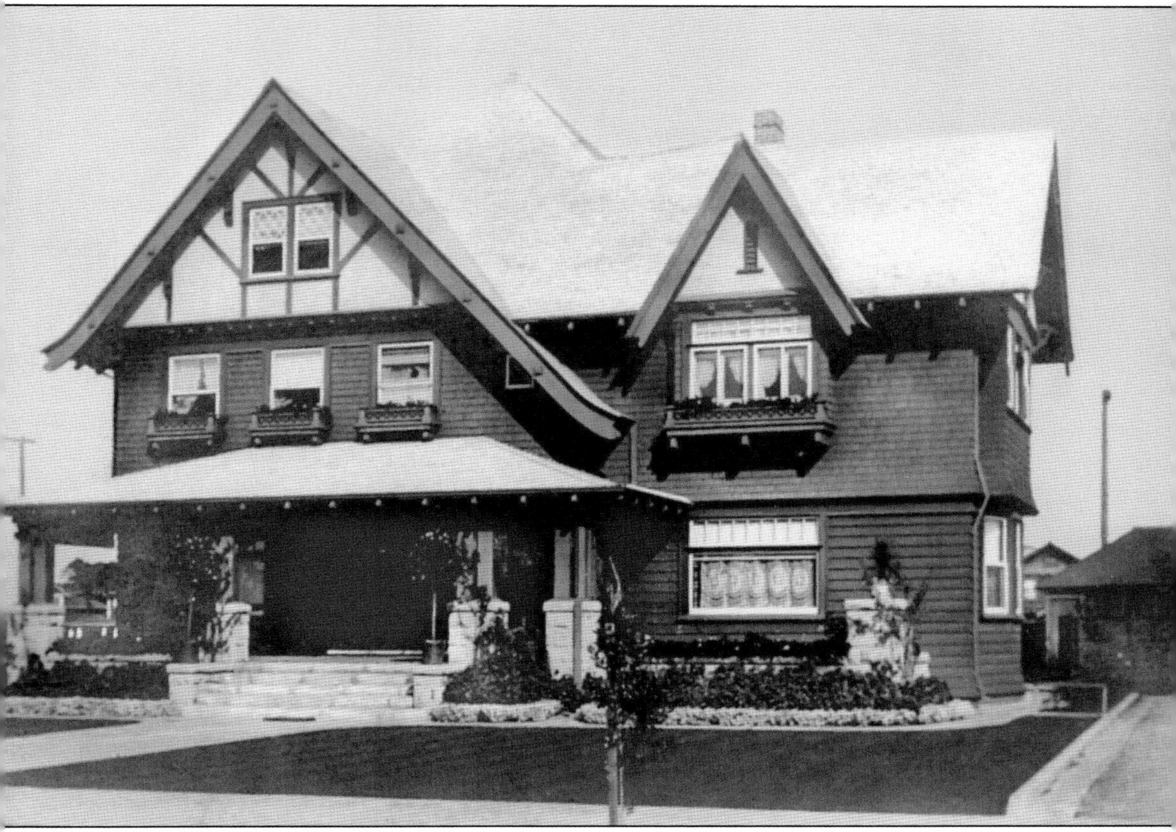

BRAUER RESIDENCE. "Mrs. Brauer's beautiful home," proclaimed the person who mailed this postcard. When clothier Adolph K. Brauer took out his building permit in December 1904, he estimated the cost of construction for a home at 2129 West Twenty-first Street at $6,000. Brauer owned at least three lots in Western Heights but chose to build here and sold the others. The house was constructed with a sun parlor and library on the first floor, tapestry wallpaper in the dining room featuring outdoor scenes, and a high-ceilinged attic, which was likely a playroom for the Brauers' two little girls.

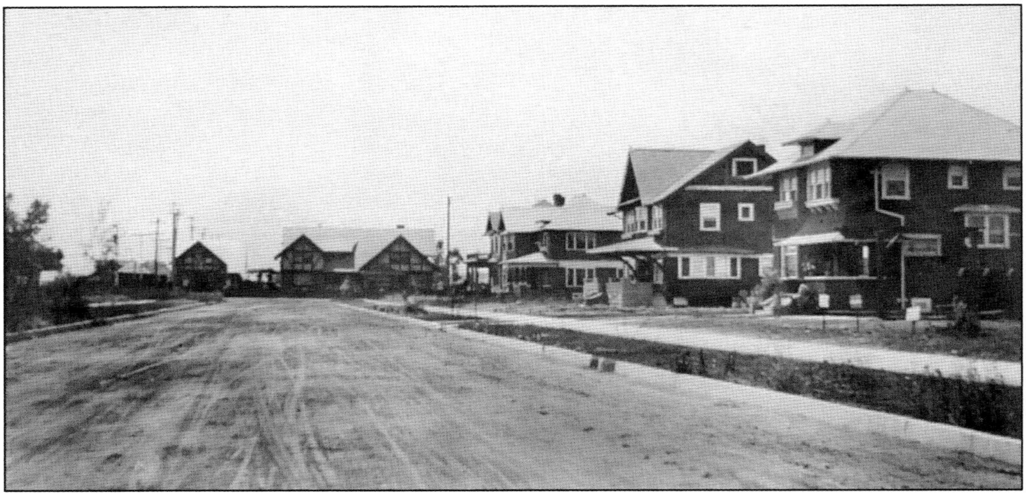

TWENTY-FIRST STREET. The 2100 block of Twenty-first Street is still being developed in this photograph, taken looking west. At the end, facing the camera, is the Asher home at 2101 South Gramercy Place. It was built in 1904 for Kentucky horse breeder Hugh L. Asher, who hired the firm of Hunt and Eager to design it. Asher did not stay long in the house, moving soon to El Monte.

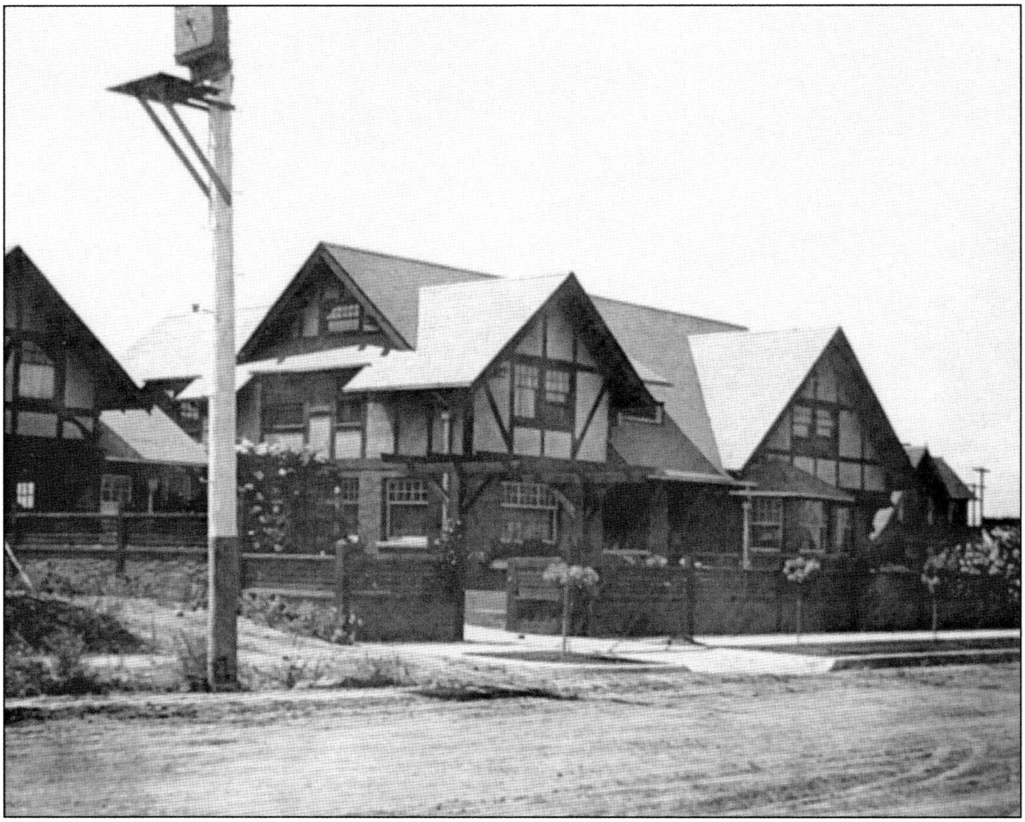

ASHER RESIDENCE. The Asher home at 2101 South Gramercy Place went through a succession of owners over the years. In 1975, singer Marvin Gaye's production company bought the house and 18 months later signed it over to Gaye's parents. In 1984, during an argument, Marvin Gaye Sr. fatally shot his son, who passed away on the front steps.

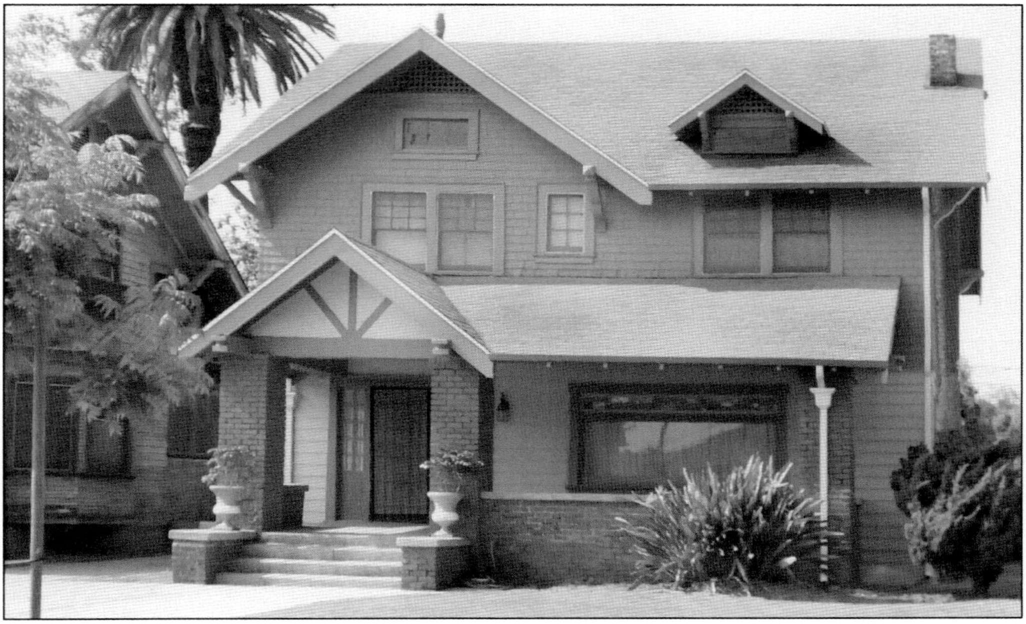

GLOVER RESIDENCE. On December 21, 1913, this home at 2219 West Twentieth Street made the national news when Roy Glover fired four shots into Boer War veteran Daniel deVilliers in the entryway. He was eventually released from jail after convincing the court he and his wife, Jean, felt threatened by deVilliers, her former husband. Glover eventually became a developer of the San Fernando Valley, giving away truckloads of holly each Christmas.

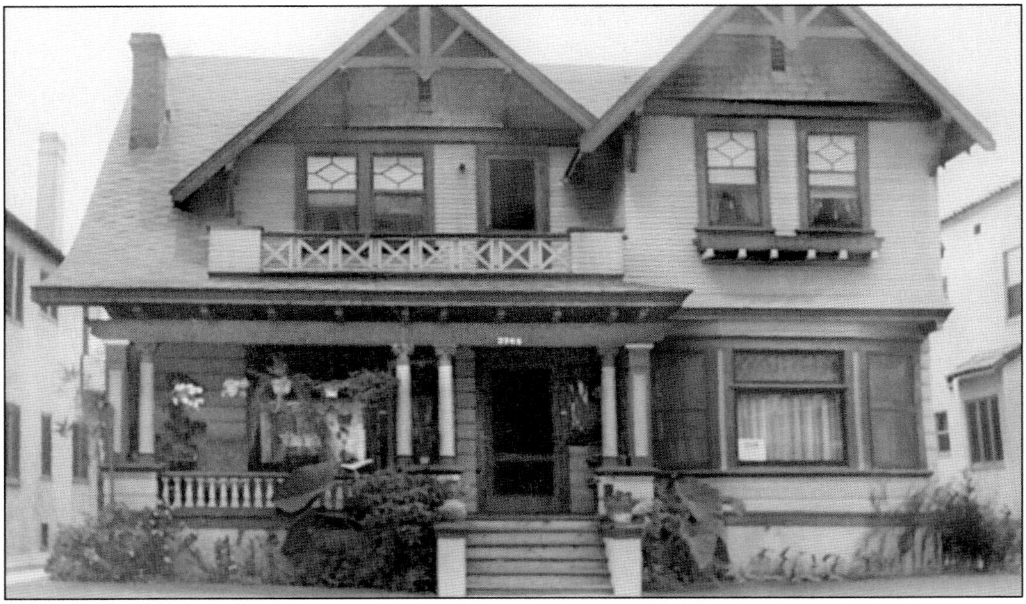

HUNT FAMILY. The Hunt family lived in this home at 2268 West Twentieth Street from 1938 until 1952. While essentially an arts and crafts–style home, it actually has some Victorian elements, such as the round columns supporting the porch roof and the machine-turned balusters supporting the porch railing. Most craftsman-style homes had square or tapered columns and balusters. Sadly, the home was later destroyed by fire and replaced with a rectangular box of an apartment building. (Courtesy of Jim Hunt.)

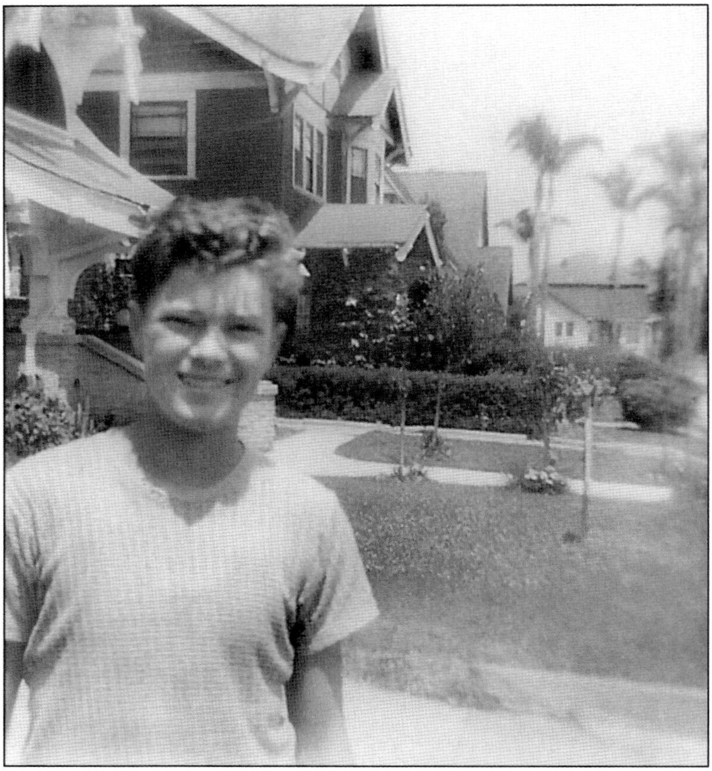

MINNEY RESIDENCE. Wayne Laudenback stands in front of his home at 2287 West Twentieth Street sometime in the 1940s. The dark painted home behind him was built for Dr. John Elder Minney of Topeka, Kansas. Around 1980, Kathleen Salisbury and Bill Washington turned it into a popular bed-and-breakfast. For 15 years, it was one of the few (sometimes only) such establishments in the city. (Courtesy of Jim Hunt.)

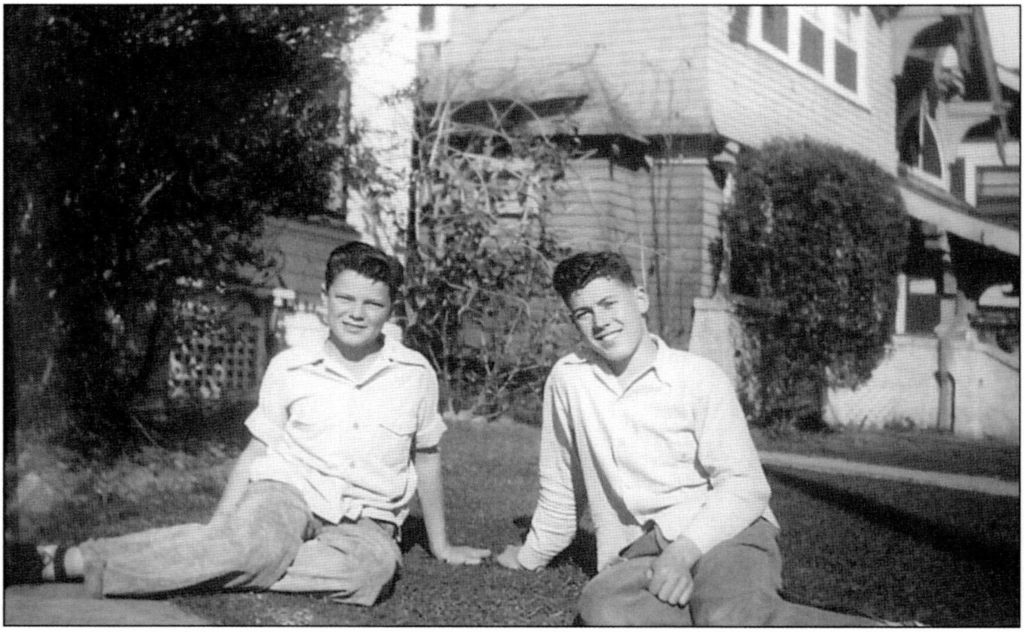

TWO BOYS. Wayne (left) and Leonard Laudenback rest on the lawn of their home at 2287 West Twentieth Street. The home behind them, number 2279, was occupied by Walter Ehlers, a D-Day veteran who was awarded the Congressional Medal of Honor for single-handedly knocking out three Nazi mortars, killing four Germans, and capturing 12 others. His older brother, Roland Ehlers, was killed in the D-Day invasion. (Courtesy of Jim Hunt.)

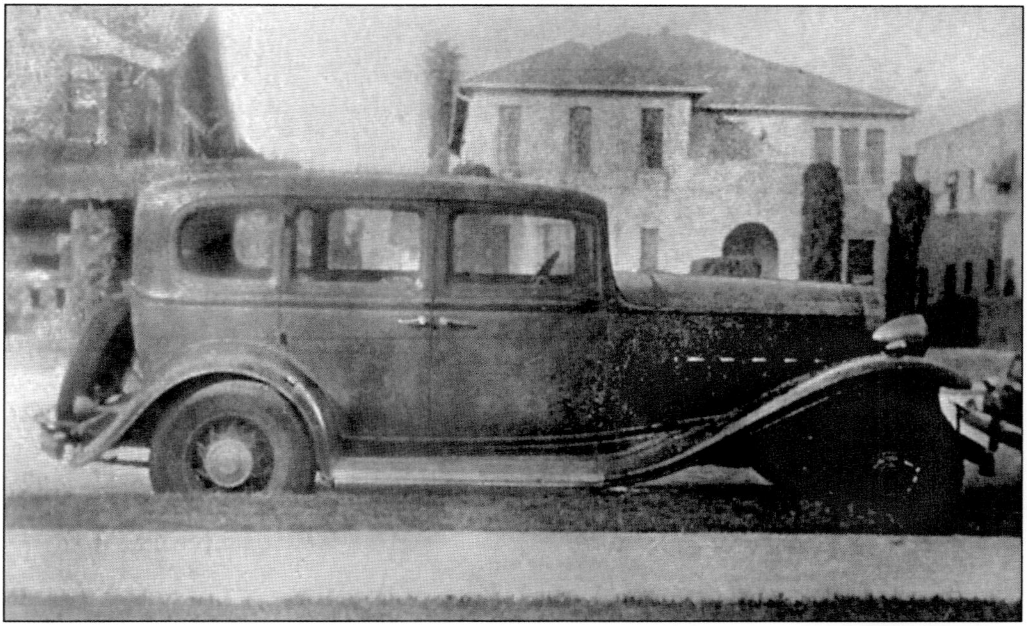

JIM HUNT'S BUICK. "This was my first car—a 1932 Buick," wrote Jim Hunt. As Western Heights, like so much of West Adams, was being developed, affordable automobiles made it easier to live farther from downtown. Other Westside communities became more desirable, leaving many empty lots in West Adams. By the 1920s, these lots were purchased for multiunit housing, such as the duplex behind the Buick. (Courtesy of Jim Hunt.)

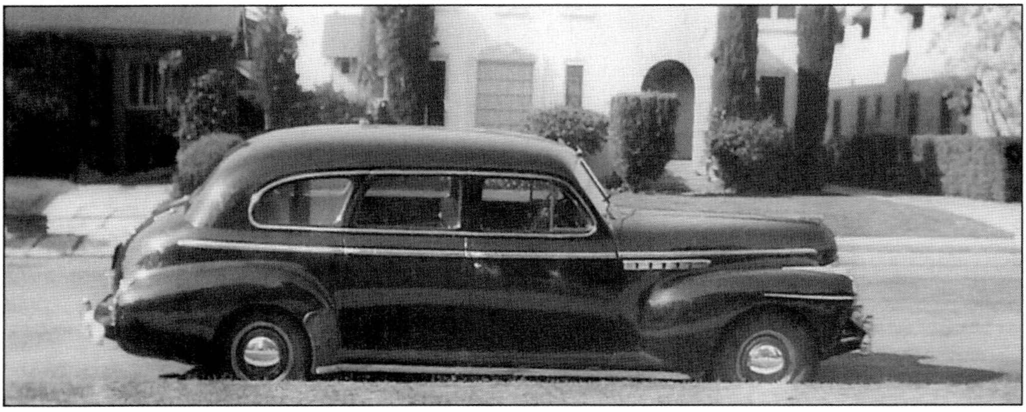

HUNT FAMILY BUICK. The Hunt family of 2268 West Twentieth Street was justifiably proud of their massive 1941 Buick, parked in front of their home. In 1927, Myrtle McNamara, a resident of the duplex across the street, was attending a tea party when two gunmen robbed her and the other ladies of $25,000 in jewelry. The mastermind was Ollie Lowe, one of the other guests. (Courtesy of Jim Hunt.)

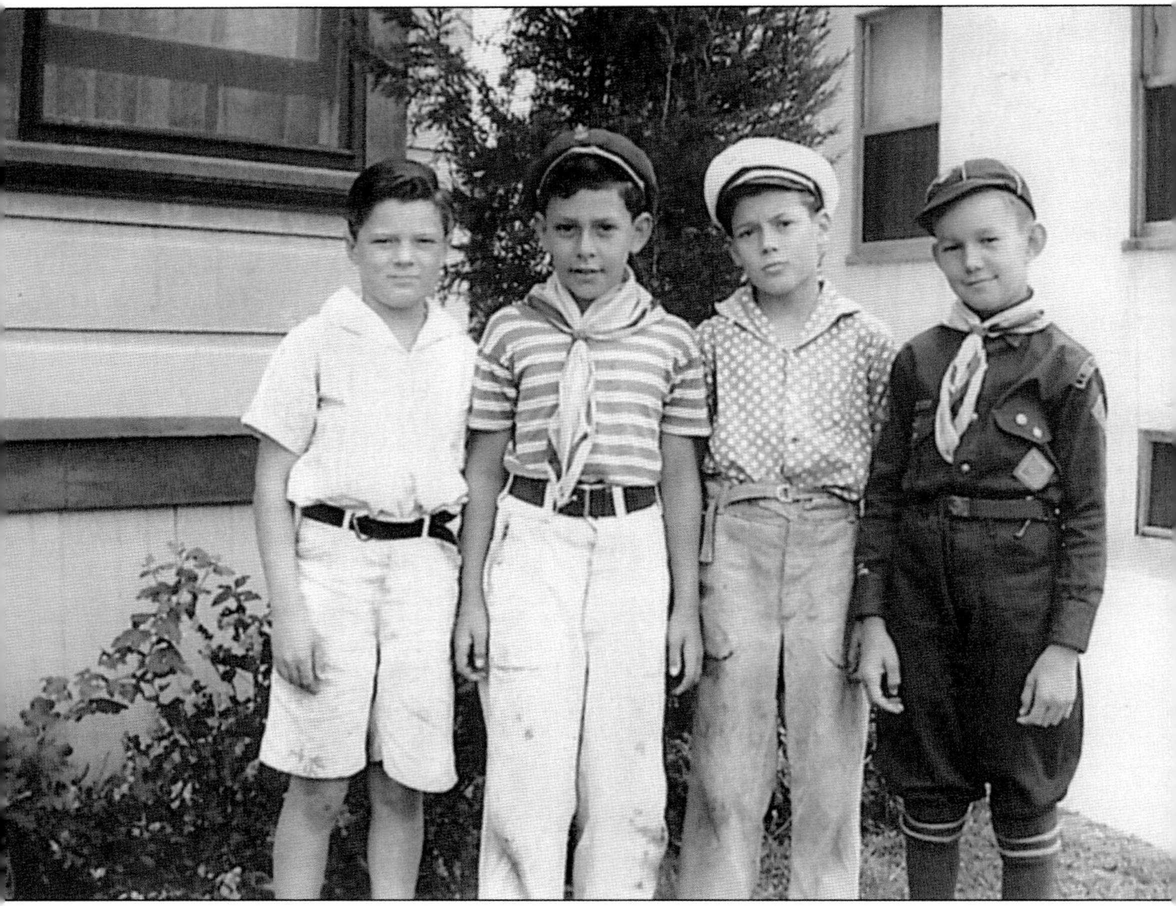

Four Boys. By the time this photograph was taken, around 1939, many of the homes were 30 years old. Residents who now moved in were more frequently middle class and were often more interested in the size of the homes than their now outdated architectural features. From left to right are Wayne Laudenback, Harvey Baron, Leonard Laudenback, and Jim Hunt, standing in front of the Hunt home at 2268 West Twentieth Street. The boys remained in touch long after moving away, and it was Jim Hunt's recent visit to his old neighborhood that resulted in a number of the photographs on these pages. (Courtesy of Jim Hunt.)

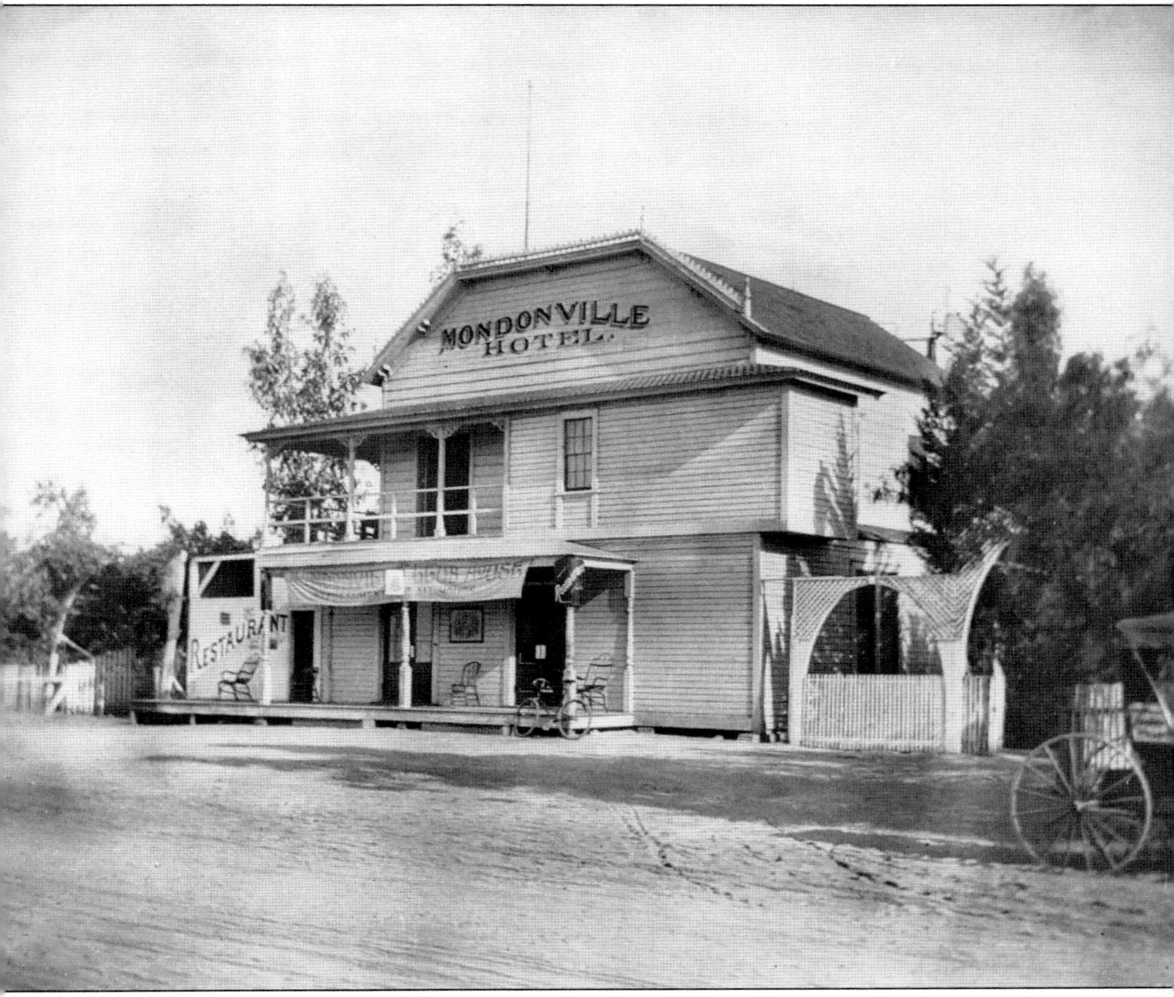

MONDONVILLE HOTEL. One would not expect the elite of West Adams to tolerate a notorious roadhouse, but in 1896, Washington Boulevard near Arlington Road (later Avenue) was mostly undeveloped land. Mondonville Gardens advertised trained goats and chicken fighting, but one scandal was not of owner P. J. Flynn's devising. Lucy Banning, one of Southern California's richest and most beautiful socialites, made a practice of eloping with various men. When fleeing her first husband (who had also eloped with her), her first stop was the Mondonville Hotel. Lucy insisted she was searching for happiness: "Most people prefer to call it a scandal. I prefer to call it a romance." Flynn preferred to call her beau, H. Russell Ward, a deadbeat who did not pay the bill. In 1902, Flynn changed the name of his establishment to the Army and Navy Club, piously claiming he legally dispensed liquor only to members. The next year, the city succeeded in closing the Mondonville, and Flynn moved his saloon to the wilds of Santa Monica. (Courtesy of University of Southern California, on behalf of the USC Specialized Libraries and Archival Collections.)

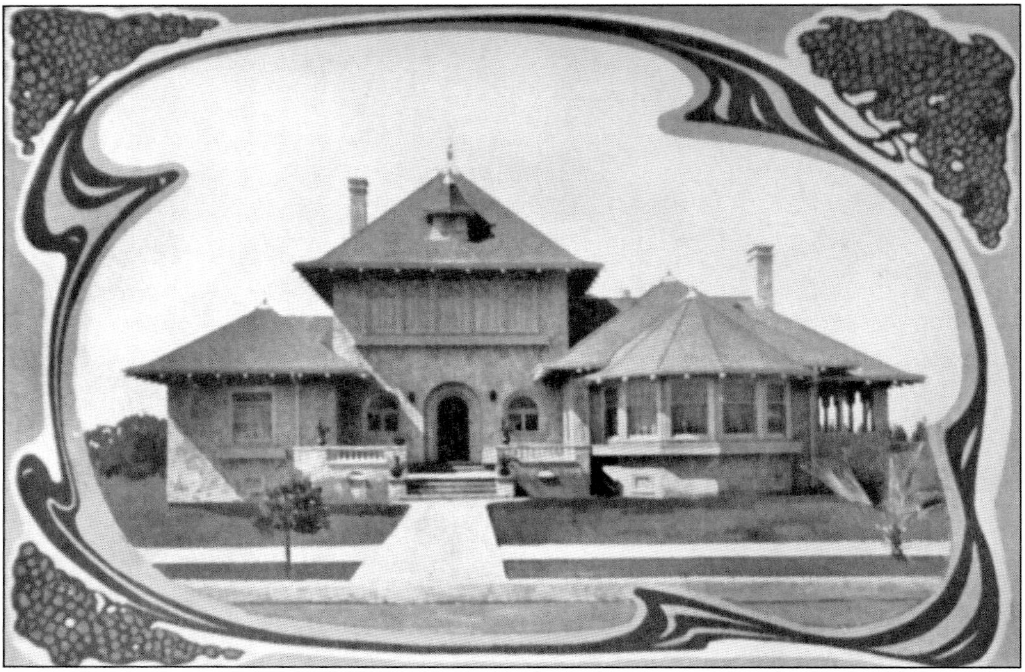

FREEMAN RESIDENCE. Archie and Edith Freeman christened their home at 1305 South Gramercy Place, designed in 1903 by Dennis and Farwell, Casa Contento. Archie, the son of Inglewood's founder, Daniel Freeman, spent his time hunting and fishing. The couple eventually relocated to France but fled to England at the outbreak of World War I. Archie returned to France as an ambulance driver in support of his new homeland.

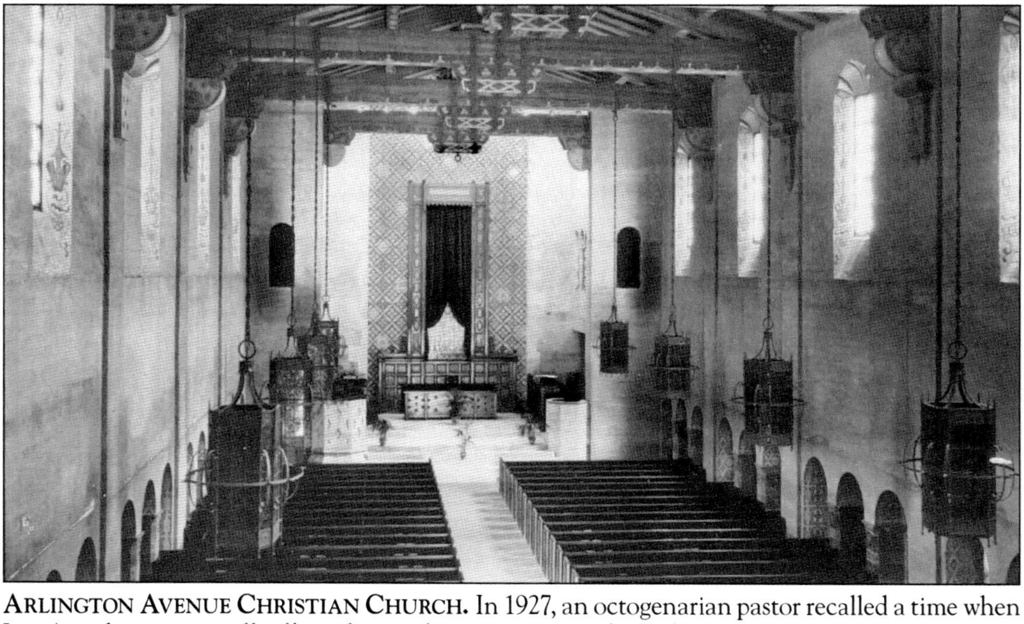

ARLINGTON AVENUE CHRISTIAN CHURCH. In 1927, an octogenarian pastor recalled a time when Los Angeles was a small village during the ceremony marking the laying of the cornerstone for a new church, designed by Harold Cross, at the corner of Pico Boulevard and Arlington Avenue. A set of 16-toned chimes donated by a parishioner was valued at $12,000, a cost surpassed only by the chimes atop the Campanile at UC Berkeley.

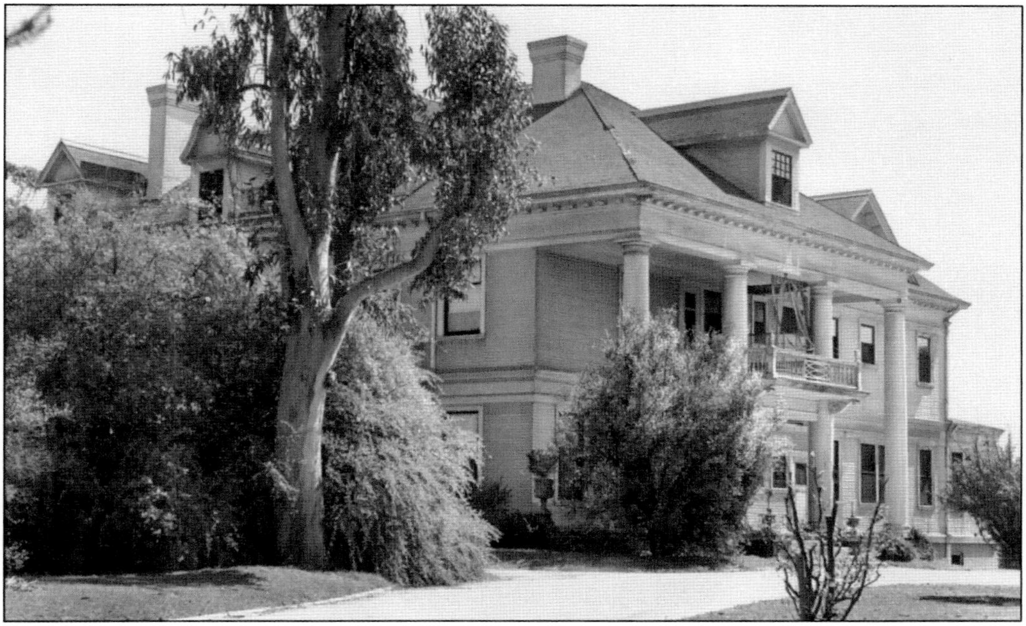

CHILDS RESIDENCE (1939). This 32-room Colonial landmark at 3100 West Adams, built in 1899, was the home of Mrs. Ozro W. Childs, born Suzanne Bate, who lived there until well into her 90s. Her husband formed the first L.A. Water Works Company and donated much of the land that became USC. The mansion later became the Childrens Home Society and was ultimately demolished in 1978 amid public outcry. (Courtesy of Bison Archives.)

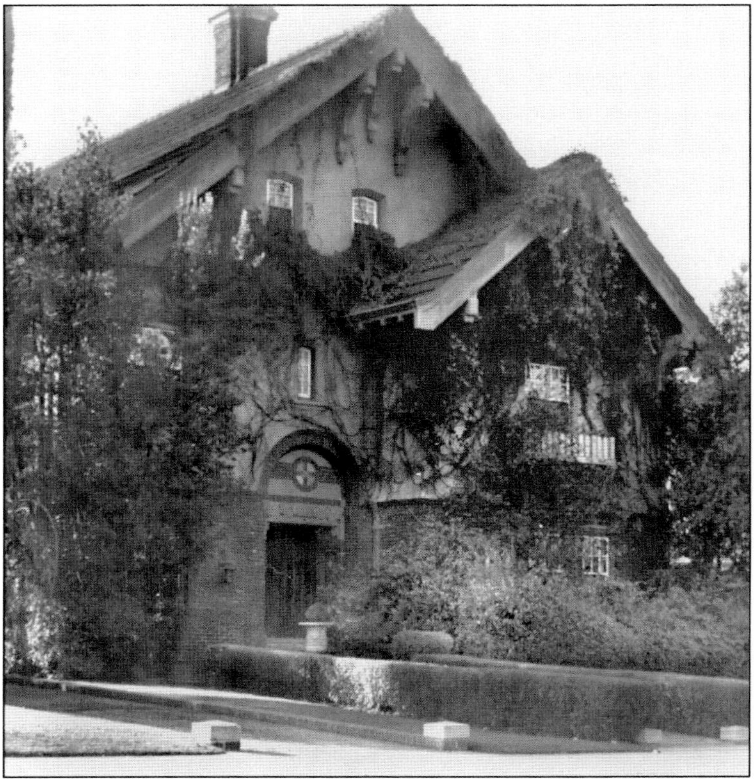

MACGOWAN RESIDENCE (1942). News coverage of Dr. Granville MacGowan tended to focus on prominent patients or autopsies of sensational murders, but social columns preferred parties given by Dr. MacGowan and his wife, Lily, at 3726 West Adams Boulevard. After he was elected president of the Los Angeles Medical Association, the press flocked to print his measured opinion on subjects like Prohibition, which he opposed as counterproductive. (Courtesy of Bison Archives.)

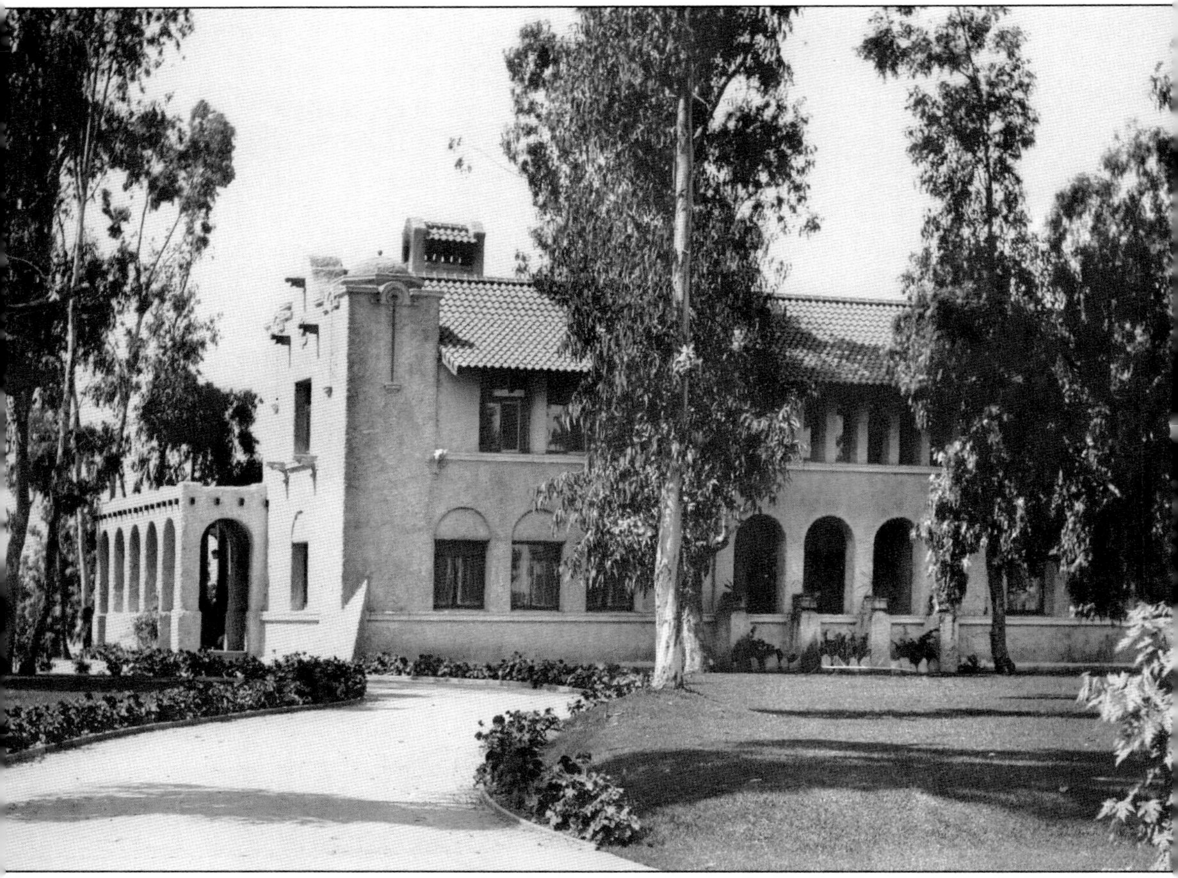

BARTLETT RESIDENCE (C. 1912). From the golden spike connecting the country's first transcontinental railroad to the finger of a West Adams resident seems a stretch, but Mrs. W. S. Bartlett (née Franklina Gray) was the stepdaughter of the donor of the famous golden spike. Besides being the proud possessor of a souvenir ring made from the bar of gold from which the spike was cast, she was also one of the founders of the Ebell Club of Los Angeles. Her husband was a banker. Their 14-room house at 3200 West Adams Street was designed by Charles F. Whittlesey around an open courtyard, with a roof garden providing a view of the city for the family's enjoyment. (Courtesy of the University of Southern California, on behalf of the USC Specialized Libraries and Archival Collections.)

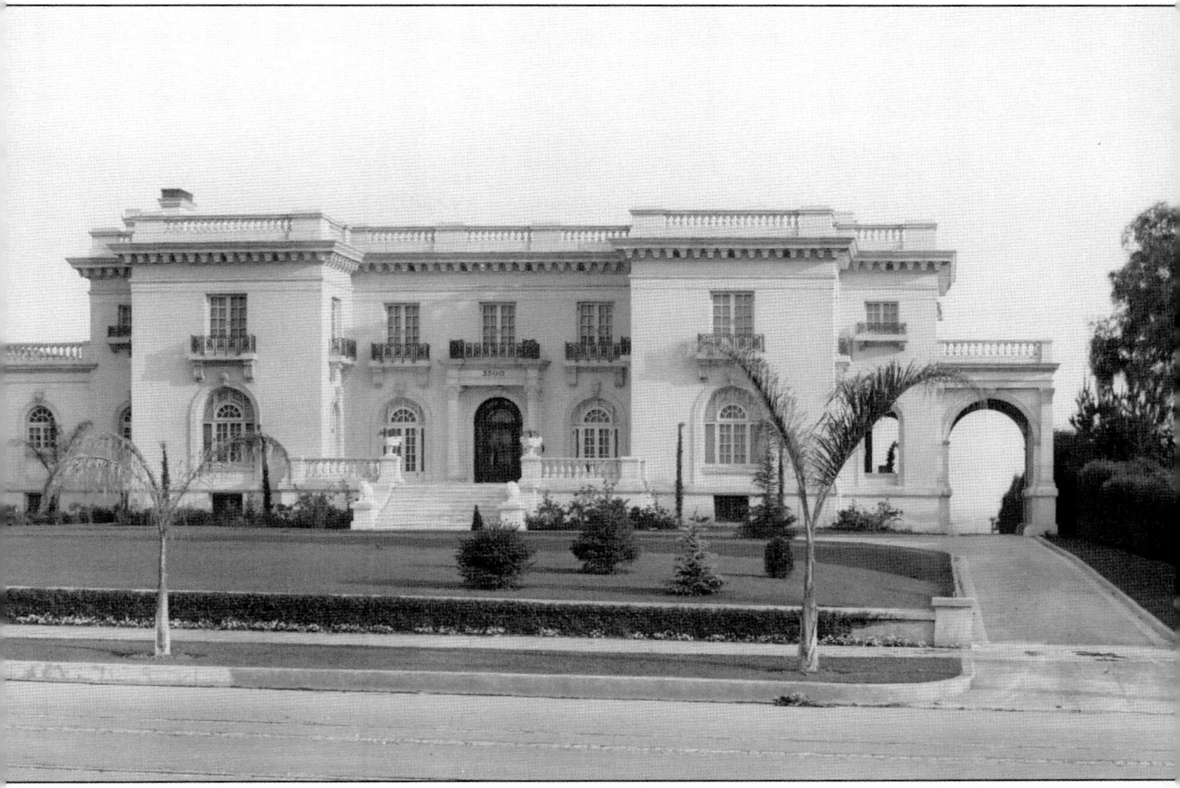

GUASTI RESIDENCE (C. 1910). In 1909, vintner Secundo Guasti hired the firm of Hudson and Munsell to design this villa showcasing pure Italian architecture at 3500 West Adams Street. No expense was spared in the use of Peruvian mahogany, oak, and white cedar for the elaborate interior. Guasti came to Los Angeles in 1883 and, with his wife, Louise, developed a small wine business at Second and Alameda Streets into a 6,000-acre vineyard at what eventually came to be named Guasti, California. When Guasti died in 1927, on his 40th wedding anniversary, the list of honorary pallbearers read like a "Who's Who" of West Adams. A later resident, Busby Berkeley, was known for his extravagant choreography, showcasing legions of showgirls in kaleidoscopic array, in musical films like *42nd Street*. During the 1930s and 1940s, he added the cachet of fame acquired by combining women and song to the house built by wine. (Courtesy of the University of Southern California, on behalf of the USC Specialized Libraries and Archival Collections.)

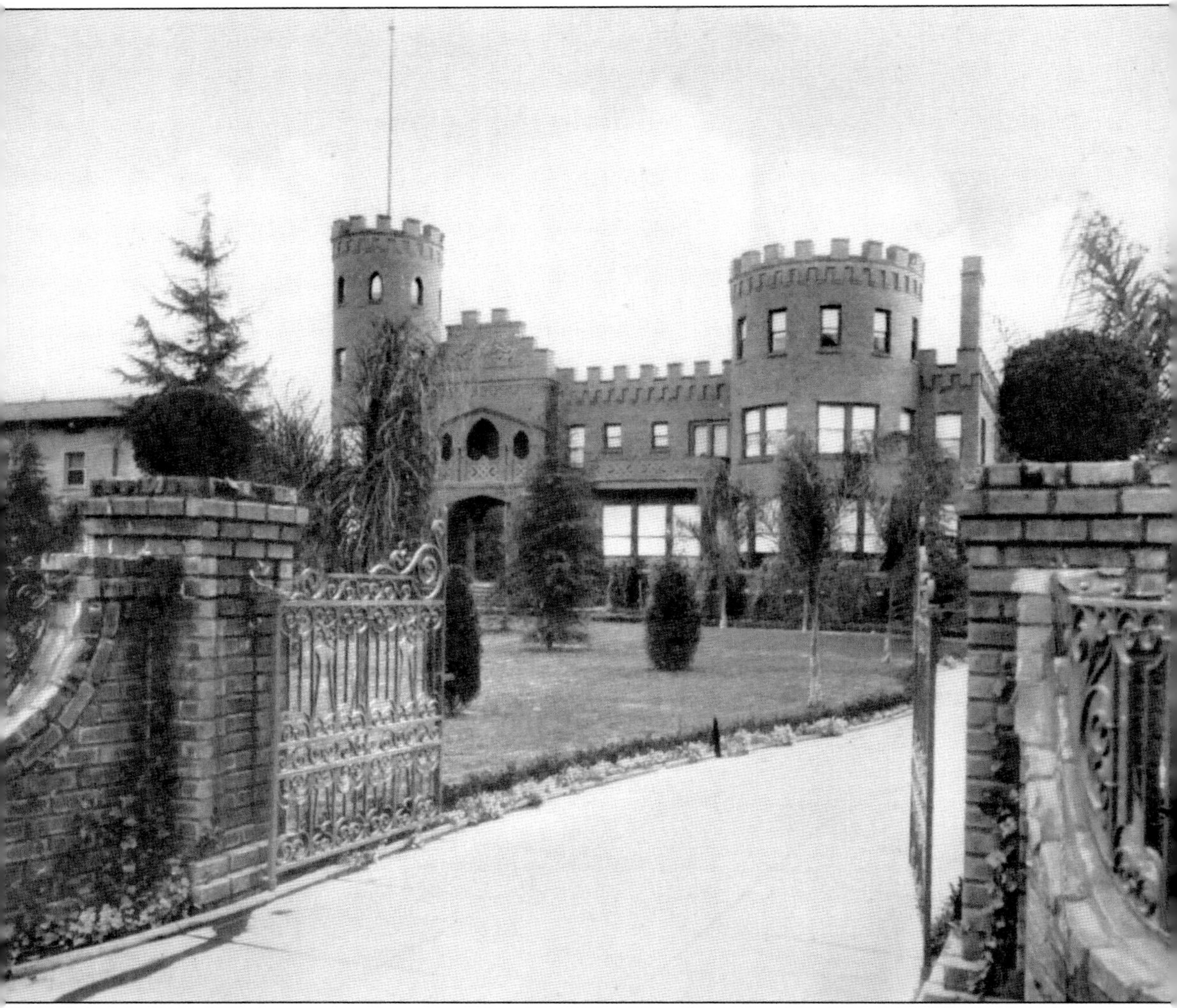

HAGGARTY CASTLE (1914). The proverb that says, "A man's home is his castle," is usually not taken literally, but apparently J. J. Haggarty did not get the message. In 1912, the Irish-born dry goods merchant had Knapp and Woodward build a crenellated mansion at 3330 West Adams Boulevard that presumably reminded him of the landscapes of his youth . . . except with palm trees. He named his $100,000 home York Castle and drew every detail from historic sources. Vases on the porch were copied from Methley Hall, while the second-story balcony was designed after the original at Windsor Castle. An adventurous spirit seemed to pervade the family. In 1912, when Stella Louise Hayden married Haggarty's son, James, her fashionably tight hobble skirt inhibited her leap onto the train. Friends tossed her onto the car, while her new husband paused in his mad flight through the station long enough to answer the question, "Trying to catch that train?" with "No, you chump, I'm just chasing it out of the yard." The happy couple finally embarked on their honeymoon, bruised but unharmed. (Courtesy of Bison Archives.)

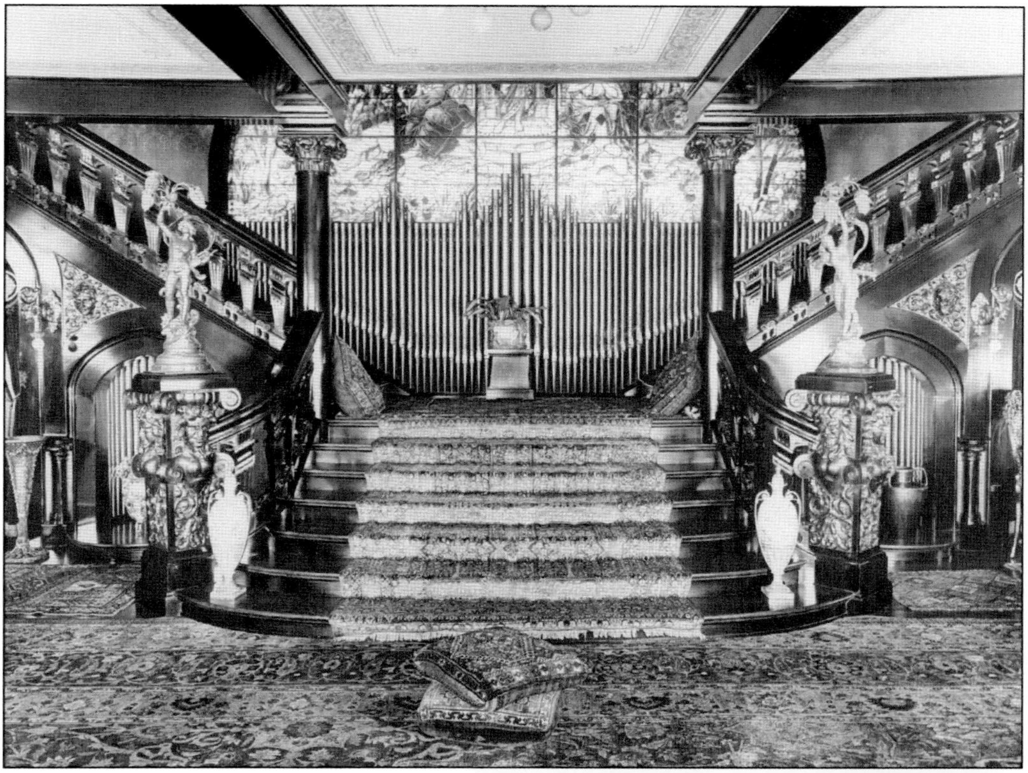

HAGGARTY CASTLE STAIRCASE (C. 1915). The castle's interior was as impressive as the outside. The massive walnut door was hand-carved with Gothic figures. Bacchus lounged in the dining room, while a Viking roamed above a fireplace. Doorknobs were teardrop crystal, and, it was said, a painting of Lady Godiva resided behind a library mirror. (Courtesy of University of Southern California, on behalf of the USC Specialized Libraries and Archival Collections.)

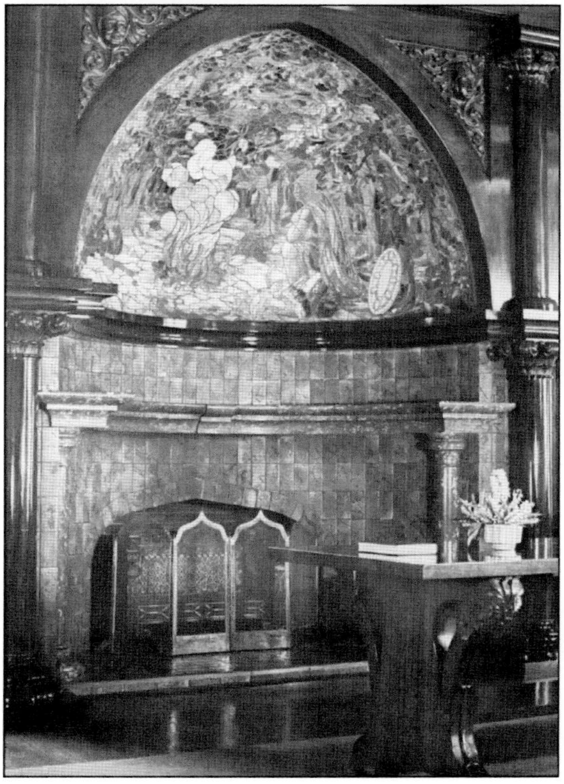

HAGGARTY CASTLE FIREPLACE (1914). J. J. Haggarty died in 1935, and in 1941, the Los Angeles Church Federation moved into the castle. Haggarty's magnificent turrets and battlements were demolished in 1971 to make way for low-income housing. The federation's executive director, Horace Mays, said, "This city needs housing and we're sitting on a piece of gold here—the market value is listed at $168,000." (Courtesy of Bison Archives.)

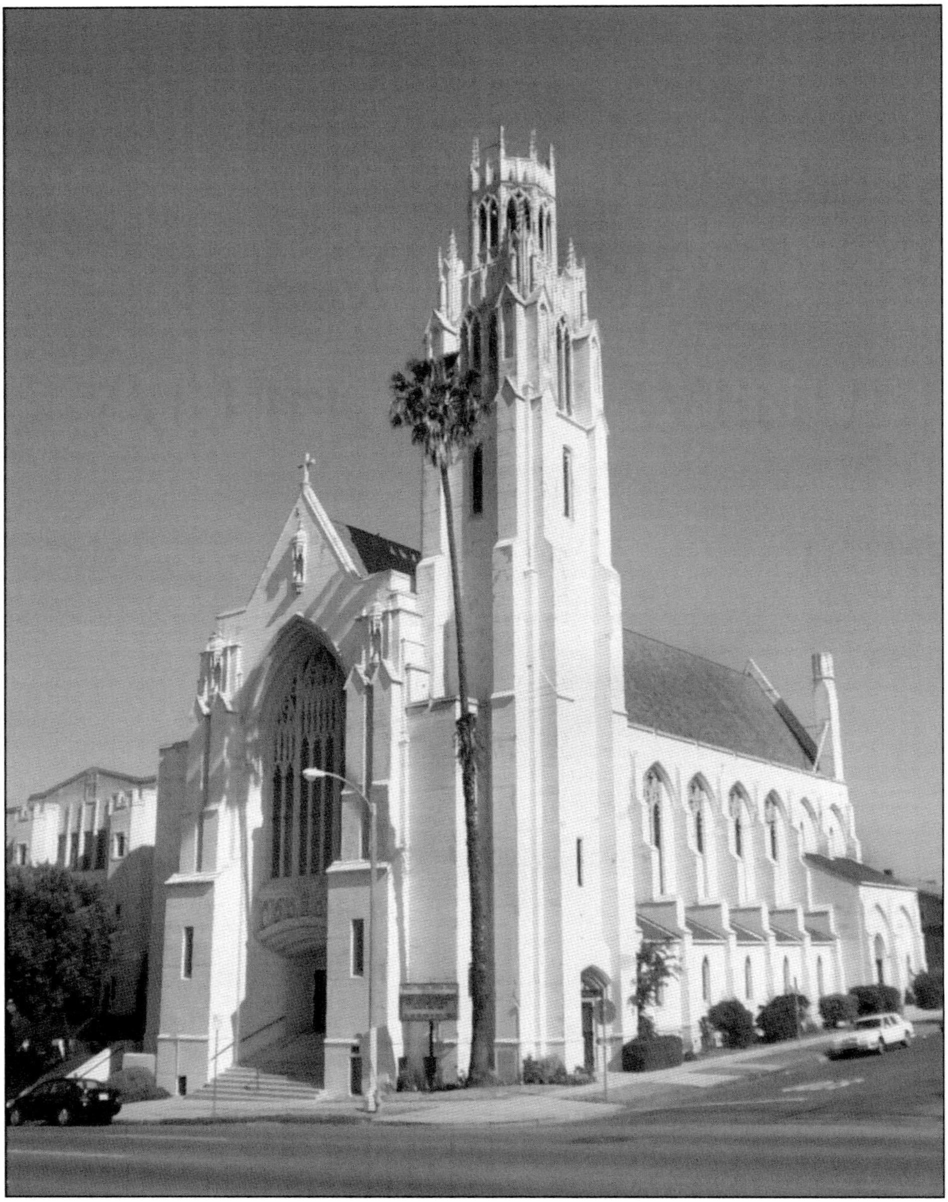

McCarty Memorial Church. "Crown him with many crowns" could be the theme hymn for the glorious McCarty Memorial Church on Adams Boulevard. Its 130-foot, diadem-topped belfry, visible from miles away, draws the eyes of commuters crawling along the Santa Monica Freeway. Dr. Isaac A. McCarty and his wife, Ona Bell McCarty, had long dreamed of erecting a church in Los Angeles. In 1931, following a European vacation, they donated $200,000 of their life savings to make the Gothic edifice a reality. Thomas P. Barber and Paul Kingsbury were the architects. Their design incorporates stained-glass windows of intricate tracery and many interior features imported by Dr. McCarty from Czechoslovakia. The dedication of the church marked the 45th wedding anniversary of the McCartys: quite a lavish gift to acknowledge a marriage. Listed in the National Register of Historic Places, the church received a Preserve L.A. grant from the J. Paul Getty Trust in 2002. The tower is also a favorite resting spot for a variety of hawks that hunt along the borders of the nearby freeway.

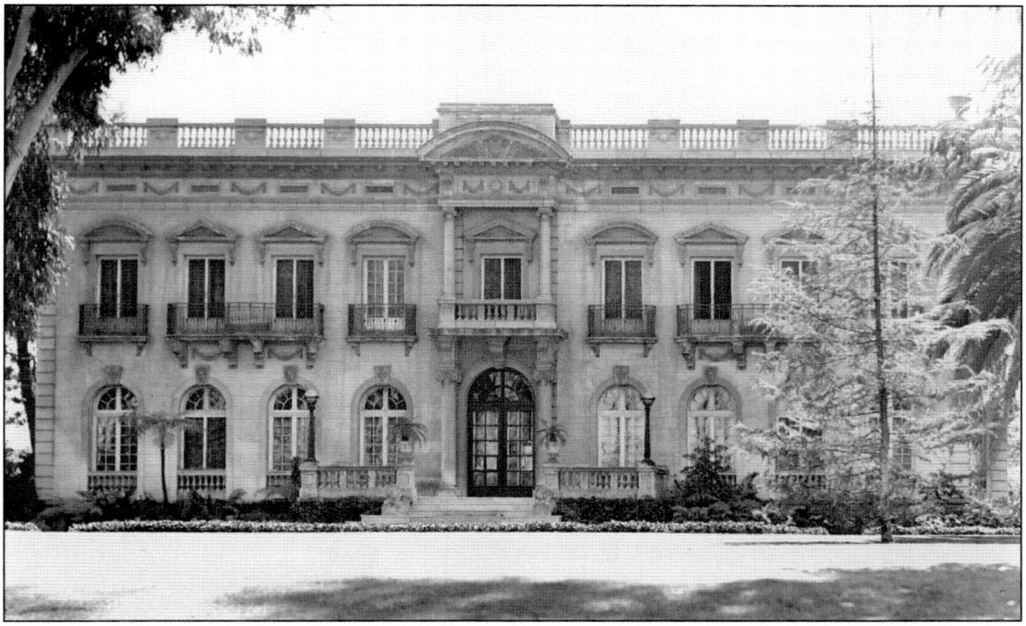

BRUNSWIG RESIDENCE (1939). Lucien Napoleon Brunswig was a French-born wholesale druggist who lived at 3528 West Adams Boulevard. Following World War I, he received the title of chevalier for founding the French Red Cross on the Pacific Coast and aiding tubercular children of French soldiers. His soup kitchen at Plaza Mission Church inspired Alma Whitaker to quip that he should be called "St. Lucien." (Courtesy of Bison Archives.)

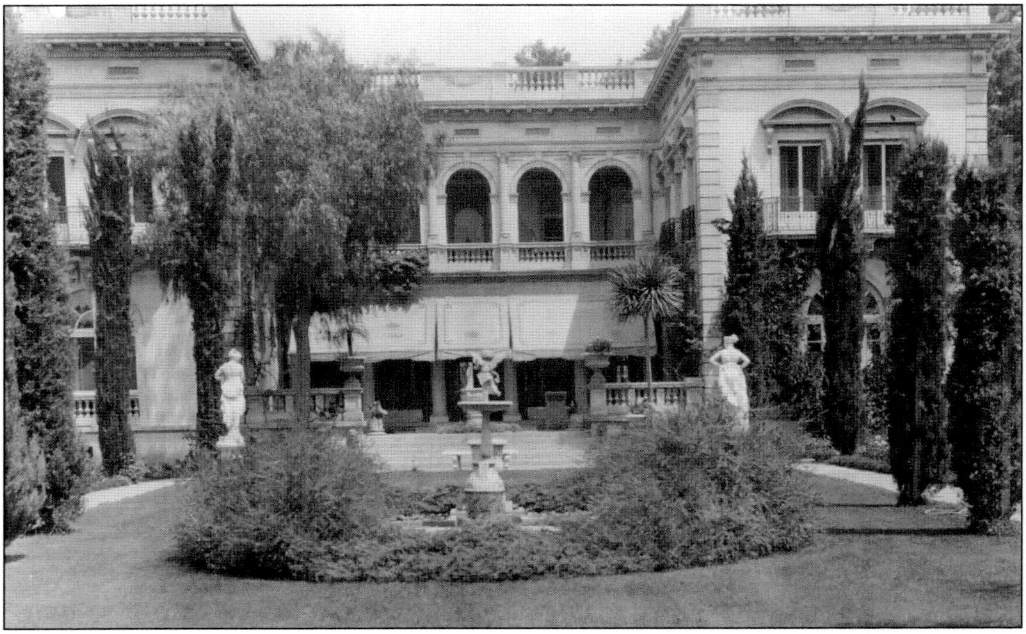

BRUNSWIG RESIDENCE (1917). Like her father, Marguerite Brunswig Staude was a devout Catholic. In 1932, inspired by her vision of a cross superimposed on the Empire State Building, she conceived the idea for a place of worship. The Chapel of the Cross, a dramatic building dominated by a huge cross nestled high in the red rocks of Sedona, was dedicated to the memory of her parents. (Courtesy of Bison Archives.)

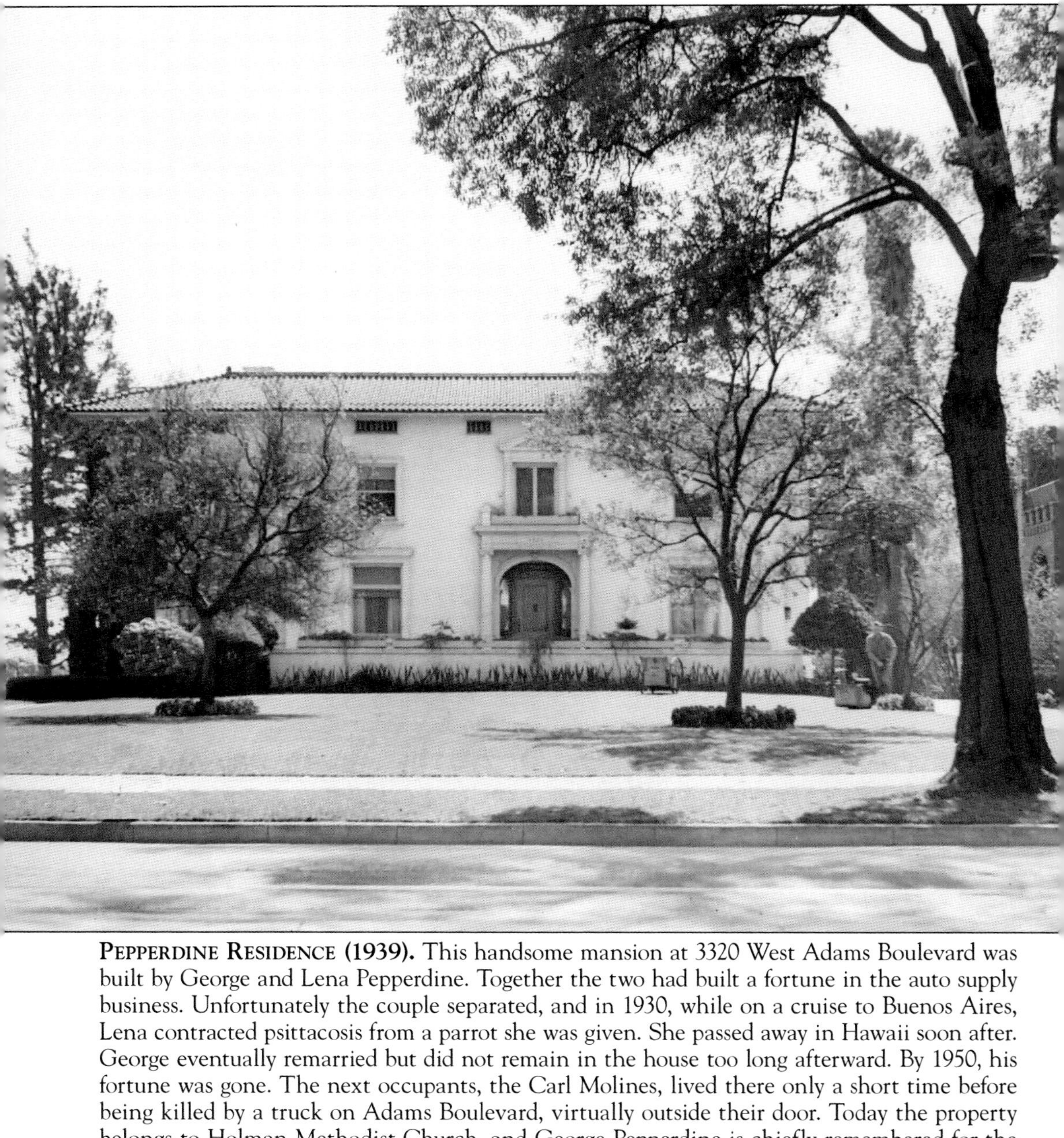

PEPPERDINE RESIDENCE (1939). This handsome mansion at 3320 West Adams Boulevard was built by George and Lena Pepperdine. Together the two had built a fortune in the auto supply business. Unfortunately the couple separated, and in 1930, while on a cruise to Buenos Aires, Lena contracted psittacosis from a parrot she was given. She passed away in Hawaii soon after. George eventually remarried but did not remain in the house too long afterward. By 1950, his fortune was gone. The next occupants, the Carl Molines, lived there only a short time before being killed by a truck on Adams Boulevard, virtually outside their door. Today the property belongs to Holman Methodist Church, and George Pepperdine is chiefly remembered for the university that bears his name. (Courtesy of Bison Archives.)

Seven

West of Arlington Avenue

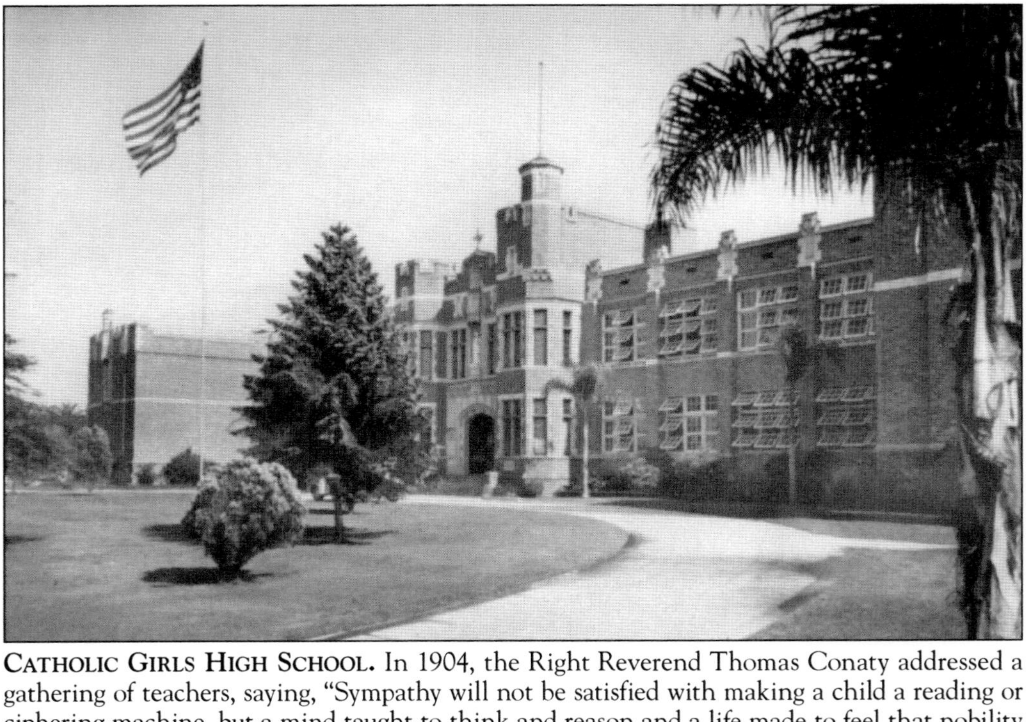

Catholic Girls High School. In 1904, the Right Reverend Thomas Conaty addressed a gathering of teachers, saying, "Sympathy will not be satisfied with making a child a reading or ciphering machine, but a mind taught to think and reason and a life made to feel that nobility of character and perfection of virtue make the true man." Or, apparently, true woman, as in 1922 the new Catholic Girls High School on West Pico Street between Harvard Boulevard and Ardmore Street was dedicated to his memory. The beautiful new school, complete with 21 classrooms, laboratories, sewing room, domestic science room, auditorium, and cafeteria, was designed by Albert C. Martin on the site of the Pico Heights Convent and was expected to relieve overcrowding in the city schools.

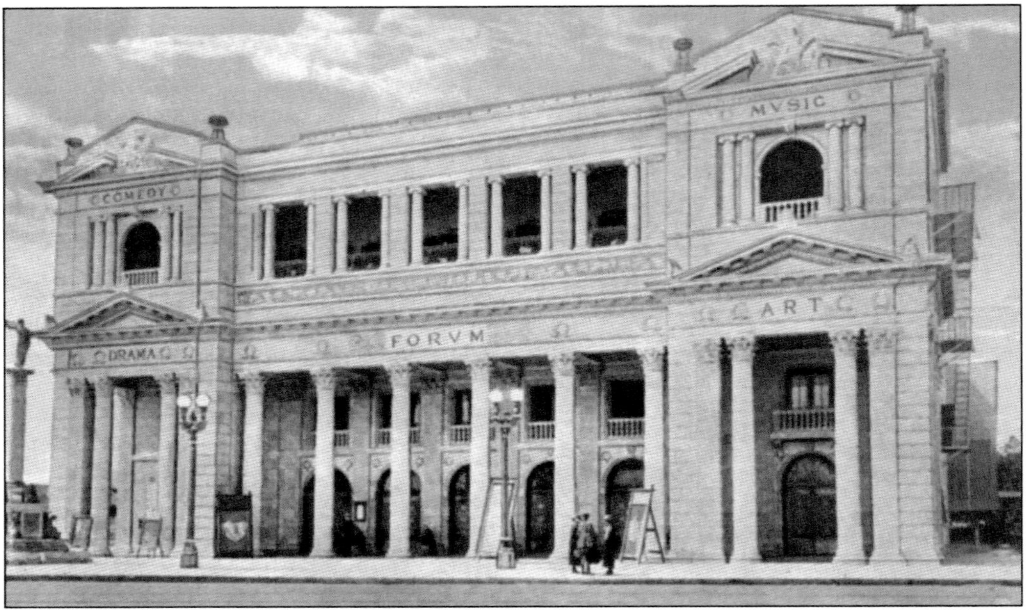

FORUM THEATRE. When the Forum Theatre opened with D. W. Griffith's epic *America* in 1924, critic Edwin Schallert mused that for the "southwest section of the city such an event as this was an absolutely new adventure." Designed by Edward J. Borgmeyer, the columns at 4050 West Pico Boulevard now guard the entrance to a church. The formerly Egyptian-style Bard's Theatre, at Adams and Crenshaw Boulevards, is also a church.

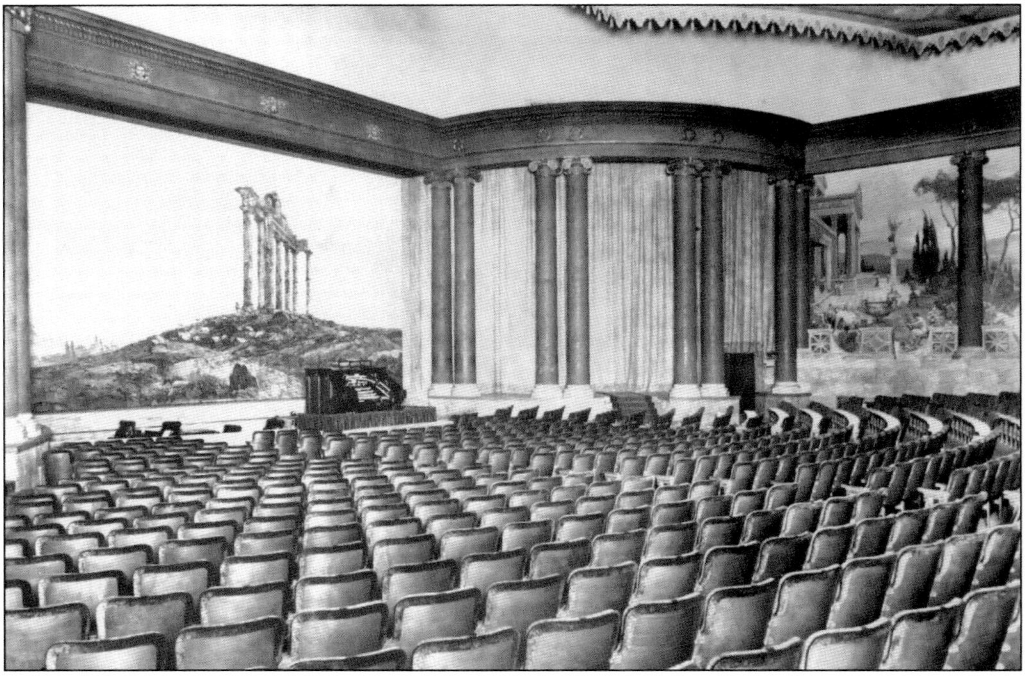

FORUM THEATRE INTERIOR. It may not have been the first movie theater in West Adams, but it was certainly one of the grandest. Another *Los Angeles Times* writer suggested, "An extra pair of eyes would be useful to those who go to the Forum for the first time," to enable them to watch the screen and admire the murals of Rome by C. Von Schneider. (Courtesy of Bison Archives.)

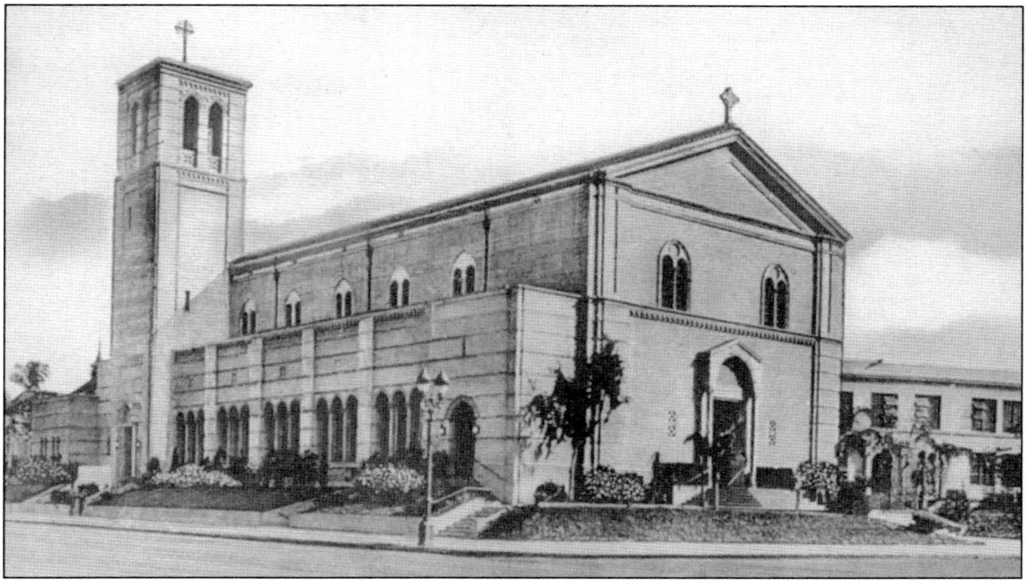

ST. PAUL'S CATHOLIC CHURCH. John C. Austin and Frederic M. Ashley took inspiration from ecclesiastical architecture of Italy when they designed a church at the corner of Washington Boulevard and Bronson Avenue in 1936. Its namesake, just outside Rome, was said to have been built on the site where St. Paul was killed by the Romans, but the location in Los Angeles meant only that the city was growing.

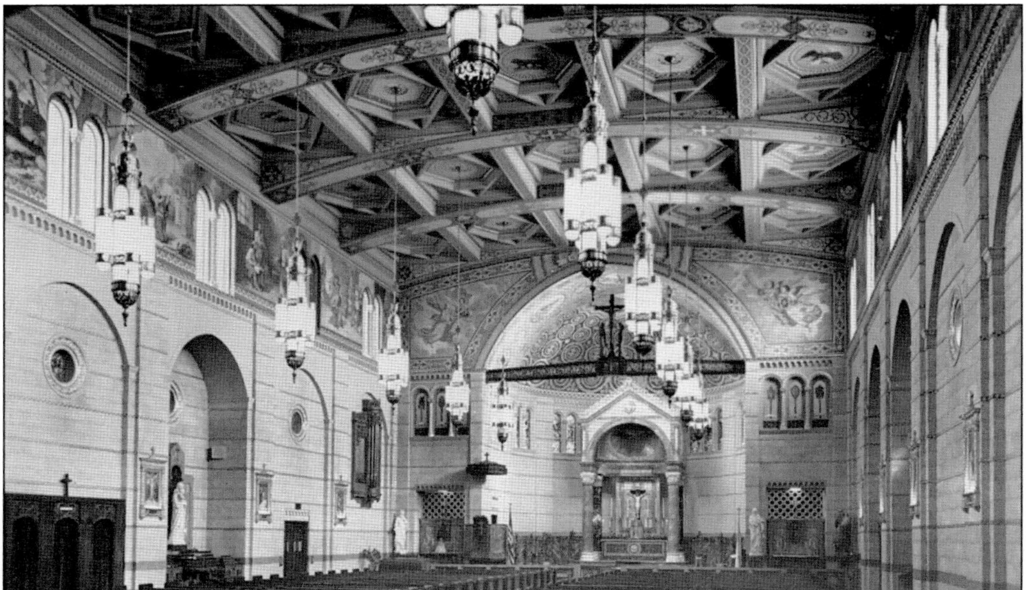

ST. PAUL'S CATHOLIC CHURCH SANCTUARY. Another difference was that, unlike its Italian predecessor, the new church was designed in steel and concrete to be fireproof and earthquake resistant. Interior design emphasized acoustics, with electrical devices installed so the hearing impaired could hear every word of the sermons.

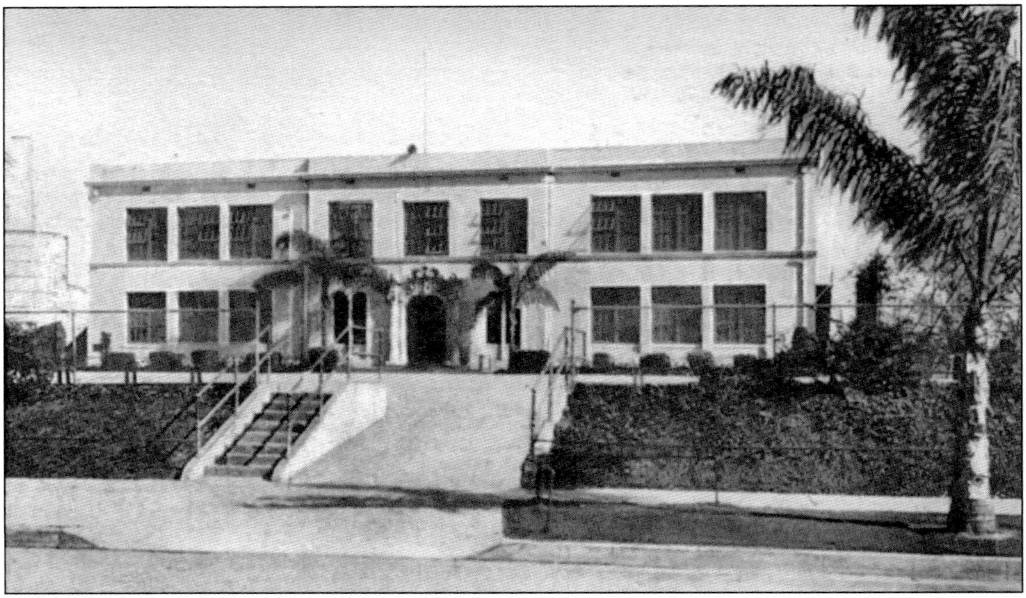

ST. PAUL'S CATHOLIC SCHOOL. Children must be educated, so in September 1922, Rev. Edward J. Hanna, archbishop of San Francisco, dedicated St. Paul's School next door to the church. A hundred pupils were enrolled under the charge of the Sisters of the Holy Cross of Notre Dame, Indiana. The school still educates about 177 students a year from the first through the eighth grades.

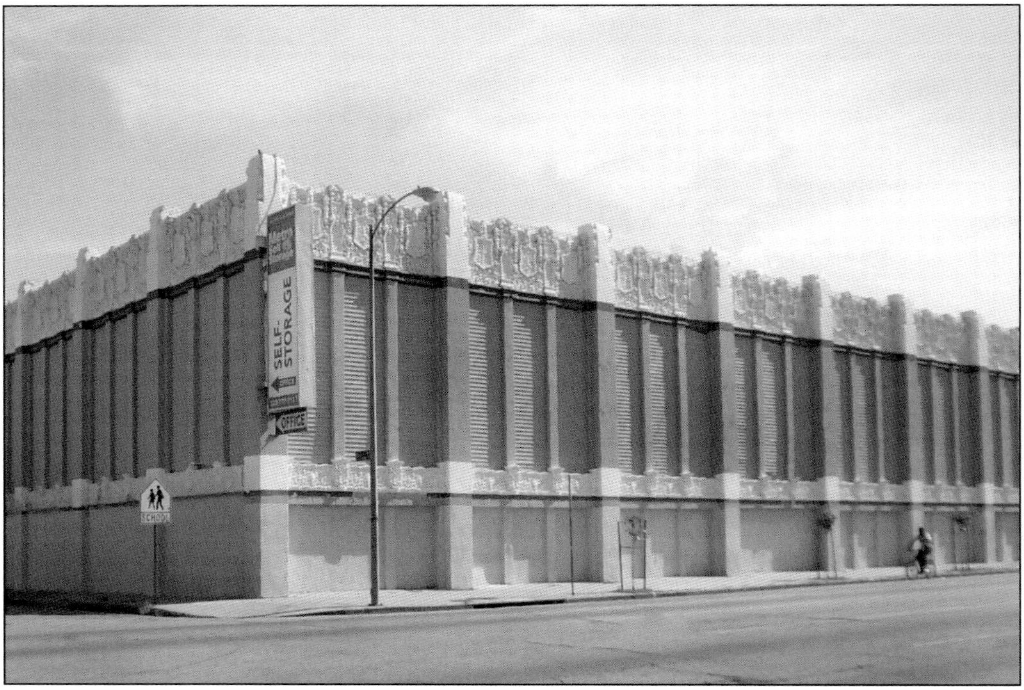

RALPHS GROCERY STORE. Morgan, Walls, and Clements designed the Ralphs Grocery Store at 3611 West Washington Boulevard in 1926, a year when the chain advertised nine different varieties of canned peas, ranging in price from 10 to 27½¢. It was the intention of the owners to build a market as exclusive in design as the high-class shops of Hollywood.

CHARLES MCGINLEY. Walter T. McGinley's diverse life included managing his own circus troupe, his chain of movie theaters in New York, his racing stables and pedigree dog kennels, Lucky Baldwin's oil holdings, and the McGinley Oil Company. Upon his death on September 18, 1932, his brother, Charles (pictured), took over the oil company's business management. Charles was said to be the godfather of Robert F. Kennedy. (Courtesy of Jean Cade.)

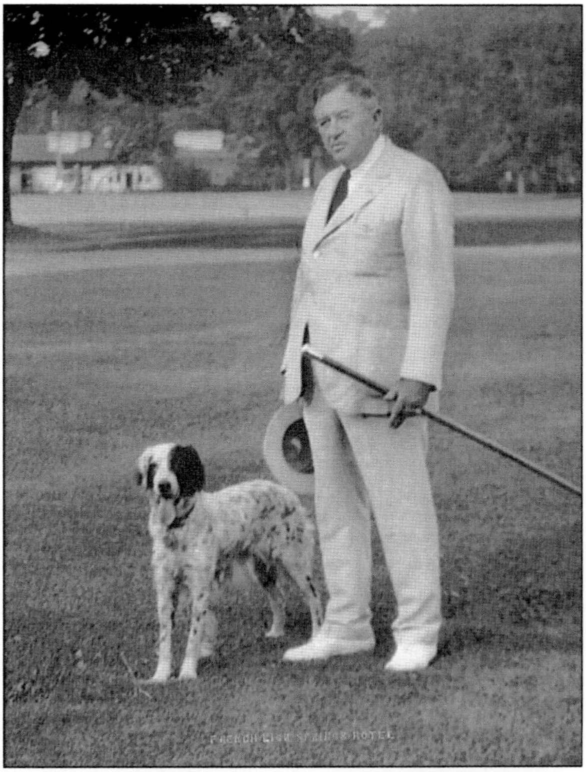

MARY, ANNIE, AND CHARLES MCGINLEY. The McGinley home was built in 1924 by architect Emmett G. Martin as a winter retreat in the posh La Fayette Square area of West Adams. Charles and his two sisters, Mary and Annie, inherited the house, and all three lived there together with a wide assortment of pets. They enjoyed entertaining outside on the grounds surrounding the house. (Courtesy of Jean Cade.)

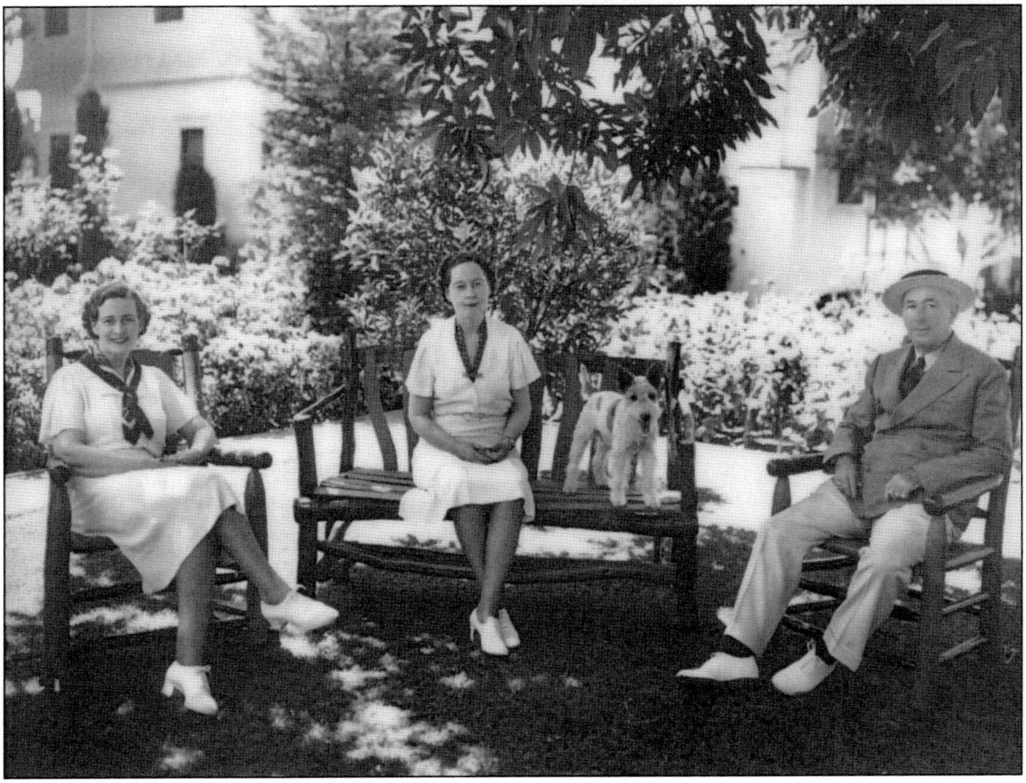

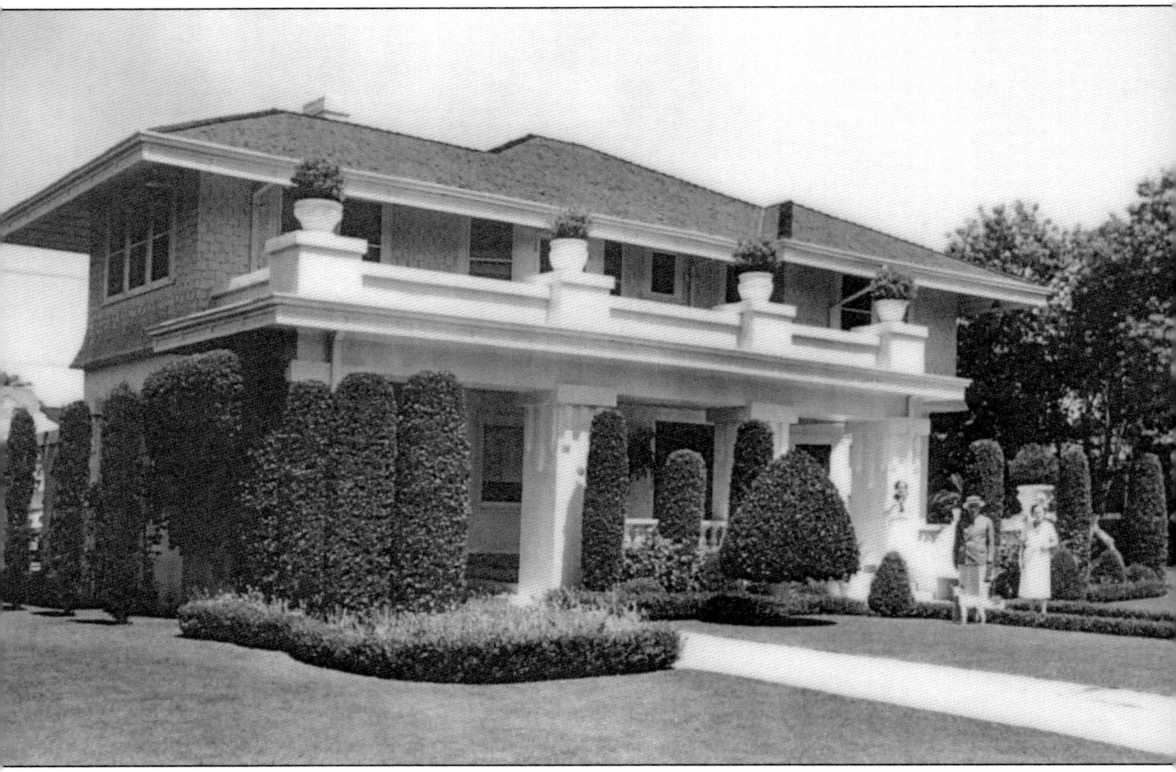

McGinley Residence. This original grand structure was obviously influenced by the Prairie School as well as the arts and crafts style of architecture. Charles expanded the original site by acquiring two adjacent empty lots, one to the north and one to the south, to form a triple-lot compound. In 1939, Charles McGinley commissioned renowned African American architect Paul Revere Williams to enlarge and update the house. As can be seen in the before and after photographs, the building permit specified a "General Remodeling and changing . . . Practically a new building on the old foundations." (Courtesy of Jean Cade.)

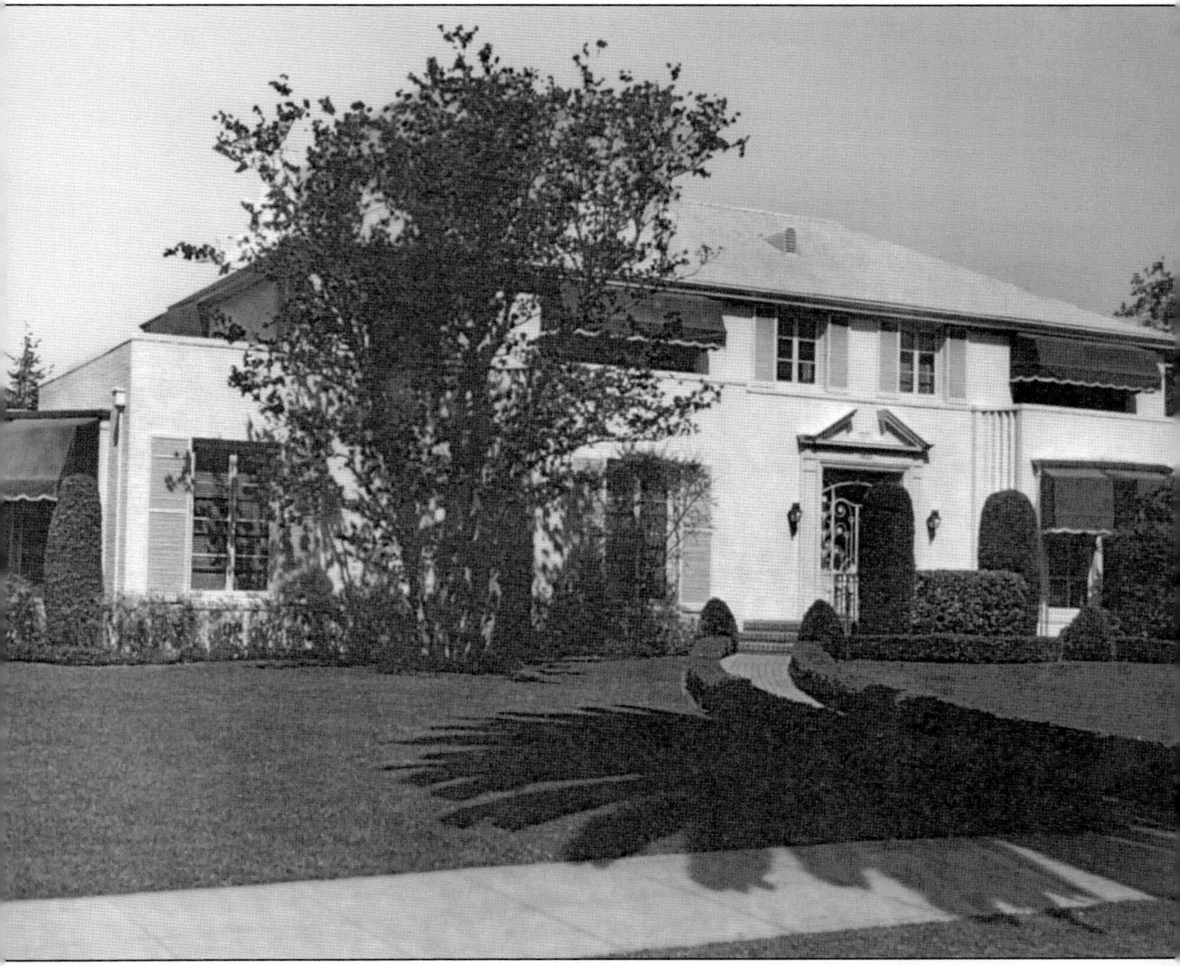

McGINLEY RESIDENCE'S CLASSICAL REGENCY REVIVAL LOOK. Williams expanded the house extensively, giving it a formal classical regency revival look, a signature style in his design vocabulary. Williams's many private home projects included his own home in La Fayette Square, as well as private homes for celebrities such as Frank Sinatra, Lon Chaney, Lucille Ball and Desi Arnaz, William S. Paley, Zsa Zsa Gabor, Anthony Quinn, Danny Thomas, Tyrone Power, Bert Lahr, Barbara Stanwyck, Lucky Baldwin, Charles Cottrell, and of course the unforgettable Zasu Pitts. He perfected drawing upside down so clients, who could have been uncomfortable sitting next to a black man, could sit across a table from him and see the drawings right side up. Besides private homes, Williams's many public buildings include the Los Angeles County Hall of Administration, Saks Fifth Avenue Beverly Hills, the remodel of the Beverly Hills Hotel, and involvement with the LAX theme building. Williams was the first African American member of the American Institute of Architects (AIA) and in 1957 the first to be elected an AIA Fellow. (Courtesy of Jean Cade.)

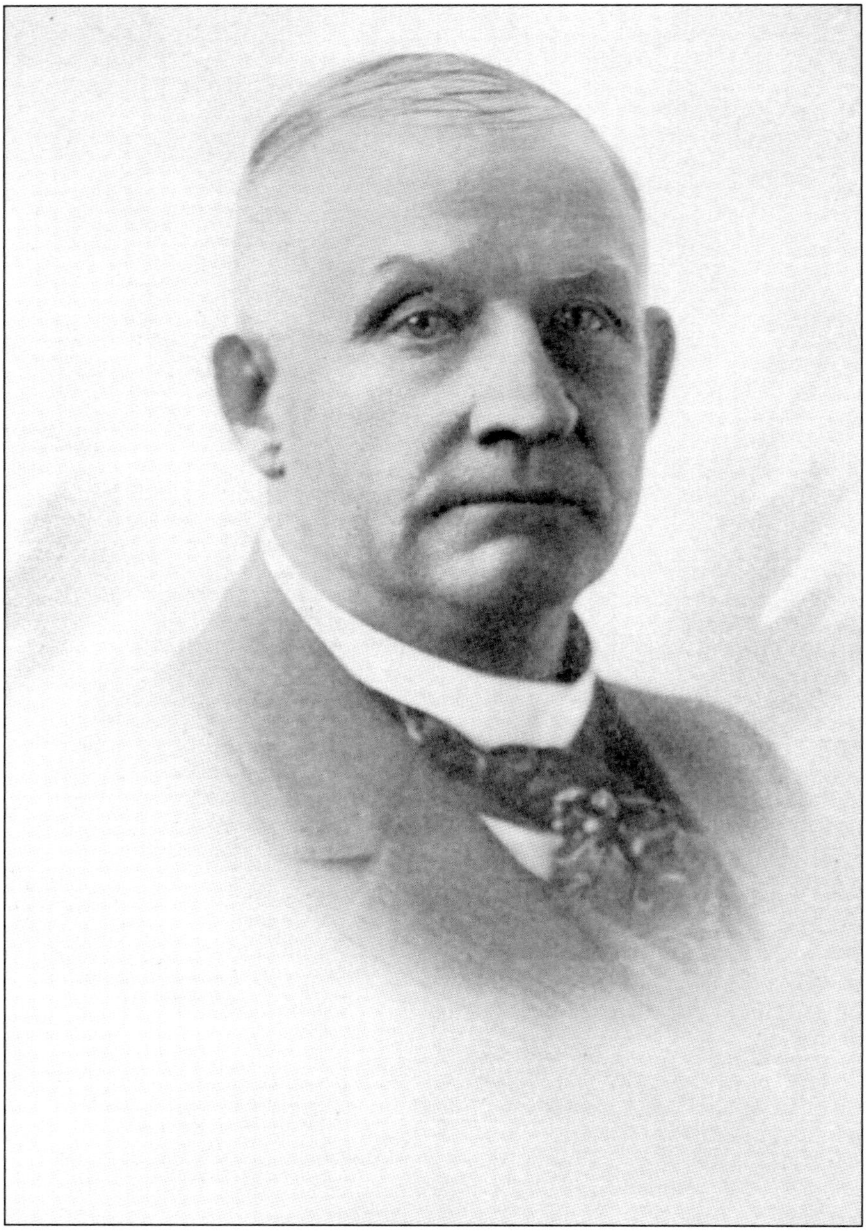

WILLIAM MILLER BOWEN. Few visitors cheering their team at the Coliseum or marveling at dinosaurs in the Natural History Museum are aware of the debt they owe to William Bowen, the man who was called the Father of Exposition Park. Although he grew up on a farm, Bowen's heart was set on studying law. He passed the bar and in 1900 was elected to the city council. While teaching at the University Methodist Church, he learned that his students were spending Sunday afternoon in the undesirable environs then called Agricultural Park. With research, Bowen discovered that the property belonged to the public and wrested it away from the alleged owners, who specialized in the brutal sport of rabbit coursing. Under his guidance, money was raised, gardens were planted, museums were built, and the Coliseum was constructed. After he died in his home at 2033 Virginia Road in 1937, his bier was covered with flowers from the famous Rose Garden, with a sprig from an oak tree he planted when Exposition Park was new.

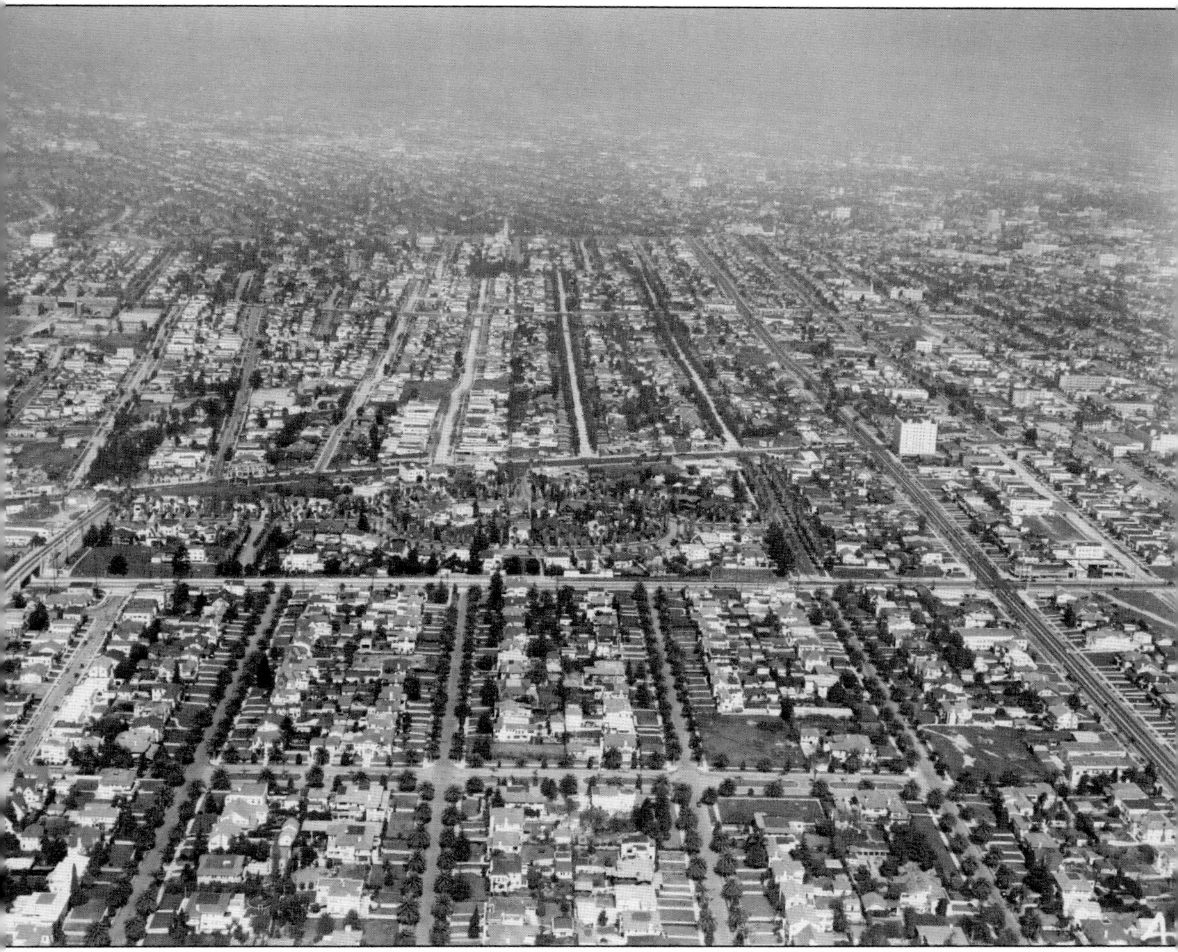

La Fayette Square and Victoria Circle Aerial (c. 1940). West Street is considered today to be the westernmost end of West Adams. In this 1940 photograph, it runs along the left side, with the West Street Bridge going over Venice Boulevard and terminating at Pico Boulevard. On the far right is Crenshaw Boulevard, and between them, in the foreground, is La Fayette Square. Laid out just prior to World War I, it was not predominantly developed until the 1920s and 1930s. Just north, across Venice Boulevard, is Victoria Circle, laid out in 1907 as an exclusive enclave by "nineteen substantial citizens," to quote the *Los Angeles Times*. The streets in Victoria Circle were 100 feet wide with "petrolithic" paving, the sidewalks were 7 feet wide, and the hilltop location featured views all the way to the ocean. (Courtesy of University of Southern California, on behalf of the USC Specialized Libraries and Archival Collections.)